THE SOUL BENEATH THE SKIN

THE SOUL
BENEATH
THE SKIN

*The Unseen
Hearts and
Habits of
Gay Men*

David Nimmons

St. Martin's Press
New York

www.stmartins.com

"YMCA" copyright ©1978 by Can't Stop the Music. Reprinted by permission.

"Erotic Collectibles," from *Rhapsodies of a Repeat Offender* by Wayne Koestenbaum,
copyright © 1994 by Wayne Koestenbaum. Reprinted by permission of
Persea Books, Inc., New York.

Library of Congress Cataloging-in-Publication Data

Nimmons, David.
    The soul beneath the skin : the unseen hearts and habits of gay men /
David Nimmons.
        p. cm.
    ISBN 0-312-26919-6
        1. Gay men—United States—Social conditions. 2. Gay men—
United States—Social life and customs. 3. Gay men—United
States—Psychology. I. Title.

HQ76.3.U5 N55 2002
305.38'9664'0973—d21

                                                    2001057894

First Edition: May 2002

10 9 8 7 6 5 4 3 2 1

To Dave F.,
whose love is manifest daily

ACKNOWLEDGMENTS

Behind every man stands a line of great men—especially if he's a bottom. Not that I'd know *myself*, of course, no siree, Bob. But to that long line standing behind and around me, some thanks are due.

Dave Fleischer, the first reader of my life, has provided constant support and love, along with an organizer's unrelenting focus on the action these ideas yield in the real world. Among those who patiently watched this book get itself dressed for the last year has been Daniel Wolfe. Lucky indeed is the writer who has a fellow writer so smart, stylish, and perceptive to think with, and these pages are far smarter for it. To my sharp-eyed and ever-skeptical friend, Dr. Lou Kushner, thanks for catching my first thousand errors, great and small. My good fortune as a writer is now yours as a reader. I thank Bryan Mathison, who has enriched these pages as he has their author. Each time your voice rings clear, I give thanks, no matter which chapter we're in.

Two visionaries, David Abbott, in Providence, and the Reverend Jim Mitulski, in San Francisco, stepped forward to help before others did, and each shaped this work with unfailing generosity. My editor, Michael Denneny, took a risk on this book when nobody else would, and hasn't stopped yet. To my literary agent, Mitchell Waters, at Curtis Brown, my appreciation for nurturing this project from the start and for the many ways you helped this book into being. Richard Burns, Dr. Ron Stall, the Reverend Penny Nixon, Terry Huwe, David Hansell, Len Hirsch, Chip Cordelli, Carlos Cordero, and the late Stephen Gendin all offered inspiration and help. To Barbara Draimin, Chris Collins, Nancy Miller, and the Toms, Morgan and Ciano, my thanks for key kindnesses at critical moments. And to my oldest friend, Mary Schmich, who has stayed reading through so many drafts of my life with a writer's keen mind and a friend's unfaltering heart, chapter 7 is for you.

Thanks also to all who have worked bringing these ideas to their local communities: Jed Barnum in Boston, Tom Dennison and Ector Simpson in New York, Ron King in Maine, the Reverend Pressley Sutherland in London, the ML gang in Minneapolis, Russ Chaffin on the Web, and Dr. Jack Doren in Fort Lauderdale. Both Eric Rofes at the Boulder Gay Men's Health summits and Sue Hyde at NGLTF allowed me to hone these ideas in workshop form, which has been vital. Scholars like Dr. John Blandford and Dr. Lee Badgett generously provided data on gay men's career choices in chapters 3 and 8. I am indebted to Tom Dennison for sharing his deeply felt views on the meanings of dance culture in chapter 8, and for providing many of the quotations in that chapter. Thanks as well to the men whose entries on the Web pages www.circuit-noize.com and www.circuitpartyinsanity.com provide many of those quotes. I am grateful, as well, to Ken Hanes's wonderful collection of gay men's observations about their lives, *Speaking Out,* some of which appear in chapter 9.

Most of all, thank you to the men in localities from Maine to San Francisco whose truths continue to breath life into these pages. You're the tops, guys.

CONTENTS

A way of life can yield a culture and an ethics.
To be "gay" is not to
identify with the psychological traits and
the visible masks of the homosexual,
but to try to develop a way of life.
—Michel Foucault, "Friendship as a Way of Life"

"We have our own decencies, our own ethics.
Our lives are a different shape than yours."
—Leo speaking to Ernest,
in Noël Coward's *Design for Living*

1 | Unseen Hearts and Habits

"You meet the most interesting people on Christopher Street."
—Betty Comden and Adolph Green, *Wonderful Town*, opening number

If you have ever had a hunch there was something special or different about gay men; if you have by turns felt you are glad to be gay, yet found yourself disappointed by the forms "gay community" takes; if you have wondered, "Is this all there is to us?"; if you have sometimes wished men like us could be different with each other; if you have craved more affection and tenderness in your gay social world, but weren't sure how to get it, this book may offer some new answers.

The story begins at a place called The Loft. Even if you have never set foot in it, you've been there. You enter past the Herb Ritts monochrome of that begrimed mechanic and his oversized tire (one wonders: Does some poor customer await in a gas station front office somewhere, ever hopeful?). Your eye catches the array of sassy bumper stickers ("I'm not a slut—I'm just popular"), the assorted condoms nestled beneath the rainbow baseball caps, and then settles on a fitted T-shirt ($42.00) stretched across the ample pectoral acreage of a mannequin seemingly on steroids. The display confronts the shopper with a daunting sartorial choice: Will it be the "Nobody knows I'm gay" muscle-shirt in gray, or the "What Daddy wants, Daddy gets—I'm Daddy" tank top in black?

The Loft's big claim to fame is its address: 156 Christopher Street, Greenwich Village. That puts it about one hundred yards from the Stonewall bar; you know, the site-of-the-uprising-that-marked-the-beginning-of-an-out-and-proud-visibly-organized-gay-community. The place the tour-bus driver points out to illustrate an upbeat urban fable of

how the spangled fairies bested New York's Finest (conveniently sepa-
rated in his user-friendly narrative). "Two days of street skirmishes" . . .
blah, "riot police" . . . blah, "drag queens" . . . blah blah. In his mythic
narrative—easily framed as our Boston Tea Party, in nine-inch heels—it
took those two days, give or take about a quarter century, for that social
movement to morph into an entity shorthanded as "the gay community."
Which, of course, is why this straight married bus driver from Newark
knows to tell this story at all.

The Loft is one of those places where the community he refers to goes
to buy its boxer shorts and muscle T's. This is where one comes to
scratch the itch for a box of penis-shaped pasta, locate a cowboy-with-a-
rope birthday card, or find that special lube gun shaped like, well, a
lube gun. If you can't find what you want at The Loft, try Rainbows and
Triangles on Manhattan's Eighth Avenue, Gay Mart in Chicago, A Different Light in Silver Lake, Castro Gulch in San Francisco's Castro, Lobo
in Houston's Montrose. In Boston, your receipt will read Copley Flair;
in Raleigh, White Rabbit. In Portland, Maine, it's Drop Me a Line, and
in Portland, Oregon, Rainbows. You'll find such venues from Seattle to
St. Louis, from Atlanta to Anchorage, in Columbus, Chicago, Des
Moines, Phoenix, on rue de la St. Croix de la Bretonnerie in the Paris
Marais, on Madrid's Chueca Plaza, lining Amsterdam's bustling Reg-
ulierstraat.

That familiarity is, in fact, the point. You can count on finding the
same iconic inventory: a faux-outrageous jumble of carnality, Carnivale,
and kitsch that mocks one set of bourgeois values even as it re-inscribes
another, onto refrigerator magnets, coffee mugs, baseball caps, and key-
chains. Whether the address is L.A. or London, the display window
offers an accustomed iconography of rainbows and triangles, flags and
flesh. On the shelves inside, the saints repose in their accustomed niches.
St. Tom of Finland, St. Quentin of Crisp, St. Raymond slaying the
Dragon. In stacks by the door, you can be sure to find the local bar rag,
with newsprint pages and a glossy cover bearing the charmed face or
body of a someone who can't recall where he was when John Lennon was
shot because, well, he wasn't. You can close your eyes and know by feel
which page will have the bar and dance clubs listed, which the personals,
and where you'll find the smudgy thumbnails of doe-eyed escorts hawk-
ing their cockles and muscles like so many Victorian street girls.

This place is a cultural outpost, as certainly as East L.A. bodegas sell
rice, beans, and Virgin Mary calendars, as self-assuredly as Rodeo Drive
boutiques offer water-processed decaf and Bed-Stuy barbers vend 'fro
combs and African flag decals. These emporia, whatever their locale, are

boutiques of belonging. Here is where you say Calvin, and nobody within earshot thinks Hobbes. In such places, inventory shades into affirmation, brands become bromides. Be an International Male. Don't Panic. It's good $2^{(x)}$ist. Help yourself to a Lifestyle on your way out. Places like The Loft are the purveyors to a culture inventing itself. They stock the retail inventory that a stirring new population, a novel kind of urban man, has come to claim as his own.

From the soft-core posters in each dressing room to the underwear boxes, all seems to suggest that what lies beneath the skin is . . . just more skin. The very walls speak in an eloquence of muscles and flesh, whispering a thousand seductions to one killing illusion: that this detritus, this skintight swirl of testosterone and camp, has something essential to do with what you're made of.

But shopper beware. Retailers of rainbows are rarely what they seem. If only what was most powerful in this place was merely skin deep. In truth, what most counts here is not what hangs inside the window, but what strolls on the streets beyond it. Because whether this store is in Madrid, Silver Lake, or Madison, it demarcates homospace. Look in its mirrors and you peer into an enchanted looking glass. This place is an entry portal to the world's newest culture, a tribal homeland where the defaults and protocols of social life shift subtly, and where new rituals and norms hold power. It is a place of different rules and language, where customs and values are not what they seem.

It matters little if you are gay, straight, or somewhere in between. Cross the threshold, walk past the Bears 2002 poster, and step out onto Planet Gay. Here, the clothes fit right, the men are men, and the Joint Chiefs are nervous. Glance back over your shoulder. Your one clue was that T-shirt in the window: "You're not in Kansas anymore." Nobody in this shop has been in Kansas for a while now. Memo to the Joint Chiefs: You have good reason to worry.

Some people say we're just the same as straight people except for what we do in bed. I say what we do in bed is the only place where we're the same.
  —Harry Hay, founder, Mattachine Society

In the early 1950s, when homophile leader Harry Hay got up to speak before a room of Mattachine Society activists, few of those listening could have imagined how profoundly the following five decades would confirm his words. By the time, more than a quarter century later, the French philosopher Michel Foucault could speak of "developing a way of life,"

one group of American men had been doing just that, and calling themselves "gay." (Readers with an interest in Queer Theory might want to
glance at the theoretic note on page 221 about the use of "gay" in these
pages. For less academic types, who hear the term *gay subject position* and
think "doggie style"—go pour yourself a drink and we can get started.)

In the last fifty years gay communities from Mendocino to Maine have
undertaken a range of profound, spontaneous social experiments. These
men set simmering a series of radical cultural transformations, scarcely
recognized and even less understood, even by themselves. Few could
imagine all that this set of experiments would come to mean.

As they grew, these innovations were not very evident. Under the
shadow of a plague, many of these changes bubbled unseen. Cultural
practices and rituals that first glimmered on blocks with names like
Christopher and Castro began to sprout in towns with names like Liberty, Tennessee, and Ukiah, California. As they did, they left their
imprint on America's life. The innovations taking shape in these male
communities would come to shape mass cultural institutions from prime
time to the Pentagon. They put into play fundamental assumptions and
givens about how men work. Now these changes and shifts reverberate
in the larger American society, bringing the potential to redraw the map
of American maledom.

Yet the power of the cultural experiments now taking shape in these
communities of men has been little recognized, either by those of us who
participate in them or by society as a whole. These changes have largely
drifted in below the cultural radar. Their import has been obscured by a
set of truths commonly held to be self-evident. Most who (for better or
worse) take an interest in commenting on gay lives have adopted an all-
too-familiar conventional narrative. As a consequence, that one-dimen-
sional view has been accepted by many of us—gay as well as straight—as
our accurate, if depressing, story. You know: that we live in a body-
obsessed, shallow, sexually profligate, consumerist culture. That gay cultural values inculcate competition and isolation, narcissism and
hedonism. That our community practices—especially in gay enclave
cities and neighborhoods—recapitulate a ruthless competition of the
flesh as they discourage any true intimacy of the heart. Most of all, just in
case you've missed it along the way, the inevitable moral of the story is
that, if gay men don't pay heed, we will party, dance, and sex ourselves
into an early oblivion.

Most of us have at one time or another wallowed at the trough of this
conventional caricature. If we are gay, we roll our eyes about our fellow-
men: "You know how gay guys are," we smirk. Sometimes feelings boil

into hurt, despair, or bitterness at how "gay men" seem to treat each other. We bemoan the "lifestyle," wonder if we will be happy. Will we find a place that feeds our hearts and hopes in this thing called gay? If we are straight onlookers, we may be the parents who fret over a son's safety, the siblings who wonder at our choices, the friends and colleagues who cluck and matchmake and shake their heads.

The pages ahead propose that this particular fairy tale is profoundly incomplete, and that a careful reading of facts supports a far different conclusion. As we will see, a wealth of evidence powerfully contradicts this narrow version of gay male lives. That evidence includes a growing body of fact from public health and epidemiological studies, sociological and psychological inquiry, marketing and public opinion surveys, anthropological texts, and ethnographic studies. More powerfully, it arises in personal stories, anecdotes and community knowledge, the lived experience of these communities of men. It echoes in the range of cultural practices and new kinds of institutions gay worlds have developed. Taken together, the facts raise the distinct possibility that all of us—gay and straight alike—have overlooked the most telling aspects of the story. Along the way, we may have unwittingly adopted a shared view of gay men and our habits that obscures a set of far deeper, more important truths about the experiments now going on in these lives and communities. In short, we may have profoundly missed the point of us.

A radically different interpretation awaits. We need to remain open to the possibility that this accustomed gay narrative is both factually incomplete and grossly misleading. That, at best, the stories told by and to ourselves, by and to the larger culture, are stunningly incomplete and inaccurate. That, at worst, our accepted narrative bristles with unexamined, willful, deliberate distortions. For complex reasons, and at great cost, we have allowed ourselves to see only a part of the story about ourselves and our ways of life.

Much empirical evidence suggests that self-identified gay men are engaged in a striking range of cultural innovations in social practices. Our levels of public violence are vastly lower. We volunteer more often, demonstrating levels of altruism and service quite distinct from other men. Our patterns of intimacy and interpersonal connectedness take new forms. We are redefining gender relations in powerful and novel ways. We have distinct patterns of caretaking in sexual and communal realms. We are enacting new definitions of public and private, family and friends, as we are vastly transforming relations of pleasure, community, and authority. We are pioneering a wide range of untried intimate relationships, with new forms, rituals, and language.

The chapters ahead chronicle some unseen habits of identified gay male cultures. They rely on words and stories from many men talking from their own lived experience, as well as on the scholarly literature. Whether you are a gay man or just care about one, you are invited to step through the looking glass into a new world and to take a clear-eyed look at what is to be found there.

These pages offer our story, half-told. They document a set of social innovations and experiments the likes of which have no clear precedent in our culture. Taken together, these experiments compose what can only be termed a distinct new code of male love and nurture.

Collectively and individually, however, we do not always realize the full potential of these experiments. All too often, adopted gay cultural habits can rub our hearts raw, leaving us feeling more lonely, isolated, and wounded than we would like. We confront that problem in the book's final chapters. There, we examine our world, half-made, moving beyond data to discern the larger meaning of these cultural experiments. Those pages examine the notable chasm between the public aspects of gay culture and our unmet needs of heart and soul.

If you are a gay man, the first chapters may surprise you. You may, at times, wonder just what gay terrain is being mapped, especially if you have not experienced all that is being described. The later chapters open a radically different view of gay male "community," one where we find more sustaining ways to be with and for each other. They offer one vision of how we will build the kind of gay world we most wish to inhabit. That is, where the practices and habits, the language and debate, the customs and rituals, the institutions and organizations, better reflect our values and hopes, which now so often go unmet. Especially if you are wondering if this book speaks to your own personal experience, I hope you will take the time to read chapter 9 before you decide.

Throughout, one cornerstone fact remains. Coming out and into gay community is at its core an impulse of hope. It is a dream shared, of finding an intentional community of like-hearted men. We were drawn into this thing called gay, and found ourselves originally called to each other, in pursuit of a dream of love. Although that hope may often feel betrayed and bruised, we have a unique opportunity to adapt our shared cultures to more truly celebrate and deliver on that hope.

That undertaking is the heart and soul of this book, and of the movement called Manifest Love that is now growing among gay men in various locales. It holds that, far from inhabiting an ethical wasteland, we are evolving a new community whose practices are without any clear modern precedent, one whose core values resonate deeply with a range of spiritual traditions. Our communities of men are experimenting with entirely new forms of public life, with a potential to radically change ideas of power, love, and the nature of American community. Until now, these experiments have remained largely unseen, hidden in our hearts and habits, obscured by what we think we know about ourselves.

It is time to explore the meaning for the larger culture of the radical experiments now arising in gay male worlds. We are undertaking an evolution of values, one that lives in our rituals, practices, and norms. That will have enormous implications and effects as it becomes more widely understood, celebrated, and embraced in the broader American family.

The more closely we look at the variety of cultures gay men have created among ourselves, the more it is clear that we do many deep and important things differently. Obviously, those differences are not exclusive, consistent, unique, or monolithic. Not all the men described here necessarily live in "gay ghettos" in cities, or even label themselves "gay." Not all gay men do these things, any more than all heterosexuals don't.

Thus the picture is far more complex than some homo-supremacist "gay-guys-good/straight-guys-bad" chauvinism. For example, one cannot discuss the significant caretaking and nurture of heterosexual men without talking about spousal and parental bonds. For those men, in American culture, that's where nurture is most easily manifested and channeled, experienced and enacted. Yet what is demonstrably different about nurture in gay worlds is the way male caring and service translate in our communal practices, institutions, and rituals.

Another clear difference involves the role of public violence in the constituted cultures of gay male worlds. The point is not that most straight men live in a milieu of public peer violence—they don't—but that virtually no gay men do. In the places where we settle in sufficient density, we have built a public sphere markedly free of interpersonal violence among our own. (The situation is more shaded in the case of domestic violence, which we tackle in chapter 2.)

We find similar innovation in our patterns of intimacy. It is no surprise that familial and social expectations channel and constrain heterosexual men's range of permissible intimacies. The affectional and intimate attentions of heterosexual men tend to turn inward, duly vested in the sacred trinity of family, career, and children. It occurs in their relations with women, with other individual men, and with communities of other men. As we will see, the gay male habit tends to more diffuse and expansive forms of intimacy. We extend intimacy in novel forms like care teams and "buddies," with more porous kinds of relationships like fuck buddies, communal homes, and three-way loverships, and innovative community practices, such as the touch and massage networks spawned from Body Electric or the historical development of j/o clubs as a communal solution to AIDS. When one considers heterosexual men's constraints on explorations of sex and sensuality, the poverty of opportunities for the pursuit of bliss and creative play, you see a different set of constraints and conventions from those that operate in gay communities. The same is true of gender roles, where it seems self-evident that the *paterfamilias* is more apt to anchor gender expectations than to trouble them. So go the differences, on down the line.

The focus here is less on innate, essential, *individual* differences than on remarkable cultural, *collective* patterns and practices found in the interlocking male worlds, so easily—and wrongly—labeled "the gay community." Obviously, any reckoning must include enormous variance and diversity. As one scholar put it: "Assertions about complex societies must necessarily be statistical distributions, not exceptionless pronouncements. However . . . it seems necessary to stress that there *are* evaluative norms and statistical ones in urban gay communities."[1] Sociologist Gilbert Herdt writes of "a distinctive system of rules, norms, and attitudes and, yes, beliefs from which the culture of gay men is made."[2]

As Australian sociologist Gary Dowsett has written of the gay world of Adelaide, Australia, such enclaves are far better described as a "tartan rug," a complex patchwork shaded with different colors and hues, intersecting stripes, as interwoven as they are distinct. They are not all white, all pumped, all employed, and all in the same Castro zip code. But as we gaze deeper into this rich male mandala, read the studies, sift the weight of factual evidence accumulating in sociology, criminology, anthropology, public health and epidemiology, hear men's stories and dreams, hang out in the watering holes and the Lofts of the world, one cannot help but be struck by the variety of uncommon practices in the lives of these men.

If gay men were simply finding new ways to be with *each other,* it would hold some descriptive sociological interest, like a treatise on Mennonite or Hopi Indian customs. But the pages ahead suggest a deeper story in several ways, for upon examination it becomes clear that the breadth and scope of gay male social innovations have no clear parallel in contemporary culture. To put this into relief, imagine that another group of men, say a previously little-known order of devout monks, has been discovered living scattered among the populace in our major cities and countryside. Social scientists document that these brothers are characterized by a virtual absence of public violence, high levels of service and volunteerism, and novel forms of caretaking with strangers and each other. Researchers further note that they manifest an uncommon amity across gender lines, enjoy distinctive rituals of bliss, worship, spectacle, and public play. Their patterns of friendships are distinctly powerful, with wide-ranging networks of intimate and intertwined social relations, whose members often live in closely woven networks of intentional communities.

If such a hypothetical band were indeed found, its discovery would arouse great excitement. The brotherhood and its members would be lauded, lionized, if not canonized. They would be hailed as role models. The President might cite them in his State of the Union address; the Pope would praise them as moral exemplars. Before you know it, *Time* magazine would put them on its cover and they would be trooping onto *Oprah* for their fifteen minutes of media spotlight.

Yet although every one of those attributes has been well documented among varied communities of gay men, no such attention has materialized. We've gotten no calls from *Time,* no invites to the White House, not a peep from the Vatican. Not even a message from our pal Oprah. The wider culture seems to have missed the story that these homosocial laboratories are brewing a set of values experiments without modern precedent.

Objectively, we are innovating in areas of male care and nurture, altruism and service, brotherhood and peacefulness. We are crafting powerful changes around bliss and ecstasy; gender roles and sexuality; intimacy, friendship, and communalism. Yet because it is gay men who are both the innovators and subjects in these experiments, their dimensions have gone largely unremarked, their meaning virtually unseen. We have paid little heed to the most interesting implications of it all.

The metaphor of the monks is closer to truth than it might first appear, for one would have to examine highly determined male cultures—religious orders, intentional spiritual brotherhoods, fraternal organizations, places where rules and codes are formalized and enforced—in order to observe such similar male patterns. These habits, customs, and practices in our communities, this gay culture of male care, pacifism, intimacy, and service, recall a range of spiritual teachings. Yet in gay neighborhoods from San Diego to San Antonio to Seattle, one sees these habits arising natively as everyday social practice, the indigenous manifestations of chosen social norms.

It would be easy, and wrong, to read this as a smug brief for gay men's superiority. Instead, this book attempts a more nuanced set of claims. First, that the lives that many gay men have been building do indeed hold demonstrable, culture-changing implications both for ourselves and for the larger society. Second, that we have long overlooked them in part because the accustomed stories offered to, told among, and accepted by gay men dangerously obscure central truths about the values evolution we are engaged in. Third, that viewed together, these queer cultural experiments can best be understood as a new, evolving public ethic. They are complex and contested, they do not happen everywhere nor uniformly, and not all of us are included in them. But throughout, they have a rich ethical basis in thought and theory, in action and relation. At its core, we are witnessing the birth of a new set of male possibilities, outlined in lavender.

The fourth implication may be, to some, the most provocative of all. Far from describing some latter-day Sodom, a society of sluts and sybarites, many of the customs of gay enclave cultures echo traditions of Judeo-Christian brotherhoods and intentional communities. Stroll down Eighth Avenue, La Cienega Boulevard, or Halstead Street, and you can just hear echoes of utopian philosophic traditions of *caritas* and beloved community. Wipe your eyes in the sweaty and smiling crowd at 2:00 A.M. at New York's Roxy or South Beach's 1771 or Los Angeles's Factory, and you may well feel you've stumbled into a postmodern rendering of Whitman's "dear love of comrades." One might almost imagine that we were a society of friends, if only we knew it.

Queer-inspired practices, from Radical Faerie gatherings to AIDS volunteer buddy teams, shimmer with notions of communal caretaking and altruism. At their best, they recall nothing so much as New Testament teachings of *agape* and *caritas,* male embodiments of service and nurture, nonviolence and gender peace, brotherhood and friendship, all spiced with equal dollops of sexuality and spectacle. Only in this case, the apostles are wearing Calvins or Abercrombie and Fitch . . . and sometimes not even that. Yet look at the soul beneath the skin, and you see we are rewriting the defaults of what a culture of men can be with and for each other.

The time has come to note the experiments of heart and habit now arising in gay worlds, to discern what they mean for gay men ourselves and for the shared world culture. Because our cultural practices don't just differ from those of the dominant society, they shape them. America is a synthetic culture, with a long history of cultural borrowing. In that light, this people—public, self-identified gay men, gathered in communities—are just a few short decades off the boat. But ours is an odd niche, for we are emigrants and immigrants both, all without ever having left our own shores. Perhaps we are more accurately understood not as immigrants at all, but as a recently emerging indigenous American culture. We are still in the process of becoming, the ink still wet on our ways and practices. But we have already proven ourselves a prolific source of societal change.

It turns out that the T-shirt was right: We're not in Kansas anymore. And because we're not, neither is Kansas. Many aspects of gay male values—social, moral, communal, and sexual—powerfully challenge those in the dominant culture. As we see norms and practices born in West Hollywood and Chelsea take root in Wyoming and Chattanooga, we are already shifting deeply held practices of majority culture. They open a larger question: Do these practices offer any pragmatic hope? In a culture where male violence is endemic and male nurturance and caregiving contested; where gender relations roil with confusion and distrust; where faith in community wanes and we struggle to support volunteerism and service; where one marriage in two ends in divorce; where isolation crowds out intimacy and the pursuit of pleasure arouses suspicion—are there lessons to be gleaned here? Abundant data suggests that gay men's communities are inventing a new mode of male. Can our nation find gifts here, a cultural patrimony for our shared life as a people? Might not these cultural innovations hold potential to address some of the best—or redress some of the worst—of what daunts contemporary America? The experiments of these men may catalyze wider change in the broader American family. Who stands to gain, and how, if they do?

Philosopher Michel Foucault once spoke of gay social worlds as "unique historic opportunities for an elaboration of personal and ethical creativity analogous to that practiced by certain moral athletes in classical antiquity. Only now such creativity need not be restricted to a social elite or a single, privileged gender, but could become the common property of an entire subculture."[3] Here, on homo home turf, it has. Here we get to write our own codes of conduct, codes that are themselves being invented through the rich social experiments we undertake. Together such codes compose, proclaim, and celebrate, then transmit and enact, a newly chosen social ethics.

Such is the world one enters at The Loft. This book is an open invitation to step beyond the looking glass. It is written for every mother who has always sensed something special about her gay son; for every straight woman who has shared late-night secrets with a man she will never sleep with; for every single heterosexual guy who has envied our getting so much sex; for every teenager who has ever danced at our clubs because she won't get hassled; for every husband frustrated that his wife seems to speak some foreign language; for every woman who's asked why all the cute guys are gay; for every tourist who has walked our streets and found herself agape; for every straight couple who has ever laughed at drag; for every grandmother who shares a special bond with her unmarried grandson; for every frat brother who calls up his gay college pal late at night when he really needs to talk; for every neighbor who wonders what those guys do when we leave the house all dressed up at 1:00 A.M.; and, most of all, for all the men like us, who are engaged in something so big we may not have realized it. For all of us who have noticed a different kind of man in our midst, step through the mirror. Welcome to Planet Gay.

Chaos erupts in Los Angeles after the Lakers win the N.B.A. championship. Mayhem follows the Puerto Rican Day parade in Manhattan. All hell breaks loose in the aftermath of a European soccer match in Belgium.
    —*The New York Times*, June 21, 2000

In a menacing gauntlet, 59 women were attacked, sexually assaulted, groped, stripped, or fondled. . . . 29 men were arrested. . . . 17 more are being sought.
    —*The New York Times*, description of Puerto Rican Day parade, 2000

At Gay Pride 2000 there were no arrests for violent crime, assaults or physical injury.
    —Sergeant Andrew McKinnis, New York Police Department, Office of
      Public Information

Vanessa Ferro is a seventeen-year veteran of the New York Police Department, and wears its sergeant stripes proudly on her lapel. Pugnacious, street-smart, and 100 percent Brooklyn Italian, Ferro has learned a thing or two after almost two decades in uniform. "Look, every Friday and Saturday night for years, every bar here in the Village and in Chelsea is packed. All that booze, all those guys, all the hormones and sexual tension, you'd expect to see a lot of fights. But you know what? It's funny, you don't."

It is an open secret known to every cop who walks a beat in America. In the roiling life of the streets, the level of violence committed by gay men is astonishingly low. One would be hard-pressed to name another male culture in America—one, that is, outside formal structures of religious orders or intentional communities—whose public realm is so notably free of assault and aggressive violence among peers. If there's one thing most gay men instinctively know about the world we have constructed with each other, it is that here we are uncommonly safe from public attacks perpetrated by other gay men. Simply put, no other province of American maledom—not sports teams or fraternities, not all male colleges, certainly not the armed forces—is as pacific in public as ours.

All by itself, the low incidence of violence in the public cultures of men might seem remarkable. Yet it goes almost completely unremarked. The conspicuous absence of public violence among gay men seems not to have made it onto the radar screens of scholarly inquiry or into popular debate. One might expect those whose business it is to register such things, criminologists and sociologists, to have chronicled this. Yet the scholarly literature shows almost no systematic study of this area.

This simple daily truth, felt deep in the bones of gay men, has somehow not registered in the common cultural mind. Oddly enough, America has a vast peaceable kingdom in its midst, yet has scarcely noticed.

Actually, one group *has* noticed: the cops. These front-line workers see just who they are busting, who and where the rowdies are, who makes trouble and who doesn't. Look at where gay men gather, compare police calls to gay clubs and straight events, examine arrest records of mass gatherings, and some stunning patterns begin to emerge. In New York, the Sixth and Tenth precincts cover some of the queerest blocks in town. The former takes in the Village, running from Houston Street to 14th Street, all the way east to Broadway; the latter includes Chelsea. The Sixth covers seven-eighths of a square mile in the nation's most populous city. It boasts the highest concentration of licensed liquor premises—both gay and straight—of any precinct in the state, and by extension, of almost any place in America. That dense mix makes it an ideal laboratory in which to sample how violence patterns differ across sexuality lines.

For the last ten years, NYPD Sergeant Tim Sikorski has done just that. Like most urban cops, his business is mayhem, violence, and the forms they take on the streets of the nation's largest metropolis. As the sixth precinct's "cabaret officer," he covers the late-night streets. Sikorski tracks what happens in the boîtes and bars, the clubs and cabarets, the discos, watering holes, restaurants, pubs, (sex) clubs, and after-hours dives. What he knows would not be accepted in academic journals. He has made no formal study. But the evidence lies in a tattered green logbook on a dusty shelf. There is a book like it sitting on the shelf of every precinct in every gay neighborhood, and they tell pretty much the same story.

Sikorski's logbook goes back years, and it lists each time police were called to a watering hole. There, neat blue pen scratches chronicle the names of the establishments and the nature of each complaint. Compare just the last three years, all police calls to gay and straight venues, and which calls involved assault and mayhem. Personal altercations, fights, assaults, knife and gun attacks were counted. Excluded were minor possession arrests, infractions by the establishments themselves, or other nonviolent offenses. Attacks committed *by* gay patrons were counted; attacks perpetrated *upon* gay patrons (gay bashing by outsiders) were excluded. If anything, this technique biases the sample by undercounting straight male attacks.

Even so, the data speak eloquently. In 2000, thirty-seven calls to clubs were recorded, of which twelve involved violence. Eleven of those were straight, one gay. In 1999, of thirty-six violent calls, thirty-three were straight, three gay. In 1998, of eight violence calls, two were by gay men. Sikorski shrugs: "In my ten years here, we get very few gay bars causing problems for us. Usually, if anything, it is spilling out of domestic disputes, but it is far less common for it to turn into a fistfight."

Police Calls for Assaults at Drinking Venues—Greenwich Village

Year	All Assault Calls	Straight	Gay
2000	12	11	1
1999	36	33	3
1998	8	6	2
Total:	56	50	6

Another New York police sergeant, Edgar Rodriguez, has watched the scene for a dozen years. He puts it bluntly: "I'd rather go to gay clubs as opposed to go to straight clubs. There, you're not concerned that you look at somebody's girlfriend or step on someone's Pumas and get shot for it. At the gay clubs, there's drama once in a blue moon, but it's very, very rare. You almost never have any problems with these clubs." It is a truth known to most beat cops around the country—certainly those whose beats include a significant slice of gay world.

A few cops' hunches do not necessarily a pattern make. It is instructive to examine whether the trend holds elsewhere. To make a valid comparison between public violence in social venues, it helps to have concentrated neighborhoods with enough straight and gay clubs so the sample will include even infrequent occurrences. Chicago's Boystown is just such an area, where the police records tell the same story. Officer Kathy Dore has been a Chicago cop for thirty years, the last eighteen in Boystown, the Windy City's gay district. "We see a lot more trouble in straight bars than gay, for sure." Again, hard numbers bear out what three decades of police work have shown her. The Twenty-third police district runs from the north end of Fullerton to the south end of Lawrence, from Lake Michigan to the east side of Clark Street, neatly taking in Boystown. Officer Jorge Lopez provided police data taken from gay and straight nightspots across the Twenty-third. The sample covered exactly the same one-year time frame, and an equal number of gay and straight nightspots, demographically matched according to age of clientele and size, popularity, and hours of business. All reported incidents of assault and battery, with and without weapons, were counted; again, domestic disputes were not. In that year, the straight clubs had a combined forty-six events; the gay bars had twenty-four, barely half as many. Three of the straight premises reported a case of an aggravated assault (using a weapon); only one gay venue did. Lopez muses: "You know, that place is really an exception. Gay guys normally don't react this way. Cops basically know the gay community is very much law abiding." (Interestingly, if that "exception" is taken out, the district's gay clubs together reported only a total of thirteen events, the same number that occurred at one of the straight venues, all by itself.)

Police Calls for Assaults & Batteries—Boystown
(23rd Police District)

Venue	Assaults	Batteries	Clubs Reporting Aggravated Battery	Total Events
Gay (10)	1	23	1	25
Straight (10)	6	39	3	48

(Sampling period: Oct. 10, 1999–Oct. 10, 2000)

Lopez himself used to cover a beat in the thirtieth sector, the predominantly gay area between Addison and Fullerton. "That sector is slow, virtually no robberies, no homicides. It has the reputation as more of a 'friendly officer' walk-by type of thing. You even get cops who ask to transfer to the other sectors because they are faster beats, more police work to do." It is, in other words, exactly the kind of low-crime quarter that all the get-tough, quality-of-life policing experts across America are spending hundreds of millions of dollars trying to create.

In city after city, the same striking pattern emerges. In Denver, police department records show the same disparate levels of public violence by gay men. Again, the sample covers the same time (1997 to 2000); bars were selected in the same area (Broadway) and matched by demographic similarity. Once again, police were called for almost twice as many assault and fighting complaints in the straight clubs as in the gay ones. The number of armed assaults was almost three times larger.[1]

Fighting and Assault Calls—Sampled Denver Bars, 1997–2000

	Straight Establishments		Gay Establishments	
	Assault/ Fight Events	With Weapons	Assault/ Fight Events	With Weapons
1997	4	1	2	0
1998	13	4	5	0
1999	14	2	6	2
2000	8	1	9	1
Total:	39	8	22	3

Such peaceful practices are not limited to central gay neighborhoods. Tulsa, Oklahoma, is not usually on anyone's short list for gay meccas. Smack downtown, on 17th and Main, The New Age Renegade is a bustling gay bar. It was there, on one June Saturday night, that a local patrolman found himself summoned to file an insurance report on a fender bender in the parking lot. Soon, he fell into conversation with several patrons and a local drag queen. What, they asked, does he see from his vantage point? "Truth is," he reflected, "we almost never get calls for violent situations at these bars. The straight places—that's usually where guys are fighting. Things get out of hand and we get called in." Gay bar owners know that when the men in blue show up at their door—assuming it's not uniform night, of course—it's far more likely to stem from homophobic assault directed *at* their patrons than from an assault committed *by* their patrons.

In no other community does such a large proportion of men congregate every Friday and Saturday (not to mention Sunday, Thursday, and Wednesday), get so well lubricated with alcohol, and hang out in rooms awash in testosterone and muscles—yet manage not to habitually injure their peers. By the codes of maledom, such men-only gatherings, their ambiance charged with competitive libido, should be a surefire recipe for rowdiness. Yet in the queer male version of the recipe, the missing ingredient is mayhem.

Ever notice how when you see drinks being served in plastic cups, ten to one you're in a straight bar? The owners know to serve on tap, not bottles, because put a bunch of drunk straight guys together with sharp glass objects, one guy gets smashed and some other guy gets slashed. It's only in gay bars they trust us enough to serve drinks in glasses and beer in bottles.
—Craig W, Los Angeles

The same truth echoes from an entirely different category of informants. These observers bring great expertise in our bar violence patterns, because they watch them unfold every night from behind the row of beer taps and maraschino cherries. They are the all-seeing, long-suffering eyewitnesses, bartenders like Bob Nelson. Bob is a happily heterosexual man who tended bar at several straight bars in central Florida for the better part of a dozen years. "Well, maybe not the better part"—he grins wearily—"but the longer part, for sure." His gay brother, Michael, recalls several conversations they had on the subject. "When I told Bob I'd never seen a brawl in a gay bar, he laughed. He said he couldn't count the number of fights he had witnessed, dodged, joined, or broken up. For him, it was a rare weekend when there *wasn't* a brawl. Fighting was all in an evening's work. Bob couldn't believe it when I explained that I had stood in gay bars for years and never seen a fight, let alone been in one. In his world, that is unthinkable."

The Roxy has for years been one of Manhattan's premier dance venues. On Friday nights it serves a young, straight, bridge-and-tunnel crowd, and on Saturday nights the gay men descend. One of club's managers says: "It couldn't be more different. The bouncers know to be very aggressive on Fridays, intimidating—you've got to set rules. Saturday nights, there's not the same energy. You can treat the crowd totally differently, because the crowd acts totally different. Everybody can relax."

I see similar patterns in speaking engagements before rooms of gay men in cities and towns around the nation. Often audiences range from thirty to 150 men, and more than 2,400 men have attended such events. The presentation almost always includes a show of hands: "How many of you have ever been in a fight at a gay bar?" "How many of you have been publicly assaulted by a gay man?" The results are the same whether the audience is in California, Indiana, or rural Maine. Rarely are more than two hands raised in the room of fifty, eighty, one hundred men.

Clearly this is not a random sample. But it holds more power than might at first appear. This comprises what's known as a longitudinal sample, because it represents hundreds of men's experiences *over time*. These are rooms of men who have traditionally gathered, socialized, and met in bars, in some cases more than once a week, some of them for decades. After all, bars remain among the most accessible and popular gay social institutions. A room of eighty gay men likely represents several hundred thousand hours of participant observation at a minimum, sampled in different times, venues, and locales. Now fights, brawls, and assaults tend to be dramatic events, not easily forgotten. So it is all the more striking that in room after room, these men recall witnessing so remarkably few episodes of public violence. Again, it suggests the pattern is quite well established, a durable norm in the cultures gay men have built as our own. It is, in short, a piece of our public ethics.

Try this experiment the next time you are with a group of gay men. Ask five gay and five straight male friends about their experience. I expect you'll hear what I hear in these rooms. Most often, gay men's own lived experience confirms what cops, bartenders, desk officers, and hospital emergency room nurses know. For whatever reason, the social contract on these streets has given rise to a culture of men who don't take their business outside and whose differences don't escalate into public brawls, shoving matches, or bar fights.

MASS GATHERINGS, HOLD THE MAYHEM

The same intriguing pattern we see in our nightspots applies more widely. Fights, as the old saying goes, don't break out at the opera. They also almost never erupt at large public gay gatherings: dances, pride parades, rallies, campgrounds, vacation communities, or marches. The pattern emerges from an entirely different set of law enforcement statistics. Hundreds of cities and towns now have gay pride events, often associated with festivals, dances, and parties, often including tens or even hundreds of thousands of gay men. Again, no academic or criminological source has systematically examined the police records of our mass gatherings. But walk into the precincts and examine the logbooks, and you see exactly the same pattern.

Police Officer Bredet Williams works as a community affairs officer in the Third District in Washington, D.C. Before moving to D.C., Williams walked a beat in West Hollywood, then the epicenter of the Los Angeles gay male world. In both places, the statistics for assault and violent crime among gay men are remarkably similar. In Washington, D.C., a city of large mass gatherings, Williams compared arrest statistics for the largest public events held over the same time period. In calendar year 2000, the D.C. Caribbean Festival attracted 25,000 partiers, with one assault arrest. Adams Morgan Day, a primarily Latino cultural event, drew some 50,000 attendees, with two assault arrests. Those two events *combined* equal the size of that year's D.C. Gay Pride, where there were no arrests among an estimated 75,000 attendees. The two largest mass gatherings in Washington that year were the Fourth of July, which numbered half a million, and the Gay Millennium March, which drew 750,000 attendees—50 percent larger. Police statistics show that the Fourth had seven assault arrests, including one felony attack against a police officer; the gay event, stretching over four days, had no such arrests.[2]

Washington, D.C., Public Events, 2000

Event	Date	Attendees	Arrests
Caribbean Festival		25,000	1
Adams Morgan Day		50,000	2
Gay Pride	June	75,000	0
Fourth of July	July	500,000	7
Gay Millennium March	April	750,000	0

The same holds true at the nation's largest gay Mecca celebration, New York City Pride. The police department's own central statistics tell the tale, says Sergeant Andy McKinnis in the NYPD Office of Public Information. "Gay Pride 2000 had no violent-crime arrests reported, no arrests for assaults or physical injury. For the most part, it was peaceful." Arrest data for the last several years confirm the pattern, showing no arrests for violence or assault behavior among the several hundred thousand parade participants. The 2000 record is especially noteworthy when compared with another large New York festival which occurred only one month before Pride, Puerto Rican Day. In that crowd, fifty-nine women were sexually attacked—surrounded, groped, some even stripped and assaulted, all in public. The ensuing police investigations identified more than forty individual male assailants. The point is not that all the straight parades turn ugly—the vast majority don't. It is rather that there is one parade that never does: the one where the guys are parading in jockstraps and sequins.

"You want proof? Just ask any New York cop," says NYPD Sergeant Rodriguez. "They traditionally say Gay Pride is one of the more enjoyable events they attend. Cops will tell you they love doing it. Some cops will do anything to not work certain parades in the city but they are happy to work Gay Pride. Sometimes you get an initial homophobic response, sure. But once they've done it, they realize it's a safe day." Sikorski agrees. "At Pride, it is very, very rare to get violent incidents. Since 1990, there has been basically nothing. It's a dream compared to other parades and festivals." His counterpart in the Tenth Precinct, which covers Chelsea, is Officer Duffy. "In the nine years I've been here, there may have been maybe one or two incidents. Usually, Gay Pride is a very calm day, very few arrests. Other parades give problems to the [police] department, but this is definitely not one of them. The people walking, marching in it, it's usually a very peaceable crowd."

In Boston, roster captains in charge of the precinct duty schedules know that, given the choice of signing on for St. Pat's day or Gay Pride parade, there's no contest. "They call it easy money," says a cop with eighteen years seniority policing all manner of public gatherings on Boston's streets. "St. Patrick's Day is a mess. You have to deal with the drunks, it escalates. It gets hairy. Gay day is all about having fun, so it's a parade they like to work. Officers know they won't have to do a lot of work in terms of law enforcement. There are not a lot of issues around the gay people themselves. You don't have to grow eyes behind your head, which is way it different than some other parades." The pattern holds true in Chicago's Twenty-third District, says Officer Lopez. "They post sign-up lists for motorcycle duty on Gay Pride. They fill up right away, in order of seniority. People want to work that day." As a patrol officer in Atlanta put it, "Even a rookie knows you won't get your nose busted with these guys. The gay parade, there's no stress involved, you don't have to worry about negative confrontations. The crowd's interacting with the cops in a nice way. And if the cop's good-looking"—he smiles—"in an extremely warm and nice way." In city after city, it's the same picture. Stack up Gay Pride parades next to St. Patrick's Day marches, Gay Games next to soccer matches, and it is hard to escape the conclusion that the gay male social contract places a different valence on violence.

As far back as the 1980s, this trend was remarked upon in municipal circles. Dr. Len Hirsch, a political scientist now at the Smithsonian, recalls a meeting of the National Conference of Mayors in Tampa many years ago. "One of the city executives there actually counseled their counterparts that gay neighborhoods were good for cities, because he had noticed those areas require lower law enforcement resources." The truth we see reflected in newspaper reports and police testimony is echoed in what scholarly literature does exist on gay criminality. A quick search of sociological and criminology databases under gay violence will unearth some 140 citations. Of those, all but about five concern domestic violence and hate crimes committed *against* gay people. It seems that only one study has directly compared patterns of violent criminality in gay and straight men. Published in 1990, "Sex, Sexual Orientation and Criminal and Violent Behavior" appeared in the psychology journal *Personality & Individual Differences.* Sampling 470 men and women, the authors examined links between involvement in violent crime, scores on aggression, and sexual orientation. In their words: "Among males, heterosexuals were more criminal and violent than homosexuals . . . scores revealed several significant relationships with sexual orientation."[3]

It seems odd that we haven't read these statistics before. While such arrest records are freely available as public information, nobody has much looked at them. There seem to be no published comparative study of mass gathering events, and no criminologists seem to have documented this rarity of public violence in among gay men. Repeated inquiries among criminologists and law enforcement agencies—local, state, and federal—reveal that they do not collect data in a way that permit systemic comparisons of assault behavior across sexuality lines. It remains an invisible truth about our lives, known only in our bones.

We're so inured to the sight of straight men responding violently to the mere idea of another man finding them attractive that we don't pause to consider how bizarre this reaction is.
   —Michael Lewis, in *Speaking Out*

To get a feel for how different it is, it is an interesting exercise to scan national press reportage on the topic. The national media over the past years have carried stories about two Laramie men who left Matthew Shepard to die on a Wyoming fence; the assailant who beat James Zappalorti to death on a lonely Staten Island beach; the two God-fearing Alabamans who took Billy Jack Gaither to a remote forest in Coosa County, Alabama, beat him to death with ax handles, and burned his body on a pile of tires; the hunter who stalked and gunned down a lesbian hiking with her mate on an Appalachian trail; the gang of several men who lured Julio Rivera into an alley in Queens and killed him with a claw hammer; the Vietnam veteran who was so ashamed that his last name was "Gay" that he opened fire in a Roanoke bar, killing Danny Lee Overstreet and wounding six others; the two Nebraska men who shot Brandon Teena to death in a weedy field; the New York man who shot and killed his nineteen-year-old stepson, Steen Keith Fenrich, for being gay, and then wrote "Gay Nigger #1" on the boy's decapitated skull; the two teenagers in Fairmont, West Virginia, who stomped Arthur Warren to death, then drove over him repeatedly in an effort to mask the crime; the Oregon man who murdered a lesbian couple in their pickup truck; the two young men in Happy Valley, California, who entered the home of a middle-aged gay couple who had befriended them and killed the middle-aged men in their bed; the gang of Idaho men arrested by the FBI as they attempted to blow up a Seattle gay bar with pipe bombs; the two Oregon men who firebombed a Portland home, burning to death the young gay man who lived there; the three men in Tyler, Texas, who took twenty-three-year-old Nicholas West to a remote gravel pit and pumped nine fatal gunshots into him. The ghastly chronicle goes on and on. Yet in the same sampling period, the same national database contains no article about an event where a gay man, whether singly or in a pack, murdered a heterosexual for being that way.

So where are the marauding gay teens assaulting straight guys over their orientation? Among the male population at large, young men commit the huge majority of bias and gang violence. If you wanted to locate gay assault behavior, you would examine the patterns of younger gay men. Yet even among this most violence-prone age group of males, gay men stand out. Several studies show that more than three-quarters of gay college-age students have experienced verbal threats and harassment, and a quarter have been physically attacked for being gay.[4] Yet even under that provocation, we do not read of gay teens pummeling heterosexual peers senseless. When was the last time you heard about a vengeful roaming pansy band ambushing a seventeen-year-old jock and his cheerleader date on their way to the prom? The example's very implausibility only punctuates the point. We are not the men who attack strangers for being what they are. We seem not to attack them at all, no matter whose team they play on.

By itself, the rarity of gay men's aggressive behavior stands out as an anomaly among crime statistics. But scholars of violent criminality note two other factors that make it all the more so. The first is that we are, after all, communities of males. If there is one truism in criminology, it is that males are far more likely to engage in violent crime. One study went so far as to label being male a "universal correlate" of crime.[5] Such research implies that the more men, the more violence. If anything, in all-male milieus like gay bars, dances, or clubs, one might expect the crowd to be *more* likely to solve matters with their fists. That makes it all the more notable that we don't.

The second finding comes from psychology, where it is well established that children in families with physical abuse and violent behavior are more likely to grow up to engage in violent behavior. A study in the *Archives of Sexual Behavior* studied violent physical abuse, finding that "gay males were found to have suffered physical abuse at the hands of their fathers during adolescence," often "related to a history of childhood femininity, [and] to having poor relationships with fathers."[6] The researcher suggested that effeminate boys and teens are more likely to be abused by fathers who are anxious their boys are not "man enough."

Chuck had one of those fathers. Seeing him at thirty-seven today, Chuck seems the very model of the tough Italian guys who saunter down the streets of his native Brooklyn. Burly, muscled, and tough, sporting a two-day growth of beard, he is every inch the opposite of a girly man. It is hard to imagine he would ever get picked on. But he did. "My dad would wake us up at 5:00 A.M. in winter and make us do pushups outside. He would throw me down in the mud, and make my older brothers fight me till I bled. He kept a horsewhip hanging above his place at the dinner table and he used it on us. It was all about toughening me up, making me 'more of a man.'" If, as the study claims, a higher portion of gay men are like Chuck—that is, more apt to have had such relationships with toughen-'em-up dads—it predicts that a roomful of such guys would, if anything, be *more* likely to resort to public violent behavior as adults. That is because in most men, violence begets violence. Violence experts report that boys raised with violence tend to grow into violent men. Yet in gay lives, this truism about male violence doesn't seem to apply in the same way. Combining these two findings—gathering in male milieus with potentially higher fractions of men whose family histories might make them *more* violent—should suggest huge levels of violence. That it is actually far lower underlines how different a path has been blazed in the public square of gay America.

By themselves, bar assaults, Pride Day arrests, police testimonials, precinct records, academic journals, psychological measures, do not make an ironclad case. But weigh the evidence, listen to those who know, and you see a clear pattern. The mayhem quotient of gay bars—

like gay parades, gay neighborhoods, gay lives—stands out simply because it looks so markedly different from the larger culture of men. What is striking is not that so many straight men live in a milieu of public peer violence—they don't. It is that virtually no gay men do.

Now lest some aggrieved reader swagger over to punch out the author, a disclaimer is necessary. What about domestic violence? Isn't that a tremendous problem in the gay world? Most of us have heard and read about it. Doesn't that explode any theory of a more peaceable gay kingdom? To answer that requires us to take a closer look at what we do know. The consensus in gay domestic violence circles echoes in the words of Jeff Montgomery, executive director of the Triangle Foundation, the primary gay anti-violence agency in Detroit: "What literature we do have says that the incidence of domestic violence in gay community is not significantly different than in the straight community." Patrick Letellier, considered one of the nation's founding authorities on domestic violence among gay men and the co-author of a seminal book on the subject,[7] agrees. "Statistically, we think rates of domestic violence rates among gay and straight couples look far more alike than they look different." Almost in parentheses, he adds: "I don't think that gay men kill their partners nearly as often as straight men. We just don't see the astronomical homicide rates you see in heterosexual domestic violence. I see dramatic differences there." Rachel Baum, the policy analyst at the National Coalition of Anti-Violence Projects, concurs: "What data I have seen don't suggest there's much difference." Data cited by Baum, Letellier, Montgomery, and other experts suggest that rates of gay domestic violence largely parallel those of straight relationships.[8] Even *The New York Times* paints a picture of parity. "Researchers believe abuse is as prevalent among gay or lesbian couples as among heterosexual ones."[9] Indeed, further research may prove that domestic violence is the area where gay male patterns most closely resemble normative heterosexual male patterns.

Yet behind this seeming similarity may lie a nuance. While aggregated intimate violence rates for gay people don't differ much from heterosexuals, one 1997 study looked at it more closely. When the researchers took gender into account, they found "lesbians reported an overall perpetration rate of 38% compared to 21.8% for gay men." They conclude that "lesbians were more likely to be classified as victims and perpetrators of violence than gay men."[10] This is only one paper, but if this suggestive finding should be confirmed, it could imply that gay men do have lower domestic violence rates than their straight brothers. Some cops think they have noticed just such a difference. "When I was out on the street, I only responded to two gay domestic violence incidents in an entire year of patrolling," says an officer in Chicago. In Boystown, the Twenty-third District's designated domestic violence officer has commented on the difference to fellow officers. "Gay domestic violence incidents seem very low to me, and I think the other cops recognize it."

As the experts and studies make clear, and beat cops well know, the point is not that queer men are immune from all peer violence. Gay domestic violence is well documented, with tragic consequences for some percentage of gay men. Any domestic violence is too much, and for those involved, the human cost is as real and hard as a clenched fist. Still, two facts ring with absolute clarity. First, that it is hard to make the case that our levels are any higher, and they may in fact be lower. Second, and more important, when one expands the analytic lens to include the *full* range of violent assault behaviors—not just domestic violence but public violence, street violence, and bias violence—one conclusion emerges clearly. We have created one of the most peaceable populations of males on the planet. Why, do you suppose, would we do that?

"*We are a gentle, angry people.*"
  —Holly Near

There's a scary thought. What if Holly Near was right? In fact, a number of academic analysts have offered a number of interesting theories on that question of "why?" One provocative school of thought proposes that gay men actually may be different at our core. That body of natural and social science findings leaves many unanswered, but interesting, questions. To put them in context, some background is helpful.

For more than twenty years now, thinkers in academic circles have squared off in two largely opposing camps. On the one hand, the "essentialists" claim that there is such a thing as gay folks and see evidence that we may be deeply, intrinsically different. Among these, some would count Dr. Simon LeVay's research on the "gay brain" (to be precise, the gay interstitial nucleus of the hypothalamus, which to brain scientists goes by the catchy name of INAH3).[11] In that tradition, one finds Dr. Dean Hamer's research at the National Institutes of Health on the gay gene,[12] brain anatomy work from Allen and Gorski at UCLA suggesting that a key cortical connecting nerve bundle, the *anterior commissure*, is physically different in gay men;[13] auditory studies that show gay men process sound differently;[14] studies that show differences in brain processing locations in gay and straight men;[15] twin studies that show being gay occurs more than twice as often among identical as fraternal twins, who are in turn twice as likely to have a gay sibling as are gay men with adoptive siblings.[16] One can find a study suggesting that gay men's fingerprints show a different pattern of fingerprint ridges from straight guys'[17] (I think it's all about moisturizer, myself). A recent study found seemingly systematic differences in the ratio of index finger length among gay people, and my all-time favorite finding was that a higher proportion of gay men are more likely to have the left testicle hang lower than an equal number of straight guys. (This, of course, requires that one count frequently and diligently. You can try this at home.) To greater or lesser degree, all of these studies share a common view that there are subtle differences in our essential makeup and attributes.

Arguing against them are the social constructionists. They argue that the closer you look at the modern Western notion of gay, the more it evaporates. They point out that there really is not any one such thing as gay people, that the forms of expression that same-sex attraction takes are immensely changeable, malleable, and immensely varied across cultures and time. They remind us that our notions of gay and homosexual—even of gender itself—are best viewed as socially constructed boxes. They are the product of a modern, industrialized, white, first-world perspective. In this view, "gay" says far more about what's in the brains of the classifiers than anything about the brains of the classified. For decades now, these two factions have faced off, like homo Hatfields and McCoys. Each seems to explain things the other can't, and together they make up complementary poles of our understanding of this thing called Queer.

With that as background, how best do we interpret the set of studies on gay male aggression? One study, summarized in a paper by Blanchard, Sanders, and Langevin, found that adult male homosexuals scored significantly lower on a scale of violence than male heterosexuals did.[18] Other investigators have found that gay men report less violence in interpersonal relationships than do their straight counterparts.[19] Another study compared a range of personality variables in gay and straight men. While the authors found none of the differences they predicted, they did report an unforeseen—and statistically significant—fact: "The heterosexual group was significantly more competitive both physically and interpersonally."[20] Another typical paper, "Measuring Physical Aggressiveness in Heterosexual, Homosexual, and Transsexual Males," defined aggressiveness as "a generalized disposition to engage in physically combative or competitive interactions with male peers." The authors created a physical aggressiveness measure, taking into account things like boyhood athletic interest and proficiency, fighting, and anxiety with male peers. Among their sample of 197 adult males, gay men scored significantly lower than heterosexuals on aggressiveness. The authors suggested these findings in adults might reflect "underlying factors . . . that relate this erotic preference to anomalously low levels of physical aggressiveness in childhood as well."[21]

These scientists in turn cited a growing body of childhood studies that they argue make a provocative case for an essential component to gay gentleness. Several papers show that boys who *later* come to identify as gay *may behave differently as young children*. Clearly, such boys do not grow up in a gay subculture. So why, a decade before they are old enough to offer a fake ID at a gay bar, do they already appear to be playing a different game? UCLA psychologist Richard Green pioneered this area, coining the "Sissy Boy Syndrome" to describe these special boys.[22] In the words of one social scientist who reviewed this literature: "As children and young adolescents, homosexual males recalled having been involved in significantly less rough-and-tumble play and fighting episodes (both self-initiated and in response to provocation by others) than heterosexual males."[23] Such tendencies to step beyond norms of boyhood rough-and-tumble play has been observed, not just in America, but also by anthropologists working in Guatemala, Brazil, and the Philippines.[24] The notion of a network of amiable boys dotted across the world's villages, cross-dressing and playing with dolls while their pals roughhouse—it's all sweetly spooky. It also puts in relief the more accustomed nexus of male violence throughout the world's cultures. Scholars surveyed more than two hundred farming and foraging cultures, and found that in 99.4 percent of them, males were the designated hunters and killers.[25] Male violence—whether in the hunt, in warfare, with women—seems ubiquitous and universal. All of which makes some people wonder what's happening with those village boys. Clearly, in the myriad ways the male roles get constructed in those cultures, some boys and men do the male thing just a bit differently.

In our own culture, another paper, "Juvenile Aggressivity and Sissiness in Homosexual and Heterosexual Males," followed a group of American boys who would later grow up to be gay. It stated: "No prehomosexual Subject had the type of juvenile aggressive encounters that the heterosexual Subjects experienced. It is suggested that male-male peer aggressive competency learned after the juvenile period will not alter homosexual orientation."[26] Translation: All those anxious dads tormenting your sissy teens to make them "real" men can just give it a rest. Turns out we're already really men, just really different. That difference may go far deeper than dear old Dad can imagine.

Findings like these childhood studies have led some thinkers to even more fanciful surmises about gay male aggression patterns. German endocrinologist Gunter Dörner proposed not only that gay men might be biologically a gentler species of male, but even explained one way this might happen. Dörner, in several papers analyzing homosexual birth patterns, posited that more gay men are born in wartime than in peace-time.[27] He suggested that the interaction of stress hormones during pregnancy created, in effect, a self-regulating biological or cultural mechanism. That is, in times of war and stress, the human body and society self-regulates by birthing a higher percentage of peaceable males. It is an intriguing idea, that human cultures might have a built-in species curb on excessive male violence, and we are it. (In a 1995 critical review of this work, a paper titled "Does Peace Prevent Homosexual-ity?", two other German doctors applied a more rigorous analysis to Dörner's thesis and dismissed it: "Our data do not reveal the slightest evidence that wartime stress . . . increases the incidence of homosexual behavior."[28] In an odd afterthought, however, they did conclude that "homosexual men can go on loving peace and getting involved in the peace movement.")

In truth, science doesn't explain why the cops don't end up often at our parties. Whether one views it as an innate disposition or a cultural norm or some combination, we do not yet fully understand the low lev-els of public aggression and mayhem in gay male worlds, nor why we seem to commit so much less public violence. The evidence from sociol-ogy, criminology, anthropology, psychology, biology, and animal behav-iorism suggests it is likely too simplistic to frame these differences as an innate tendency of a gay species. But whether you come down on the side of nature or nurture, say it's bred in the bone, constructed in our cul-tures, or both, a wealth of observed facts and lived testimonials converge with clarity on one inescapable fact. Gay men enjoy one of the least vio-lent male cultures seen in the contemporary world.

So the next time you watch the bears leaning against the wall watch-ing *Queer as Folk* at the local bar, or gaze out over the crowds of shirtless boys dancing their hearts out on the dance floor, think of yourself as a witness at a precious watering hole. These animals before you, all strut-ting and preening and pumped, are among the most peaceable flock of males on God's green earth. Then as you sip, ponder all that implies. Much evidence says that the gay cultures that we enjoy, create, and enact with each other seem to have made progress around one of the gravest, most intransigent problems facing the globe. If the men in gay worlds did nothing differently except work and play peaceably with others, it would merit note. If our shared male norms have succeeded only at drastically reducing the public violence committed by our gender, it would be radical accomplishment enough. After all, the evolution of peaceable mores is the sort of thing for which they award Nobel prizes, found religions, and canonize saints. The fact is, though . . . we didn't stop there.

The next domain of difference is distinct from these pacifist patterns but may be related. Over the last twenty-five years, social scientists have documented a wide range of systematic differences between gay and straight men's habits, practices, and attitudes around tolerance and bias. Many studies over two decades have found that gay men hold more tolerant attitudes and behaviors than other men do. Some focus narrowly on sexual tolerance, no surprise. One study of 4,251 university students found "Individuals with homosexual experiences, compared to those without, tended to be more liberal in their views toward socially deviant sexual behavior in general."[29] A researcher named Lumby found "significant attitudinal differences" between gay and straight groups, with us being "significantly more liberal than heterosexual Subjects regarding the propriety of masturbation, extramarital sexual activities, and the sexual activities of their teenage sisters."[30] Kid sisters? Diane was one of them, although she wasn't even alive when those studies appeared. "When you're from rural Ohio, there aren't a lot of people to talk to about stuff. Dave is my older gay brother. He was always the cooler one. Growing up, he was the only relative I would ever consider talking to about guys and everything." That same study found gay respondents were both consistently more accepting toward sexual behavior in general, and more comfortable about such views, than were their heterosexual counterparts.

Studies also show that sexual conservatism is generally significantly associated with higher social prejudice and more negative attitudes toward gay people, blacks, and women.[31] That anxiety, it seems, isn't all between the ears. A 1999 study, guaranteed to frost the 'phobes, took a group of highly homophobic men and measured their penis circumference when viewing gay porn. Homophobia, they found, "is apparently associated with homosexual arousal that the homophobic individual is either unaware of or denies."[32] Dirty work, but someone's gotta do it.

It's no big shock that we're less judgmental in the sexual realm. But more provocative is the range of studies showing that this tolerant attitude is reflected in a wider social ethic in our lives. Corbett, Troiden, and Dodder directly compared bias and tolerance by measuring attitudes toward various unconventional groups among 150 subjects, gay and straight. Gay men, they found, showed "significantly more tolerant attitudes toward defiantly labeled groups" and were "significantly less likely to place social restrictions on those who opted for unconventional alternatives."[33] Five years later, a study by psychologist C. A. Mallen found that gay men "held less rigid sex-role stereotypes" than straight men did.[34]

A decade later, researchers saw similar tolerant attitudes being reflected in our chosen social patterns. "Attitudes Toward Minorities: A Comparison of Homosexuals and the General Population" surveyed almost one thousand subjects about their attitudes toward groups different from themselves: women, Jews, blacks, recovering alcoholics, gays, even communists. Gay men were "more likely to count some or many friends in all six groups," breaching lines of color, gender, religion, and politics, than was the general population sample. Gay men were also significantly more likely to perceive discrimination against all six groups.[35]

A 1999 study took the question of homo tolerance one interesting step further. Where previous researchers had surveyed homophobia, this one turned the question around, to ask gay men about to their attitudes toward heterosexuals—what the authors termed "heteronegativism." They found gay subjects held fewer negative attitudes about those across the sexual orientation divide, despite having endured more actual negative experiences, than did their heterosexual counterparts.[36] In that same year, Bliss and Harris found that children of homosexual parents were "more mature and tolerant" than the matched heterosexual students in their sample.[37]

If there is a difference in tolerance, it may simply come from having experienced the sting of stigma. Would that not after all make any individual more tolerant? If so, one should find it in other stigmatized groups. Yet there is no real scholarly consensus that stigmatized groups are significantly less likely to hold biased attitudes.[38] Dr. Stuart Oskamp, a nationally respected researcher who has authored a dozen-plus studies on bias, notes that "it is a fair conclusion that other minority, ethnic and social groups are not necessarily more tolerant than the white majority." For example, one 1999 paper surveyed almost two hundred white, African-American, and Latino subjects, ranging in age from eighteen to fifty-six years old, and concluded: "African Americans were significantly more homophobic than White students."[39] Approaching the question from another perspective, if stigma truly begets tolerance, they reasoned, then those who carry a double stigma ought to be more tolerant than those with only one. In 1991, just such a study was conducted, surveying both women and men, African-American and white. Again, researchers found that "less social tolerance of homosexuality exists in the black community," but interestingly, they found the difference *more* pronounced among women. "Analyses of gender, educational achievement, religious preference, and marital status revealed that the racial difference in condemnation of homosexuality was derived almost exclusively from a difference in attitude between black and white females." That is, the African-American women they spoke with (who endure double stigma) actually showed *more* homophobia than did the African-American men in the study.[40] Such studies lend no support to the idea that any greater tolerance in gay male samples derive solely from our having have suffered discrimination.

Any such preliminary hint of increased tolerance among gay male cultures is noteworthy for the same reason that our relative rarity of violence is. It is so different from the aggregate norms of heterosexual men. In the case of bias (specifically anti-gay bias), several dozen studies show that men consistently hold less tolerant attitudes than women do.[41] One study reviewed the literature, including nine different studies, and put it bluntly: "Males have more negative attitudes than females toward homosexuals."[42] Another compared samples from 1986 and 1991 and found "men expressed significantly greater negative attitudes toward homosexuality than did women."[43] The same in 1996, this time with a sample of 377: "Results indicated that males were less tolerant than females of gays" and "suggested that anti-homosexual responses lie primarily within the realm of prejudice."[44] The next year a study surveyed 700 more people and reported: "Females endorsed fewer homophobic attitudes, beliefs, and behaviors than males."[45] The year after that, the *Journal of Sex Research* published a study of 270: "Results indicated that men held more negative attitudes toward homosexuals than did women."[46] This male pattern of what one researcher called "homoprejudice" has been found whether the male subjects were hotel clerks and innkeepers,[47] salespersons,[48] devout Christians,[49] or trained psychoanalysts.[50] And, of course, among whole herds of college undergraduates.[51]

On the subject of tolerance, it is tempting to interpret the levels of tolerance researchers find among gay samples as reflecting spiritual values like those espoused in, say, the Christian gospels. But ironically, research has repeatedly shown that strong Christian religious affiliation is significantly related to being *less* tolerant—at least of us.[52] In the words of one study: "Religiosity was significantly correlated with more biased beliefs about the origins of homophobia, greater affective discomfort around gays, less endorsement of human rights for gays, and greater homophobia."[53] Wrote another: "Subjects with more traditional male role attitudes, a religious fundamentalist orientation, and a parent who had completed fewer years of education were significantly more likely to express homophobic views."[54]

As with the prior evidence on violence, it is important to recognize what these studies do and don't say. They do not imply that gay men lack prejudice. Nobody can credibly claim that gay worlds as now embodied are as multiracial as Benetton ads, a homo Hallmark card free of bias and intolerance. Like any set of communities, we have discrimination around issues of race, ethnicity, class, age, ability, and religion. Not to mention chest hair, waistline, sexual kink, dog breed, haircut, and bathing suit. Don't mistake West Hollywood for Mister Rogers' Neighborhood (well, he may *live* there, but you get my drift). Rather, these data on tolerance raise a subtler point. They offer a preliminary, tantalizing hint that one subculture of men has been observed to dance somewhat differently with Lady Tolerance and her ugly cousin, Prejudice. For whatever reason, we seem to differ from other men in some measurable, repeating, if unseen, ways. We don't know if that has any connection to the lower levels of violence in queer cultures. All this research tells us is that, when it comes to boys and bias, tolerance is for pansies.

There is one other possibility hidden in this stack of studies on tolerance, a possibility that may be important. If these scholars are right, then *many gay men may hold a set of personal values that are not yet fully manifest in many of the most visible, accessible parts of the collective gay world.* That is, in this realm, gay worlds as they now exist have not yet fully lived up to the values we cherish, nor do they yet fully reflect the personal values and public ethics that many of us as individuals hold dear. Put another way, perhaps such studies of individual gay values are a first clue that we have it in our hearts to do better with each other than we do—and far better than we think.

Much data for this hunch about gay aggression relies on negative findings like our comparative absence of assault and violence, lower levels of intolerance or bias. But if gay men have truly chosen to place ourselves in a different relationship to male mayhem, we should expect to see it reflected in affirmative ways, all over the place.

And so we do. Gay men have fashioned a remarkable breadth of organizations, institutions, networks, and groups dedicated to the proposition that all men are created peaceable, or can at least act like it for a week. Given enough free time and airfare, one might spend a year attending the Blue Heron gathering ("A gentle gathering for gay men and their friends"); camping at Radical Faerie sanctuaries in Wolf Creek,

Oregon; Liberty, Tennessee; Zuni Mountain in New Mexico, or Camp Destiny in Vermont; breaking bread with the Make-It-Beautiful Tribe on Penobscot Bay, Maine; communing at the Gay Spirit Vision gathering in the mountains of North Carolina; or attending a gathering of the Sweet Williams in rural Northern California. In aggregate, these gatherings involve thousands of gay men.

"The same gentle-hearted spirit is reflected," says Les Wright, "in the 400-plus groups of gay 'bears' now in existence." "Bears" are, of course, the groups of gay men who have built an accepting subculture around being stocky, large, hirsute, friendly, or some combination of the above. Les Wright, a professor of humanities and cultural studies, is perhaps the nation's best-known scholar of bear culture, the bear community's unofficial "bearstorian," and hunter-gatherer (a.k.a. archivist) of a vast collection of bear-iana. "Male gentleness and community are often at the heart of how men understand what the bear movement is about. Strong but gentle, playful—it's very much there in the archetype."

Even smack-dab in the center of me-first Manhattan, reputed as the pinnacle of take-no-prisoners-get-ahead-ism, you could find yourself attending a group known as Gentle Men. This group of gay men has been living up to that name on alternate Friday nights for the better part of a decade. The group was founded "to promote intimacy and trust among gay men without the posturing or threat that sometimes exists in the bar scene." Owen, the group's long-time facilitator, explains: "We use gentle touch, fully clothed, and emotional check-in sharing exercises. Often we spend time in silence, stressing eye contact, gesture, and touch."

Similar organizations exist among queer men in every region of the country. Chapter 6 explores the radically distinct ways gay worlds organize male intimacy and community, from friendships to fuck buddies. For now, we can just note that the gay world offers a social smorgasbord of groups which celebrate values of male nurture and gentleness. This cultural truth is summed up in the words on a sign greeting the newcomers to New York's Lesbian, Gay, Bisexual, and Transgender Community Center: "Within these walls, we expect to be treated with consideration and kindness. We expect our persons, our property, and our opinions to be respected. We expect to be free from violence and the threat of violence. We expect our disagreements to be resolved with sensitivity and goodwill."[55] Visit gay community centers from Nova Scotia to Orange County, California, and you may see strikingly similar language adorning the walls. Just as the Statue of Liberty's invitation to "send me your huddled masses" stands for something larger about the idea of America, so do these words embody something bigger about the idea of Gay World. This small sign is just one of the ten thousand ways that a culture's norms and expectations get proclaimed, modeled, and transmitted. Here, as in so many other areas, our ethic around male violence and tolerance looks very different than the norms of the world just outside these rainbow-striped doors.

An eye for an eye leaves everybody blind.
　　—Dr. Martin Luther King, Jr.

These tender tendencies are not just evident in the violence we don't commit, but in a wealth of acts we do. In 1999, a cover of *Time* magazine bore the stark picture of the lonely Wyoming fence where Matthew Shepard was beaten and tied to die. When his murderers went to trial, gay communities nationwide seethed with national vigils, demonstrations, and anti-violence marches, amid a torrent of media coverage from local papers to the evening news. In those weeks during the trial of his murderers, eleven national gay and lesbian organizations issued a forceful statement on the death penalty for the defendants in that case. It was small surprise that they took a stand. Given popular support for the death penalty, their shared policy interest to deter anti-gay violence, the glaring media attention, and their own fund-raising base, one would expect that. What one might not have expected was that these organizations—among them the National Lesbian and Gay Task Force; Gay Men of African Descent; LLEGO, the national Latina/o LGBT Organization; Lambda Legal Defense and Education Fund; and New York's community center—resolutely, unanimously, *opposed* it in the Shepard case. When eleven leading national organizations issue a joint statement, it may be seen to reflect the values of their constituents. In this case, a value of compassion. The view was summed up by Richard Burns, of the Lesbian, Gay, Bisexual, and Transgender Community Center of New York: "This is one of those moments when we, as a community, should lead. We consider this a teachable moment. The death penalty is no way to deal with anti-gay violence. The answer to homophobic violence is not more violence, it is education." (The contrast in attitudes is put in relief by a statement made by the on-air host on KBRT-AM, a "Christian owned and operated" radio station in Costa Mesa. Barely a year before Matthew Shepard was killed, the host urged death for gay people.[56] A few years before that, in the town of LaPorte, Colorado, not two hundred miles from where Matthew Shepard was killed, a similarly devout fellow,

Pastor Peter Peters, issued an earnest broadside: "INTOLERANCE OF, DISCRIMINATION AGAINST AND THE DEATH PENALTY FOR HOMOSEXUALITY is prescribed in the Bible." You can pick up your copy from an outfit called Scriptures for America.)[57]

Sometimes, of course, it gets hard to tell the faithful from the fags without a scorecard. In July 2000, *The New York Times* reported that a group described as "Christian hecklers" crashed a funeral of a murdered African-American gay man. Equal parts rage and righteousness, they waved placards reading "God Hates Fags" before the grieving family and mourners, issuing biblical condemnations of the murdered man's lifestyle. But then, the reporter wrote, a gay man stepped forward and something extraordinary happened: "David Strickler, a husky, forty-eight-year-old local resident, knew what he had to do. He strapped on a oversize pair of theatre-prop wings" to block the protesters' view of the otherwise peaceful evening memorial. . . . 'They say they're coming in the name of God, but they are coming in the name of hatred,' he said quietly among the protesters' din." This role of the protective angel, the article noted, "is being seen increasingly at gay rights gatherings. He helped reduce the small band of antigay visitors to a minor nuisance on an extraordinary night in this rural county seat, where hundreds of gays and lesbians, blacks and whites, stood together in the streets and demanded justice for the murdered man."[58]

This haunting image—a burly man, angel wings outstretched in supplication, protecting the communal peace against hatred—has entered the iconography of the millennial gay world. A flight of such guardian angels was also in evidence at Matthew Shepard's memorial, sheltering the mourning family from the clutch of angry bigots. They are a chosen cultural symbol, embodying the ethic of gentleness and nonviolence that is being cultivated in gay worlds. It is a deadly earnest piece of our people's guerrilla theater, precisely the sort of symbol Dr. King or Gandhi might have deployed to make a similar point. Like the bedside vigils we kept together just a decade ago, it is the work of angels in America.

Everything you know is wrong.
   —Firesign Theatre

Let's make one last stop at the issue of domestic violence, because it offers an object lesson for an issue we will meet often in these pages. The fact that a disclaimer on the subject should even be called for—that a smart, skeptical, and informed reader even thinks to object about domestic violence—is telling. It suggests that you, like many of us, have incorporated in your descriptions about gay men, a belief about our supposed domestic violence "problem."

Of course you have. We have all read the dramatic headlines like the one given prominent display in *The New York Times* lead section: "Silence Ending About Abuse in Gay Relationships."[59] The phenomenon is described as having been "shrouded by silence," and finally "coming out of the closet." Yet it offers no data to demonstrate that domestic abuse is any more common in gay relationships than in straight ones. We have absorbed those dismal statistics as gospel, so much so that one academic writer could characterize domestic violence as "by some estimates, the third largest health issue facing the gay, lesbian, and bisexual population."[60] Such reportage leads many of us to believe that it is a *more* frequent problem for us than it is in the straight world. This, despite the fact that experts find no real evidence of higher rates of domestic violence among us. Yet we all too easily add it to the list of our "problems," and readily accept it as gospel. Thus we weave a thread of dark fable into our common lore.

Yet consider this. Why have you never read or heard about our pacific propensities, for which there is actually a great deal of evidence available, from many diverse sources? Can you recall reading *those* statistics in your local gay paper? When did your gay magazine last discuss our notable lack of violence in public culture? Where was the bestselling book noting that gay circuit parties are among the most peaceable mass events of their size? Which enterprising reporter or academic has documented this aspect of our lived gay experience? What local agency investigates, celebrates, or teaches it?

It is fair to ask why we know so little about this aspect of our truth. The question is even more vexing if you stop to consider your *own* personal lived experience. You don't have to scratch deep to find that gay men know this about gay male spaces. We sense it intuitively from our own lives. How many bar fights have *you* been bloodied in?

These are facts we sense deep in our bones. Our habits of harmony are woven into our own native knowledge about our gay cultures. As queer men, we know the rules of our bars, because we made them. In fact, this pattern could not exist if we didn't constantly re-enact it each Saturday night we get together. We experience, and expect it to be this way. We *create* it. What we don't do is acknowledge it.

When was the last time you sat around after dinner with five friends and mused over why we so rarely beat each other up after a few beers? That scene isn't likely to crop up in gay movies or sitcoms. Quite the opposite. The conventional habits of gay mind, the received truths of our culture and media, leave most of us far more able to fret over our presumed crisis of gay domestic violence—that "third biggest" scourge of the gay world—than to tell this part of our lived and familiar truth.

But what if it turns out that we have this part of our story precisely backwards? Perhaps the first set of facts isn't so true as we thought, or the latter is truer than we knew. Who might we be then? In the domain of male violence, as we will see on many other topics, we consistently adopt a narrative that obliterates the very values we enact every weekend. We have accepted a gay story that says we are kinda good with flowers, kinda bad at contact sports, and—did I mention?—kinda major sex pigs. Yet we uniformly fail to give voice to this peaceable part—as we will see, to many parts—of our shared norms that roomfuls of gay men know to be most true.

So, why do we trade in fable instead of speak the facts? When I stand before rooms of gay men and ask that, heads shake. The most common response is: "You know, of course that's true. I just never heard anyone say it before." Somehow we agree not to mention that we live together in ways virtually no other men seem able to. And then we hardly notice it ourselves, even as we do it. Eventually, despite the truths we know from our own lives, we largely collude in omitting that fact from our shared picture of ourselves. We obliterate it from our description, delete that part from our collective personal ad—*even though most of our lived experience and intuition tells us it rings true.*

While we're staying mum and modest about our uncommon experience of male violence, nobody else is. The question of public violence has become America's prime national obsession. In the last presidential election, as in every congressional session, we heard much anguished wailing and loud gnashing of teeth over how our nation must curb violence. Senators harangue about censoring the Internet, regulating violent TV content, imposing mandatory prison terms, supporting the death penalty. Blue-ribbon panels wring hands and blame Hollywood or liberals, drugs or permissive parenting. Professional harrumphers decry assault weapons, mandate trigger locks, defend metal detectors. Should we try juveniles as adults or fund conflict-resolution courses? No matter, so long as we "get tough on violent crime."

How odd then that nobody pays much heed to the one group of men who seem to have evolved some better answers. No senator has yet recommended that criminologists sit down and talk with those well-groomed guys in the tank tops. No presidential commission has dispatched a fact-finding mission to Castro and 18th to study the habits of those peaceable guys with the piercings.

In 1999, all across America, the word "Columbine" conjured images of teenage males bringing high-powered rifles to a high school and slaughtering fellow students. In gay lives, it's as likely to be somebody's drag name. In 2000, America spent more than $500 million on anti-violence programs to "increase the peace." Yet nobody thought to look at the one group of men who already have. Memo to Washington: Check in. Shutter Congress for a week, hop a bus to South Beach or Montrose or Castro or Capitol Hill, hang out a while, and *pay attention*. America already has a fraternity of successful peacemakers in its midst.

Research has found many societies where violence is not an accepted cultural value. Variation in the amount and type of aggression in individuals and cultures suggests that violence is socially constructed, and not the inevitable result of a biologically-determined human nature. Anthropologists seek to understand its cultural determinants.
—Dr. Jack Bernhardt, Professor of Anthropology, Elon University[61]

At the Twenty-sixth Conference on Men and Masculinity held in Denver, one presenter, Dr. Michael Kimmel, posed a provocative question: "If boys have a natural tendency toward violence and aggression, do we organize society to maximize that tendency or to minimize it?" It appears that one group of men has voted with its fists in answer to that question. Our distinctive cultural patterns make us one of the world's most harmonious cultures of men. From scholarly journals in libraries and front-line reports, from precinct houses and gay bars, evidence mounts. One day, historians may shake their heads at the irony that the twisted logic of sodomy laws could transmute this least-felonious group of men, this peaceable kingdom in pink, into statutory criminals in eighteen states. For us, our crime is not how we fight, but how we love. Of course, those future historians may not blame others for failing to recognize this subtle truth about gay lives. How could one expect that, really, when we—who live this every day, who create and enact these radically new patterns of male coexistence with each other—scarcely recognize it ourselves?

3 | COMMUNITIES OF CARING

The emotional states, which are central to the belief that the epidemic can be overcome, are unacknowledged in its discourse. There seems to be a reluctance to use words such as "respect," "caring," "compassion," "love," "spiritual-ity," or "concern" in this context. These emerging and yet to be spoken dis-courses recognize a basic truth: to understand and respond to this epidemic, one must understand daily life and human nature in all its complexity.
—E. Reid, *Approaching the Epidemic*

Cops are not the only ones who have noticed we do things differ-ently. While they have been logging the acts we don't commit, scholars like Susan Folkman have been documenting the ones we do. At first glance, Dr. Folkman is just about as far from your basic streetwise beat cop as one gets. She is a fifty-something mother of three, grand-mother of two, an eminent social scientist and an internationally recog-nized scholar of human personality. Folkman co-authored a now-classic text creating something called Coping Theory. A treatise in the mechan-ics of the human spirit, it examines how the human heart makes it through terrible times without breaking. She now runs million-dollar research projects at the University of California, San Francisco, where for a decade, the heart and soul of her work has been in this community of men.

Since the mid-1980s, Dr. Folkman has been absorbed doing just what one might expect of someone who has both an abiding interest in how humans survive dark times and a San Francisco address. She has been a front-line witness and chronicler to the gay Hiroshima that is HIV. Her scholarly work has involved interviewing couples, friends, life partners who are helping others face disease and death. In her work, she says, "the levels and richness of male caregiving we have documented in this community are simply unprecedented. There really is no other word for it. The world needs to understand what these men have been doing." Watching gay men's lives up close for almost two decades, she has been working to answer the question: What is it to give care in a cataclysm? Can the world learn anything from the way these men have responded?

Since 1981, when a new disease was first seen among gay men, literally thousands of research studies have probed, documented, surveyed, and plumbed gay men's attitudes, behaviors, and beliefs. This work has provided an unparalleled window into the values and mores that gay-identified men enact with each other and in our lives. These papers tell a fascinating, if unrevealed, set of stories about our patterns of support and practices of communal caretaking. The research suggests that the men in these worlds are indeed doing something radically distinct, and quite different, than we imagine.[1]

The current conventional wisdom, reflected in magazines and books, gay folklore, and discourse, holds that gay men inhabit a culture of narcissism, hedonism, and self-absorption. Freed of the "burdens" of child rearing, the story goes, we focus on ourselves, our bodies, clothes, and careers, prettying our neighborhoods, amassing wealth, and most of all, pursuing sex. But a clear-eyed look suggests a breathtakingly different view. There is as much reason to think that it would be hard to find another community of males who exhibit such enduring levels of altruism and nurturance, in ways subtle and overt. What's more, it may even be that we do so in ways seen in no other group of men we know of.

Folkman's research teams tracked social circles, interviewed friends, peered over the shoulders of volunteer buddies, and sat with caregivers, couples, and patients, all the better to understand the motivations and patterns of altruism at work in the realm of the dying. What she has seen, she admits, is humbling. In a paper called "Stress and Coping in Caregiving Partners of Men with AIDS," she writes: "Rather than turning first to their families for emotional support, gay men are likely to turn first to partners and friends."[2]

She is hardly alone in this observation. The closer researchers looked, the more noteworthy the evidence grew. A 1995 study, comparing gay men and others with HIV, reported "Gay men relied on friends far more frequently."[3] A number of studies have documented the profound ways that men in gay worlds serve as each other's support and families through hard times.[4]

The magnitude of what was going on first hit in a study quietly published in 1994. Researchers from the Center for AIDS Prevention Studies at the University of California reported then that a staggering 54 percent of the men sampled in central city gay neighborhoods—*more than half*—had cared for other men ill with AIDS.[5] In the peak years of the American gay AIDS epidemic, such men were more than ten times more likely to be taking care of the sick than was the general population in those same cities. In the dry prose of social science, such a finding gets rendered in language like "caregiving rates far above typical gender norms." But that almost misses the point. *There is no known example where more than one in two men took time to care for others unrelated to them* by blood, family, or clan ties. Let alone kept doing it for more than a decade. Nor can contemporary social science document anything remotely similar among any other communities of men. Nowhere else in recent memory have half the men in a population assumed roles as care partners, to nurture loved ones, friends, even strangers. It recalls the caretaking that occurs in an army in a battle. Only in this case it is an army of lovers, and its campaign, the evolution of a new queer *caritas*.

OUR QUEER *CARITAS*

> *The largest group of caregivers in this age category are male friends of the PWA {people with AIDS}, a group not typically found among caregivers. . . .* [6]

The Latin *caritas*, variously translated as "dearness," "affection," or "high regard," has now become understood simply as "charity." But it was the ancient Greeks, with their half-dozen different words for different kinds of love, who had a word, *agape,* denoting an unselfish, brotherly love of one person for another. The term was later adopted by New Testament writers to mean the love of God or the love of true Christians for one another. Ancient Greeks and early Christians both would have recognized that value at the heart of the deluge of voluntary care that made up the first decade and a half of AIDS in gay worlds.

Images of gay men as buddies became part of the landscape of queer America. We saw buddies at bedsides, helpers bringing food, healers comforting the dying, consoling spouses and families. In those years, we rewrote the rules of volunteerism. Our flood of community caring built agencies, improvised care partner networks, created new models of buddy systems and home care, and raised the standards for community volunteerism in cities across the land.

Observers found this deep communal response so noteworthy that they began to study its lessons.[7] Researchers in altruism and "pro-social motivation" commented on "the diversity of community helping structures that . . . gay men have elaborated."[8] Soon, thinkers who had devoted entire careers to studying the finest aspects of human compassion and heroism began to ask: What is it about these communities, that has motivated so many to such uncommon commitments to others?[9]

Researchers soon noticed one extraordinary feature in this cascade of caring. It is no big surprise to have a group that exhibits low public violence, high levels of caregiving, robust volunteerism, and that enjoys sleeping with men. We call them women. In almost all societies across cultures and history, the roles of the designated caregivers, the nurturers, have been filled by women. It is a virtual gender job description, as close to a cultural absolute as one finds. Absolute, that is, except for these cultures of men. More surprising is what happens when some men adapt and transform the helping roles women have taken for millennia, refracting and recasting them in novel masculine forms.

Most caregivers were gay males caring for male partners and friends . . . subjects provided substantial emotional support and comfort . . . and most provided at least some help with instrumental and basic activities of daily living.[10]

Social scientists observed that the most remarkable thing occurring here was not simply the profusion of care, the wealth of care teams and buddies, the creativity of new volunteer structures and institutions that arose. It was that never before had such innovations in nurture sprung from the unlikely gender called males. "The literature does not provide models for male caregivers," noted one paper bluntly.[11] A researcher who reviewed fourteen separate studies of caregiving found the same.[12] Still another noted: "Females were more likely to assist with care provision tasks . . . and to experience higher levels of burden than males."[13] Another examined gay male caregivers from two large Midwestern cities, calling the phenomenon "significant because men as caregivers typically have not been studied."[14]

Even in arenas where men are traditionally seen at their most nurturing—with spouses and children—studies found real differences. Even among married cancer patients, "husbands were less likely than wives to help their sick spouses with household tasks . . . and wives tended to be the sole caregivers . . . providing approximately twice as many hours of care as husbands."[15] As one paper noted: "The absence of public support or even acknowledgment of men as caregivers is symptomatic of the non-normative aspects of being a caregiving partner for a person with AIDS."[16] Four out of five doctors surveyed agreed: Most guys just don't do this stuff.

Because experts had not observed men do this to such a degree, they began to explore what made these men act so differently. Journals began to publish papers with titles like "Altruistic Behavior and Caregiving in the AIDS Epidemic,"[17] "Informal Caregivers of Persons with AIDS,"[18] and "Women and Men in the Caregiving Role."[19] All noted that these men were behaving quite differently from the patterns of men elsewhere in the culture.

These findings came as little surprise to people who manage volunteers professionally. "Really, ask anybody who runs a volunteer program," says Jennifer Trank, who does just that in a large social welfare agency in Los Angeles. "If you want volunteers, look for straight women and the gay men—that's who mostly volunteer in these places." Clearly, the point is not that straight men never volunteer. A thousand little league coaches, scoutmasters, and soccer referees disprove that every weekend. Such men's volunteerism is a valued part of the American male mythos, from volunteer fire departments to barn-raisings, in church groups and fraternal organizations. What's notable is that, even outside these structures, one group of men appeared to be volunteering significantly more time, more often, and in different ways.

During the height of the plague years, America grew used to images of gay men at vigils and staffing hotlines. Touching *pietà*s of buddies at bedsides became part of our AIDS iconography. Soon a growing body of research began to hint that males in these queer worlds were demonstrating striking patterns of altruistic behavior well beyond AIDS. Look close, and you see it manifest in everything from our service to our sexuality to our serostatus.

Dr. Lee Badgett, a professor of economics at Amherst and researcher at the Institute for Gay and Lesbian Strategic Studies, conducted the first large-scale, systematic study of gay altruism. She examined our giving and volunteerism patterns in more than 2,300 people in Milwaukee, Philadelphia, and San Francisco. Badgett found her sample volunteered 61 percent more time (twenty-nine hours per month) to nonprofit organizations than the heterosexual group, and above the eighteen hours a month typically worked by volunteers in this country. One might be tempted to think that this is just a matter of our taking care of our own, and it is certainly that. But the study also found that we divide our charitable contributions—in both time and money—almost equally between gay and non-gay causes.[20]

For ten years research showed our extraordinary rates of care volunteering. As recently as 1999, a public health survey in Rhode Island showed that 62 percent of the gay men surveyed had participated in an AIDS-related event, a quarter of them had provided caregiving services, and a similar proportion had volunteered at an AIDS agency in the prior six months.[21] A national magazine poll reported exactly the same numbers in 2000, asking about men's volunteering over the previous three months.[22] Our practices of care and service extend far beyond the AIDS bedside, of course, including anti-violence patrols, volunteer-run counseling groups, the nation's burgeoning network of community centers, and generations of HIV prevention volunteers taking to the streets and sex clubs to help save lives.

It is interesting to consider just how many of the high-profile gay legal challenges of the last years have contested *our right to volunteer*. We have fought to be permitted to give service as blood donors, sports coaches, Big Brothers, scout leaders, in the armed forces, as foster parents, and as Salvation Army volunteers. Lambda Legal Defense and Education Fund, the leading gay and lesbian legal advocacy organization, has brought more than two dozen legal actions to *simply allow us to follow our best instincts to serve others*.

Even when the matter is life and death, we have to fight to be allowed to serve. One of the most dramatic instances concerns blood donors. Despite the fact that the nation faces a severe shortage of blood, gay men are consistently turned away. The reportage on the FDA's own Blood Products Advisory Committee in 2000 is revealing. The members "agreed that the permanent ban on gay men seemed discriminatory, lacked a firm foundation in science, and should be changed." Public statements from the Gay and Lesbian Medical Association, "various hemophilia groups, and the American Association of Blood Banks all urged a change in the policy."[23] Yet the Red Cross, an agency synonymous with American volunteer spirit, stayed staunchly on record with their policy that said, in effect, "better no blood than gay blood."

Nor are they alone. It is notable that for the last fifteen years, volunteerism has been on a steep downward slide in the larger society of Americans. Sociologists have noted significant drops in volunteered time. Nonprofit agencies from Big Brothers to churches to soup kitchens have scrambled harder and harder to find people who are even willing to help. Academic conferences, federal funding initiatives, private-public partnerships, university courses, and corporate incentive programs have all addressed the waning spirit of service in America.

How odd, then, that nobody has thought to inquire what is different in the male communities where volunteerism is still a cherished and central value. It is unclear which is more remarkable: that for well over a decade, one group of male citizens has stepped up to volunteer so disproportionately to its numbers in the population, or that so many institutions which claim to celebrate volunteerism—from the Boy Scouts to the Catholic Church, from the Red Cross to the Salvation Army, to foster care agencies and the military—so consistently reject our help. It can't be easy to preach ideals of service and volunteerism, to extol neighborliness and altruism, yet be unwilling to welcome the very gang of men most inclined to live up to those ideals.

A SHOT IN THE ARM

> *To really be a gay or lesbian citizen, you must also give back to your community. You must reach out and help it.*
> —Paul Monette

By the textbook definition, behavior is properly termed "altruistic" only if it carries a cost to the helper. How interesting, then, that several studies have found just that among gay male AIDS caregivers. Researchers have noted that these helping habits persist despite clear evidence that they take a significant toll on the mental and physical health of the men who help.[24] Another study of hospice volunteers in Texas found they volunteered despite "a significantly higher degree of threat caused by their volunteer work. Threat to health, total threat, threat to social world, and employment significantly differentiated the volunteers."[25]

That is not anywhere more clearly demonstrated than in a form of volunteerism now being seen around the nation. As of this writing, several thousand queer men across America have stepped forward to enroll in HIV vaccine trials. They are becoming guinea pigs for an untested vaccine to prevent HIV. Such men might well feel that they are placing their lives on the line—because they may just be. (Not because a vaccine is necessarily so dangerous, but because it may carry consequences that even the best scientific minds cannot predict.) For uninfected men, this particular shot in the arm means courting a series of unknown risks: possibly becoming HIV-positive, having adverse vaccine reactions, suffering unknown long-term health effects, enduring HIV-related job or personal discrimination, bearing medical costs, and bearing social and sexual stigma from one's perceived HIV status. The informed consent form for these vaccine trials leaves little doubt as to its gravity: It goes on for several typewritten pages. Plainly, this is one volunteer commitment that goes way beyond stuffing envelopes and candy striping. It resonates, quite literally, to the very cells of one's being.

Given these costs, one New York research team inquired why their gay male volunteers might consent to take such risks. More than three-quarters (78 percent) cited personal values in "helping find a vaccine that works" or "helping stop the epidemic." Six in ten (60 percent) expressed finding personal meaning in "giving to my community," and more than half (55 percent) of the men spoke of "doing something to honor people I know with HIV, AIDS, or who have died."[26] A poll published in *The Advocate* found a staggering 74 percent of the gay men they surveyed said they would be willing to help in a vaccine trial.[27]

The sentiments echo in the words of a twenty-seven-year-old Chicago man: "It's what I can do in this horrible time—to play my part to end the epidemic." In Washington, D.C., an African-American gay man named Timothy cited his own reasons: "I feel as if I am giving something back to the communities of which I am a part. I'm thrilled to be in this trial. It reminds me that we sometimes have to swim through fear to get to our islands of joy."[28] *The Advocate* printed the words of another HIV-negative gay man: "It's time for me to help my brothers. . . . I so desperately want to do something. I'm tired of watching AIDS become less of an 'issue' in this country . . . of being told the fight is over." He sees volunteering as "my way of saying to deceased lovers, to those who have just seroconverted, and to long-time survivors, 'you are not forgotten.'" He recalls telling an HIV-positive friend about his decision: "He was silent for a moment on the phone. Then haltingly he said: 'Thank you.' A soft noise rose through the receiver. Is that static, I wondered, or is he crying?"[29] After scores of interviews, the national research team leading the HIV-prevention vaccine stated the same finding: "Altruism was a main motivator for participating"[30]

Victor Zonana, former public affairs director for the International AIDS Vaccine Initiative, has seen that up close in gay men's volunteering. "The community responded heroically to the call to enroll in vaccine trials. I think that HIV-negative men, especially those in their 30's and 40's, feel a responsibility to give something back for having escaped."

At one gay event in Minneapolis, dinner table talk turned to the vaccine volunteers. Several men said they were involved. One of them was Peter, now in his early thirties. "It's funny. As soon as I heard about it, I just knew I'd be doing it. For me, it wasn't even like an option not to be involved." Across the country in San Francisco, researchers Robert Hays and Susan Kegeles interviewed more than a hundred men like Peter. Why, they asked, would they court the vaccine's risk? Why participate at all? Almost four in ten men (39 percent) felt a desire to contribute to ending the epidemic ("Because this disease is too dangerous to the human race. I want to help stop it once and for all"); as many said that they wanted to help research ("The researchers are doing a very important job, and I want to help in any way I can"). As one man put it: "As a healthy HIV-negative young man, I'd be willing to submit my body to this process." More than a fifth of the men interviewed stated frankly altruistic reasons: "To feel as if I'm doing something worthwhile for other people." One wisecracked, "I guess I'm just a regular Joan of Arc."[31] The Joan part, maybe, but there is little so "regular" about shouldering this kind of a volunteer commitment.

Connect the dots—from AIDS caregiving to volunteerism to vaccines—and a pattern starts to emerge. It is both provocative and persistent, yet wholly unacknowledged. Examine the facts, note the gay world's myriad responses to AIDS, observe the cultures, practices, and institutions of caregiving queer men have built. They add up to a documented pattern of uncommonly large numbers of men manifesting the finest and most humane values on an unexpected scale. The evidence begins to chart a surprising landscape. Maybe Planet Gay is not the arid and desolate terrain we have been repeatedly shown. Shift perspective, probe just below the surface, and what floats into view is a queer world alive with altruism.

Were that true, it should show up well beyond AIDS. Consider a market research study conducted in 2000 by market researcher Jinny Henenberg. She surveyed a group of givers to New York's Lesbian, Gay, Bisexual, and Transgender Community Center. This group, overwhelmingly gay men, she noted, "showed a very distinctive pattern. Normally, in such an institution, donors give to programs they and their peers are most likely to use. But these donors were much more willing to invest charitable dollars in programs they reported they didn't use, even ones that helped others who were very unlike them." Since the sample was never designed to test altruism, she is cautious about her conclusions. Still, she muses, it's a striking pattern. "In my experience, you don't see this result in most market research for institutions. Let's just say it makes you think twice about what was going on in this sample."

Another study attempted to directly assess the altruism in gay men and found tantalizingly significant results. Predicting that homosexual men might be more altruistic than heterosexual men, researchers decided to look at empathy, which psychologists know is strongly associated with altruistic and helping behavior. The authors assessed 127 men, both straight and gay, using a test proven to reliably measure levels of empathic response. They concluded: "As predicted, the homosexuals were found to score significantly higher on the empathy assessment." Given the strong association between empathy and altruism, they wrote in their conclusion, "There are data supporting a model predicting that these individuals are likely to be more altruistic and empathetic."[32]

From a very different methodology comes a similar finding. In 1996, a researcher from New Mexico, Dr. Daniel Nieto, gave the widely accepted Myers-Briggs personality inventory to a sample of gay men who used a computer bulletin board service. In his study of 290 men, he reported several areas where the gay men sampled seemed most different from the wider population.

Certain personality types—notably those involving "intuition-feeling"—occurred between three and ten times more often in the gay sample than would be predicted in the general population. However, gay men were up to fifteen times *less* likely to be found in categories involving extroverted sensation-feeling. (In one personality category which usually comprises 13 percent of the general population, fewer than 1 percent of gay men fell.) About twice as many of the gay men had personality styles rooted in intuition, hunches, and abstraction as relied on objective fact, logical structure, and concreteness. In the whole sample, he found the distribution of differing personality types among gay men to be almost exactly 100 percent reversed from the patterns that would be found in a general population. Terming these differences "most salient and striking in terms of their deviation from general population parameters," he characterized them as "personality characteristics which tend to be other-oriented and reflective of keen awareness of and sensitivity to *relationships* along many dimensions."[33] According to this measure, at least in the realm of empathy and relationships, these guys look really different.

If it were true that empathy is valued or practiced differently by gay men, one would expect to see it play out in relationships. In a 1983 study, researchers tested the perceptions of one hundred subjects aged seventeen to sixty-four, gay and straight. They found the gay men to be rated by the sample as "the most helpful to others, and expressive of tender feelings."[34] Six years later, researchers looked at fathers, gay and straight, and found that "gay fathers [were] more responsive to children's needs and provided reasons for appropriate behavior to children more consistently than did an equal number of matched heterosexual fathers."[35] (We were also, on balance, stricter dads. Even if dad's a poof, he's no pushover.)

That same interpersonal empathy echoes in a 1996 study from California, comparing gay and straight men in their spousal relationships. The investigator found that in our intimate relationships, gay men lied significantly less often than did the heterosexual men sampled.[36] Another researcher used a psychological test to assess "capacity for intimate contact from an existential-humanistic point of view" and found "mean scores for homosexuals were greater than were mean scores for heterosexuals."[37]

The caretaking theme arises as well in a totally different set of evidence, around where we put our energies, not just after hours, but on the job. Several studies have established that gay men make career choices that diverge in systematic ways from those of straight men.[38] The leading work in this area has been done by Dr. John Blandford at the University of Chicago. He analyzed a large sample from standard U.S. census figures, some 10,000 male same-sex partnered households. There were many significant differences in what we do for a living. The sample was "greatly over-represented" in a category called Professional and Specialty Occupations, and "some two-thirds of the gay men in this category worked in jobs that were female identified (elementary school teachers, RN's) or were associated with the arts."[39] "Female-associated jobs" are traditionally those emphasizing empathy, caretaking, and personal care and service.

Blandford's landmark findings, not yet published, tell some fascinating stories. Compared to the job pool of men in general, this pool of men was 3.6 times more likely to manage service organizations; about five times more likely to be a registered nurse; four times more likely to provide some sort of caretaking as a therapist (respiratory, occupational, speech, psychological, or physical); more than fourteen times as likely to teach education or kindergarten; twenty-seven times more likely to do private home care; ten times more likely to cook; twenty times more likely to do personal care like cosmetics or hair; five times more likely to be a special education teacher; thirteen times more likely to be a librarian; more than seven times more likely to be a designer, a writer, or teach theology. Just in the category of service occupations, they were far over-represented when it comes to food (twelve times), personal service (seven times), or health service (three times). But it's far less likely you will find this group of men taking care of those buildings, or for that matter working as guards, in law enforcement, hunting, trapping, logging, or operating heavy equipment other than our own. They were also far less likely to sell insurance, operate lathes, work as stevedores, read utility meters, deliver mail, be carpenters, or spend the day working on the rail-road. If, however, you look at what this cohort of men doesn't do—that is, occupations with a 0.0 percent likelihood of finding us—you find we avoid things that make big boomy noises ("explosives workers"); don't like long deep shafts, at least not as miners (0.0 percent chance); don't fix photocopiers, lay bricks, sort grain, fix cars, fit pipes, set type, run pick-ling machines, or ever sign up as boring machine operators (no, really, that is the job title, #708, you can check). While our husbands may be animals (with luck), animal husbandry is not these men's lot, as they are far less likely than other men to work on a farm (forget what you've seen in the Falcon videos). But the sample was two and a half times *more* likely to work in a plant nursery. Once inside the home, the statistics say, those are the guys to call for wallpaper hanging (more than twice as likely), but we don't do windows (0.0 percent chance. Trust me). And so it goes.

This sample has its limits, to be sure. It includes only men in same-sex partnered households who are willing to so identify on census forms. Until the census finds a better way to count single gay Americans—esti-mated at one half of us—we cannot have a more complete picture. But even with its limitations, one serious fact shines through these numbers. In this sample, a decided, significant, above-average clustering of gay men are found in service and caretaking occupations. Clearly, the U.S. Census Department is unlikely to be a hotbed of homo propaganda. Yet their numbers leave little doubt that we trace quite different career paths than our straight brothers do. That may be because caring professions are traditionally women's work and so are more accessible to us. It may be because the levels of intolerance are lower there than in other male-dom-inated career domains. Or it may have something to do, for whatever rea-son, with values that we find important. The point, again, is not that we are the only ones doing these things. Rather it is that, where men are to be found in them, heavy odds say it's the gay guys who are doing the job. In career choice, as in our personal lives and volunteer patterns, an uncommon number of us seem to place uncommon value on service.

A strong possibility exists that homosexuality is a distinctive beneficent behavior that evolved as an important element of early human social organization. Homosexuals may be the genetic carriers of some of mankind's most altruistic impulses.
　　—E. O. Wilson, *On Human Nature*

The thinker is E. O. Wilson, professor at Harvard, author of the landmark (and controversial) text, *Sociobiology.* Wilson, like many evolutionary biologists, has suggested that the tie between altruism and guys like us may run very deep indeed. Animal behaviorists have long noted links between altruism and homosexuality in a range of animal species.[40] The customary line of thought is expressed by David Seaborg, of the Foundation for Biological Conservation Research: "In an evolutionary sense, homosexuality is a form of altruism, because it results in fewer offspring for the homosexual, allowing the offspring of others to have fewer individuals with whom to compete. Much of the altruism seen in humans, not directed to relatives and unexplained, may be the result of the tremendous behavioral plasticity and learned component of behavior."[41]

Evolutionary biologists even have recognized the existence of what they term "helpers at the nest," animals who do not breed, but function in ways to keep the whole flock, pack, or herd humming along. The bachelor baboons who stand guard, the unmated chickadees who bring food to feed another's young, the guardian swans who watch a nest while another forages: Such helper roles exist from birds to sea mammals, from primates to penguins. That has led some thinkers to propose something fairly breathtaking. Are homos hard-wired to help the herd? If that were even partially true, it would begin to put our helping habits in a larger perspective.

Of course, nothing here proves altruism is intrinsic. The profusion of AIDS caregiving may just be a historical accident. After all, wouldn't any community so besieged have done the same? Any subculture would mobilize to take care of its own, right? When a levee breaks or a twister touches down in a rural river town, you see an intense outpouring of neighborly strength and support. Such mutual assistance is an important and valued strain of small-town and rural culture, from barn raisings to volunteer fire departments to flood relief. Consider the volunteer outpouring after the 9/11 attacks. Isn't it just like that?

Nobody knows what the response of straight men would have been had the AIDS pandemic descended in *their* midst in the 1980s. But we do know that they haven't habitually been the ones at the bedsides. Even in communities most like gay male enclaves, in terms of sheer volume of

HIV infection in their peak epidemic years (in inner cities, injection drug networks, or third world countries), the pattern seems to hold. It's not usually the boys who carry the bedpans.

Examine the forms male caregiving takes and you see some other differences. Large-scale male helping responses tend to be acute, not chronic. More typically, they seem to last a weekend, a week, a month, but rarely endure over a decade. As well, men's assistance is far more instrumental and practical than it is emotional and nurturant. That suggests a charming thought. Perhaps queer men have held on to values of neighborliness, volunteerism, and mutual assistance more than most any other group of men one can name. Call it a victory for traditional values.

We don't need to resort to biology to note the point. At the very least, a population of men has had the experience of being called to care for others, with all that teaches. If for no other reason than the happenstance of where the AIDS tornado first touched down, these men's hearts, values, and lives have been changed. As studies document, men who spent those years caring for others have learned to find significant meaning in their caregiving.[42] One study explicitly asked volunteers about how it affected them. Among these men, they found spirituality "increased or deepened in 77 percent of the entire cohort."[43] It suggests that the men involved in that era may have found a broader meaning than even we understood.

As we have seen, history records no other peacetime culture of men where so many took time over so long a period to care for those unrelated to them, nor did so in these intimate ways. The most similar culture of service among men, one could argue, is the Catholic priesthood, and more than a few observers have suggested that queer men occur disproportionately among the practitioners of that noble calling. So much so that a range of informal estimates place from one-fifth to three-quarters of the American priesthood as being gay.[44]

There's no point to enter here into that nasty thicket of numbers estimations and refutations, always a bad idea with a party that considers itself infallible. Yes, one can easily agree that such high figures may be grossly distorted. Then again, they may be spot-on. We can't really know until the Vatican is inclined to release statistics on the matter. For now, the question of whether the Catholic priesthood represents a fascinating example of ongoing queer male caregiving in our time remains tantalizingly unknowable. Of course, the very idea may be preposterous since, as everybody knows, Catholic priests are celibate.

Being gay for me means gentleness, sensitivity, warmth, and service to others. When I meet a gay person who is the opposite of those things . . . that is someone who has not realized himself. . . .
—Boyd McDonald

The peak gay male epidemic years brought innumerable examples of gay men stepping forward to help each other in large numbers in ways not seen before or since. Whether due to historical accident or intrinsic nature, many of us learned things we didn't know. In those years, these worlds of men were drawn to examine the value we place on care, service, and selfishness, the nexus between other and self, I and thou. We have been given to wrestle with the most fundamental ethical questions of meaning and mortality, and tested the limits of community in the most blood-and-guts ways. It is the sort of thing that shapes the history, the living ethic, of a people.

Yet even as our private acts may brim with nurturance and caretaking, altruism and generosity, bliss and communal intimacy, all too often the shared public habits of gay worlds bristle with attitude and exclusion, loneliness and looks-ism, defense and disrespect. In chapter 9, we inquire more deeply into that disconnect of values, and suggest some ways that our public culture could sing in better harmony with our private values.

Still, these habits of heart may hold important lessons for the larger culture. Set against dominant cultural habits of self-interest and the rule of the insular family, the patterns of communal caretaking emerging in queer communal laboratories look quite distinct. In an age of soulless cynicism, isolated individuality, and bald self-interest, some men in these worlds have experimented with a new public culture where one cares for unrelated others. That helps us all think differently about the notion of "we" and all it can hold. Who is responsible for whom, for what kinds of nurture?

Read the studies, listen to the stories, and you sense enormous numbers of gay men struggling, hungry for another way of being with and for each other. Our experiments profoundly stretch the limits of how we understand this prickly gender called men. As one researcher put it: "The broader implication from the study was, from a societal perspective, that assumptions and generalizations about men's capabilities as caregivers are much too narrowly drawn. This selection of male caregivers provided a broader perspective of the caregiving role."[45] In the domain of service and caretaking, as in violence, we are rewriting the rules of maledom.

People who five years ago were self-absorbed and hedonistic are now giving their whole lives over to serving their fellow beings. That's a tremendous and prophetic sign to the world at large.
—Andrew Ramer, *Gay Spirit*

So now we step back for a moment to consider what this all might mean. It has been said that "a person's true character is revealed by what he does when no one is watching." What we have done, unwatched, is remarkable, and the second of our half-told stories. We have seen that in no other free-living cultures have so many men taken time to so deeply, intimately, and consistently care for others unrelated to them. °

Let that idea settle in, and then behold the bedside *bodhisattvas* of the AIDS years. It is the sort of thing to make one's neck hairs stand up. When such large numbers of men in secular communities are practicing daily the nobler values enunciated by so many spiritual traditions, one might suspect that something important is going on. This part of ourselves we know from our own experience to be true—we serve. Not all of us, not all the time, not perhaps as much as we did. But we have a cultural habit of helping. Yet how often have you read headlines about gay men's uncontrollable urges to . . . volunteer? For that matter, how many of have ever discussed around a dinner table of friends queer patterns of caretaking? How often have we failed to ask the obvious: What do our patterns say about our hearts?

4 | DOGS, PIGS, AND ALTRUISTS

I have to have safe sex or I can't do it at all.
I wouldn't, me, it is just not my morals.
   —Rich, 34, HIV-positive man, Seattle

I would say the practice of safe sex speaks to you, speaks about your morals
and your values. I would seriously say that.
   —Elyssio, 22, HIV-negative, San Diego

There are also new, emergent patterns of love and caretaking, available to
them in gay culture alongside new forms of sexual behavior: a new set of
rules for the game.
   —Gilbert Herdt, anthropologist

The topic for today's sermon is sex. Now there's a surprise, right? When you're homosexual, it's kind of your middle name. Sometimes it seems two queer men can hardly meet but that the communication turns carnal. "What do you get into?" is our subcultural equivalent of "How 'bout them Mets?" Sex is what we construct as the principal domain of our difference, our favorite hobby, *terra* (very) *cognita*. It is certainly the patch of gay turf we imagine we know best, where the accepted truths and narratives are most familiar and best understood. Without question, our sex is also where the lives of queer men have been the most thoroughly prodded and poked by the watchers, and where we find the greatest wealth of information about our behavior and habits. So it may come as a surprise that, once again, a fresh reading of the facts suggests that it is precisely in the domain of our sexuality that we may have gotten our story most profoundly wrong. It turns out we don't always check our souls at the door with our pants. Indeed, in ways unseen, sex may be the arena where we enact some of our most profound habits of care and nurture.

This story properly begins, not in gay men's hearts, but about eighteen inches lower. So let's start with the one factoid you may not have encountered much of anywhere else. Pop quiz: In the first fifteen years of the American gay AIDS epidemic, roughly what proportion of gay men habitually reported high-risk sex?

_____ 45%   _____ 50%   _____ 65%   _____ 85%

None of the above.

In fact, an overwhelming weight of sexual behavior studies, well in excess of sixty studies in the first decade and a half of the epidemic, demonstrate that *the clear majority of gay men were in fact mostly safe, most of the time.* In the great bulk of studies conducted throughout the peak epidemic years in core gay communities, that number consistently hovered near the two-thirds mark.

The table on page 58 lists a sample drawn from such papers spanning the years 1990 through 1998. The sample begins in 1990 for several reasons. By then, it could be presumed that most sexually active men in core gay communities (and beyond) knew the facts about HIV, educators knew how HIV was transmitted, and, most important, the changes in gay men's sexual risk were by then reflected in published public health studies, which often lag several years. Papers published by 1990 could track behavioral changes begun in 1985, the year when gay men widely began to know their HIV status. The sample ends in 1998, because by then so many factors combine that it gets murky to make any meaningful statement about motives, altruistic or otherwise. By then, it was two years after potent combination HIV treatment came into wide use and HIV was deemed a "chronic, manageable disease." Some men had far reduced concerns about the long-term gravity of infection due to widespread use of protease inhibitors and combination therapies; many believed, in turn, that low viral load reduced danger. Others began employing a variety of popular risk management strategies, including negotiating safety or choosing partners of similar HIV status. At the same time, gay and mainstream media magnified a barebacking subculture (principally among positive men, although one would hardly know it from the papers). Together, these factors make it more difficult to clearly assess the ethical implications of unprotected sex among partners of different HIV status than in the ten years prior. As we will see, in recent years, these complexities have muddied the waters, bringing with them a rise in risk and infections among some groups.

But we start here with a cross section of studies that tries to fairly represent gay men's behavior in the peak years when we knew the facts, knew HIV to be lethal and had little effective treatment. Those were the years that ethical issues of protection and caretaking, the values of self-interest and altruism, stood in sharpest relief in thought and deed. Coincidentally, the same years also represent the time when we have a wealth of knowledge available about our decisions, behavior, and practices. The story they tell may surprise you.

Among men who have sex with men and have a risk factor for HIV transmission, approximately 65% reported consistent condom use over the prior six months.
—Diane Binson[1]

Author	Year	Place	Percent Reporting Safe Sex with Casual Partners*
Marks[2]	1994	Los Angeles	91
Paul[3]	1993	San Francisco	88
Mayne[4]	1999	New York	89
Voigt[5]	1992	Vancouver	88
Eckstrand[6]	1990	San Francisco	88
Posner[7]	1996	Los Angeles	85
Prestage[8]	1996	Sydney	84
Silvestre[9]	1993	Pittsburgh	84
Hunt[10]	1993	Britain	82
Dawson[11]	1991	American	81
Moreau-Gruet[12]	1996	Switzerland	80
Roffman[13]	1995	Smaller U.S. cities	78
Osmond[14]	1993	San Francisco	78
Myers[15]	1996	Canada	77
Perkins[16]	1993	North Carolina	77
Waldo[17]	2000	San Francisco	75

Author	Year	Place	Percent Reporting Safe Sex with Casual Partners*
Kelly[18]	1995	Smaller U.S. cities	73
Kanouse[19]	1991	Los Angeles	71
Steiner[20]	1994	Seattle	71
Meyer[21]	1995	New York	70
Bochow[22]	1994	U.K., Germany, Switzerland, France	70
Schmidt[23]	1992	Denmark	70
Kelly[24]	1992	Mississippi & Louisiana	69
Ridge[25]	1994	Australia	69
Kelly[26]	1992	16 smaller U.S. cities	69
Kippax[27]	1993	Australia	65
Hickson[28]	1996	U.K.	66
Wagner[29]	1998	New York	66
Binson[30]	1995	U.S. urban centers	65
Molitor[31]	1999	California	65
Kelly[32]	1990	U.S. cities	63
Wang[33]	1997	Barcelona	63

*Safety definitions vary but generally include habitual use of condoms. The numbers listed in the chart factor in subjects' knowledge of partner HIV status where available (e.g., Mayne, 1999).

Several things stand out in these numbers. First, that the proportion of men primarily behaving safely commonly hovers between 60 and 70 percent. It is uncanny, in fact, how often this rough two-thirds rule occurs throughout this literature. The studies listed above are just a sample of the many surveys throughout those years which cluster in this same 60 to 70 percent range. It's not that every single study in this time period found this—there were certainly exceptions—but that the overwhelming preponderance of published papers group in this same approximate range. The narrative of wanton irresponsibility, that staple of journalism both yellow and pink, that *cri de coeur* of HIV prevention Cassandras, was deeply at variance with a large body of evidence.

Second, there is little debate that gay men use condoms much more than do our straight male brothers. Alongside the avalanche of "two-thirds" studies among gay men, studies over the exact same sampling period consistently find straight guys using condoms far less often. So a paper surveying bar patrons notes, "Gay men were more likely to use condoms and the HIV antibody test than their heterosexual counterparts."[34] One study examined both gay and straight subjects and found: "All . . . homosexual men reported reductions in risky behavior." While they noted "substantial" risk reduction among straight couples where one partner knew the other was HIV-positive, they also noted "findings among other heterosexuals at increased risk were scanty and mixed."[35] The next year, a paper in *Science* reported in their straight sample, "condom use was relatively low," as only 17 percent of those with multiple sex partners used latex,[36] and other researchers termed behavior change among heterosexual young adults to be "small to nonexistent."[37]

In 1993 alone, nine different studies reported that two-thirds of gay men were being primarily safe in locales as disparate as North Carolina, Britain, Australia, Pittsburgh, and San Francisco. Yet the National AIDS Behavioral Surveys surveyed heterosexual men and found: "Among respondents with multiple partners, only 28% of men and 32% of women always use them with secondary partners . . . in general, almost half of men and women with multiple partners never use condoms."[38] Another study compared gay and straight men and found gay condom use "twice as high."[39] In the same period, as studies were documenting 65 to 88 percent of gay men regularly behaving safely in Los Angeles, New York, Denmark, Vancouver, Mississippi, Louisiana, and San Francisco, another researcher wrote of the heterosexual sample that the same percentage—65 percent—used condoms "sporadically or not at all."[40] That same year, another paper reported that heterosexuals' "condom use significantly increased from 11% in 1990/91 to 20%."[41] In yet a different heterosexual sample, "Unsafe sexual practices were common: 97% of nonmonogamous respondents did not use condoms during all sexual encounters, and few respondents consistently asked new sexual partners about previous high-risk behaviors."[42]

The divergent pattern held true among samples of straight college students: "Students do not appear to be adopting safer sexual practices";[43] among married heterosexuals having extramarital sex: "Low levels of condom use were found . . . (8% to 19% consistent users)";[44] in a study of the "singles scene" in 1997: "Consistent condom use was not the norm, with either casual or regular partners. Unprotected sex with regular partners was very high";[45] heterosexual young adults in New York, Los Angeles, and San Francisco: "Heterosexual youths appear at high risk for HIV based on reports of low rates of condom use";[46] and in a survey of four hundred heterosexual adults in 1999: "Males expressed more attitudinal barriers to condom use than females; higher HIV risk status was associated with maleness [and] single relationship status."[47] This fact, known to every family planning clinic, makes gay men's broad adoption of latex all the more notable. In 1981, some 2 percent of gay men used condoms; by 1987, the figure was 62 percent—again, our familiar two-thirds level.[48] Numbers like that inspired a team of the nation's leading HIV epidemiologists to label the changes among gay men "the most profound modifications of personal health-related behaviors ever recorded."[49] Despite challenges, backsliding, barebacking, and scores of scary headlines about rising tides and relapses and second waves, it's the poofs who place first in the condom competition.

If you slide one step further along the Kinsey scale and examine our nearest sexual relatives, bisexual men, the statistics turn out to be a complete mirror image of ours. Where two-thirds of gay men sampled are mostly safe most of the time, about that same proportion of bisexual men are unsafe. One study stated flat out: "Bisexual men with primary female partners often had not disclosed their bisexuality to female partners (75%), and 64% had not modified their behavior to protect female partners."[50] In 1996, different researchers, different men, reached a similar conclusion: "Bisexual men use condoms inconsistently with male and female partners . . . and are more likely than exclusively homosexual men to report multiple HIV risk behaviors."[51] (By way of comparison, the prior year, the National AIDS Behavioral Surveys sampled 1,298 gay men and observed that "68% of homosexual . . . men with a risk factor reported consistent [100%] condom use during intercourse over the prior six months.")[52]

The very populations where we know men having sex with men have the highest rates of infection—among the overlapping circles of bisexual men, non-gay-identified men, young men, and men of color—are precisely those cultural places where the notion of a public gay social existence may hold least sway.[53] In such places, the hard-fought cultural space representing an elaborated, out, named gay world is least accepted and most contested, often because it is perceived as white, monied, or urban. It is no surprise that in places where "queer" still means "wrong," practices may look different. In the words of A. Cornelius Baker, executive director of D.C.'s Whitman Walker Clinic: "You end up with people subverting their identity, living double lives, and putting themselves—and their partners—at risk."[54] The enormously higher infection rate in such communities may reflect that the places where our love least dare speak its name are also those where men are least practiced or prone to adopt the practices that have received such massive cultural support in more out gay environments.

The third thing of note here, as we saw with violence, is how little we hear about it. The reasons are complex. The academic and official press— public health scientists and epidemiologists, journals and symposia— gravitates to risk, not safety. So a literature search on "gay men, HIV, and risk factors" finds some 588 studies, yet the same search on "gay men, HIV and safety" yields only nine. Of those, only eight papers explicitly set out to chronicle the native strategies gay men have developed, the affirmative and creative ways ordinary people have invented to protect each other. Should you go so far as to marry the keyword search terms "gay men, HIV risk, and altruism," it will be a short read. Only one paper among several thousand has explicitly framed safer sex as an altruistic act.

What Public Health Talks About

Search Term	Number of Papers
"gay/homosexual men"	6,731
"gay/homosexual men & HIV/AIDS"	1,389
"gay/homosexual men, HIV/AIDS & risk"	588
"gay/homosexual men, HIV/AIDS & safety"	9
"gay/homosexual men, HIV/AIDS & success"	8
"gay/homosexual men, HIV/AIDS & altruism"	1

One could easily pick up the abstract of a study of AIDS in 1994[55] and despair at the abstract's conclusion: "The majority of gay men engaging in high-risk sex remain unaware of their partners' status." Now there's a moment of "omigod" epidemiology. But that abstract neglects to mention the finding that "the majority of the partnerships involved only safe sex." Again, it was approximately two-thirds of the sample.

It is not just the academics, of course. In 1996, the Maryland journal, *AIDS/STD News Report*, aimed at policy makers, ran a shrieking headline: "Reckless Sexual Habits of Young Gays Threaten to Start New Wave of HIV." The "news" in this particular report tells you that several studies, including one from Vancouver, show rates of unprotected risk at 28 percent, concluding "about one-third of gay men in their twenties engage in anal sex without a condom." Only the reader alert enough to do the math realizes that it also suggests that 72 percent of these Vancouver guys (sound familiar?) were being safe, as were some two-thirds of the studies cited nationally.[56] By way of comparison, that year, 61 percent of the American population consistently reported wearing seat belts.[57]

In the mainstream press, one could read the entire hand-wringing op-ed "HIV-positive and Careless," which ran in *The New York Times,* without ever learning that gay men with HIV have repeatedly been found to be more likely to act safely than HIV-negative or unknown-status partners. One could read the headline "'Russian Roulette' Sex Parties: Rise in Fringe Group's Unsafe Practices Alarms AIDS Experts" in a 1999 article in the *San Francisco Chronicle* without grasping that the clear majority of gay men in the study cited—in this case 61 percent, not so far from that magical two-thirds—were behaving safely.[58]

All too often, our own media follow suit. Read the article in the national lesbian and gay news magazine that reports a study of gay men in six cities around America, using words like "alarming lapse" and "rising tide of unsafe sex." Yet nowhere does it mention the finding that the overwhelming majority of men in the sample were, in fact, safe. Who is alarmed about that lapse?

Gay community attachment has proved a significant predictor of successful behavior change among gay-identifying men in response to HIV/AIDS.
—M. J. Chapple, 1998

Reading the popular press, one might never know how many academic studies have suggested that participating in gay sexual cultures is as likely to protect as to endanger. In the journal *AIDS Care,* one study notes: "Acculturation into the gay community is associated with safer sexual behavior."[59] Similar findings have come in studies from the U.S.,[60] Australia,[61] Britain,[62] France,[63] Germany,[64] and The Netherlands.[65]

So the next time you read one of those there-go-gay-boys-killing-each-other-again stories, take a breath, read the fine print, and do the math. As often as not, at least in these sampled years, you find that the invisible statistic, the number lurking behind the shrieking alarm, shows that a huge percentage of the men sampled were in fact following one of several strategies of safety. Commonly, the number approached the magic two-thirds.

Of course we do not always behave safely. Yes, we still put each other and ourselves at risk. Absolutely, even one-third of the time would be too often. Yes, we see evidence from studies and our own lived experience to suggest that unprotected sex has risen in recent years. The import of that grows complex and shaded in gray in an era of same-HIV-status negotiation, consensual barebacking, AIDS cocktails, and undetectable viral loads. The key point is not that risk doesn't occur, nor that gay men are always peerless paragons of penile protection. It is that our perspective on it has been mightily, dangerously, skewed. The public-health evidence on sexual behavior echoes the same theme we saw in the domains of violence and volunteerism. In the case of HIV safety in those years, we fashioned ourselves a cup often two-thirds full, yet resolutely persisted in calling it mostly empty. The question is, just who does that serve?

THE DEMISE OF KILLER DICK

Ever since I got HIV, people look at me and think: There he goes, Killer Dick.
   —Abraham, 29, HIV-positive, Brooklyn

It is just . . . I don't want anybody else to go down the same road the way I did. I don't want to see people go through a lot of things that they might go through if they did find out they were positive. Some people tend to overreact at first when they find out. And I'd rather save other people from having to go through that. I don't know if I was scared straight or just don't want a lot of people to go through the same thing. I don't like people to worry.
   —Lou, 34, HIV-positive, Detroit

You just don't take the chance of infecting him. I don't think it would be worth it. It is just ethically not right . . . it is like, hey, it is within my sense, it is in my policy, it is in my life book of rules. It is there. So, it is just like, my ethical book.
   —Gregory, 26, HIV-positive, Brooklyn

The picture comes into even clearer focus when we consider three other bodies of studies: those concerning HIV-positive men, partner choice, and disclosure of HIV status. In each case, in the same sampling period, one finds similar patterns of sexual caretaking, similarly unrecognized. The first set of studies suggested fairly clearly that HIV-positive gay men tended to reduce risk behavior *more* than negative men or those unaware of their HIV status, especially with partners of different HIV status.

A score of studies in the public health literature, conducted over the epidemic's first fifteen years, have shown HIV-positive gay men to be more likely, if anything, to follow safer sex practices than negative or untested men are.[66] One study itself analyzed fifty separate studies, and concluded: "All longitudinal studies of homosexual men reported reductions in risky behavior among both tested and untested men, and a few reported greater decreases among seropositive men than among seronegative men and those untested or unaware of their serostatus."[67]

A paper, "HIV-Seropositive Men's Perceived Responsibility for Preventing the Transmission of HIV to Others," studied 250 positive men and found they recognized "a special responsibility to protect others from HIV infection" and which shaped the kind of sex they had.[68] In a 1996 sample of face-to-face interviews of gay men in San Francisco and New York, the researchers reported: "Explicit concern for the safety of one's immediate sexual partner was stated by every one (100%) of the infected men."[69]

If, as recent evidence suggests, this may be in the process of changing, it is all the more vital to understand and give voice to the values that for so long motivated so many men to make such decisions. That truth does not come from neatly bound academic abstracts, but from the words, deeds, and values of the men themselves. "Before I was diagnosed . . . it was not me protecting anyone else. It was my own protection, I wanted to protect myself from my partners." Joel is twenty-four, HIV-positive, and lives in Kansas City. "But now I think the feeling has reversed. I know I'm positive, so I know I have to protect my partner."

Mike, in San Diego, has been positive for twelve years. "For me, a big part of it is an act of love. . . . I believe safer sex is definitely an act of love and caring about the other person and yourself. . . . I think sleeping with another man, having sex with another man is loving another man in some form, whether you are in love with this person or you just love them as another human being. So, expressing that love and caring comes with saying, 'Well, I don't want to put you at any risk.' There's a lot of temptation not to, and I'm not saying I always do it right. I'm not perfect. But I hold it that we can still have pleasure at the same time and I think about what could happen if you don't play safe."

Eduardo is a corporate trainer in Miami. "I enjoy having to keep conscious of that. If they're negative when they come and meet me, I want them to be negative when they leave. I have to think about them, they are not just a sexual outlet, it is a person with a life."

Even as recently as 1999, in one of the largest samples taken in the nation's largest gay mecca in recent years, only 11 percent of the 7,000 New York City men reported having unprotected sex with men with a different or unknown HIV status.[70] Yet somehow the idea that HIV-positive gay men were actually behaving *more* safely has not made it through the clamor of Really Scary Headlines. The idea that an unstated ethic may work to help men sustain practices that keep themselves and each other safe has gotten little press. Instead we watch and fret as the bogeyman Killer Dick still roams the dark alleys of the popular imagination.

In that same period we saw a pattern surface, not just in what we do, but whom we do it with, which is termed partner selection. A number of studies in the eighties and nineties suggested that HIV-positive gay men often prefer HIV-positive partners.[71] Commonly, when researchers ask why, these men say it "reduces anxiety not to have to think about infecting someone" or "just makes it easier" or "means we can be more free." A similar finding is that there are far higher rates of condom use among infected men with known HIV-negative partners than with other HIV-positive partners.[72] Ask why, and infected men in these studies usually report seeking like-status partners to reduce their own anxiety. So think about what that anxiety tells us. If you didn't care, you wouldn't worry. An HIV-positive man with such a partner preference may, in fact, be acting from an unarticulated ethic of care. To that man, whom he beds and whom he boffs may well be deeply interwoven with his notions of nurture and caretaking, in ways that he cannot even name.

Safer sex is a complicated form of caretaking. If we are truly concerned over many recent studies reporting that this care is taken less often, it is all the more vital that we explore, articulate, and honor the reasons men have found it meaningful to protect others when they do. That means we have to listen to the words of men like Kent, who is HIV-positive and lives in Raleigh, North Carolina. "I tell them. It's just easier for me. Nobody has the right to choose whether or not someone else lives or dies, especially with this disease." Erwin, thirty-eight, also positive, says, "I just, I don't feel it is appropriate for me as an HIV-positive person, as someone who wants to be responsible in life, to not inform or certainly not to infect someone else. It just isn't an option."

A similar ethic may also been seen in HIV-positive gay men's patterns of disclosure. Several studies in this same period showed that a majority of HIV-positive gay men have disclosed their HIV status to sex partners, both primary and casual.[73] Some studies even suggest that gay men disclose at levels above that of heterosexual men. Others suggest that we disclose more to intimate partners than to casual ones. It seems clear that disclosure is at least, in part, an act of sexual ethics. Despite concerns over potential rejection, it has become a common cultural habit to disclose. While the disclosure data are less complete and exhaustive than those about condom use, they raise the same question: Why?

One cannot help but be struck, in talking with men and reading the studies, by an awakening. Disclosure, partner choice, safer sex: All are forms of protecting one's partner. The conventional wisdom may say gay men and HIV-infected men don't care, but many studies show many of us behave as if we care deeply, but about something beyond ourselves. Brad, who works in a retail store in Seattle, says, "Of course sometimes I find it a struggle to do what I think is right. But for me, it's just about caring. Caring about yourself and caring about other people." To Mike, thirty, who lives and works in Harlem, "It is up to just your own personal spirituality, living healthy, mentally and physically, having safe sex. Having unsafe sex is living the negative state of mind, as far as I'm concerned. Sure, it feels like what you want to do, but having safe sex is saying: 'This is what is happening these days and I'm going to do the right thing. Do the right thing.'"

Hear their words, read a decade and a half of studies. For those years, a majority of HIV-positive gay men exhibited high levels of safety. Yet nobody much thought to ask the obvious question: Why? Self-interest—the cornerstone of much HIV prevention—doesn't really explain it very well. HIV-positive men could well see themselves as having little to gain, often much to lose, from condom use. In that case, using a condom may be less a rational act than an ethical one. In truth, rubbering up may not be an act just of rational self-interest, but also of altruism, a statement of one's values. Plainly put, it is an act of gay personal ethics.

The next time you see unprotected sex in a sex club, remember: Tapping a top on the shoulder and offering him a condom and some lube is a very powerful way to express your affection for a brother.
—Michael Callen

When these men took that personal ethic public, grassroots HIV prevention was born. The idea of men banding together to save each other's lives rewrote the rules of public health practice. In cities from Albuquerque to Augusta, groups sprang up. They had names like The Safe-Guards Project (Philadelphia); the Sisters of Perpetual Indulgence (San Francisco); Gay City (Seattle); AIDS Action (Boston); AIDS Prevention Action League (New York); RubberStuffers (London); Q Action (San Francisco); The Mpowerment Project (Albuquerque); the Latex Ladies (Atlanta). In virtually every major gay urban enclave, groups of citizen volunteers were banding together to save lives. The whimsical names covered a life-and-death goal, to encourage communal caretaking by stopping HIV.

This emerging broderbund armed itself with latex and lube. Never before had groups of men approached strangers in parks, on street corners, in clubs and bars to talk sex, distribute condoms and safety tips, answer questions, and support, cajole, exhort, and flirt their brothers into safety. These HIV prevention efforts sprung from an ideal of men looking out for each other's lives. Critics can say what they will about their effectiveness, reach, diversity, clout, competence, or skill. What is clear is that grassroots gay prevention was a tidal wave of communitarian altruism, that it rewrote the rules of preventive public health practice, and that no communities did it better than ours.

You heard it in the words of men like Tyrone, who at twenty-eight had seen HIV take a dozen friends in Chicago. "I feel it is my responsibility to educate whoever I'm with. It has got to stop somewhere. It has got to stop somehow. And if something I say can help one person, that is the part that I want, because everybody should be helping one other person. And if we all get together as a community and help one other person educate one other person. . . . They've found ways to slow it down and stop in some people. Let's find a way to slow this down and stop it in us as a gay community." Tre, twenty-six, says "I try my best to educate people as the best way I can. I'm an educator mostly." Paul, a twenty-one-year-old gay man from Hoboken, says: "What can I say? Sometimes people, just by hearing them talk, they're asking for help. If I see that, I'll just put my two cents in. I'm just an aid in this community."

Robert belongs to an extended friendship network of young men from Central American immigrant families near San Jose. "My friends and I are really, really close," says the twenty-three-year-old with a smile. "I would really kill somebody if they gave my friends something. Most of my friends, because we really care about each other, it is kind of like we try to keep each other, like always bring up condoms everywhere and everything. If I did something risky, I know they would have a big old temper tantrum. And like if someone starts to go with someone I know is trouble, you know, or messy, I say something. We sort of watch out for each other." We always knew gay men were dogs. It just never occurred to us that we might be watchdogs.

The dirty little secret of this epidemic was that we were saving each other's lives every night of the week. Not just during sex, handing out condoms, or when we attended ACT-UP meetings, but also in a thousand quieter ways. It happens with the trick who explains how to use a condom; the friends who chide each other about staying safe; the fuck buddy who brings new condoms to try; the roommate who imparts a safety lesson.

"I have images in my mind," says Kevlin, a muscular twenty-eight-year-old who calls Santa Rosa home. "My lover, Brad, is fifty." At that point they had been together just over three years, but Kevlin recalls a night that happened about two months after they started dating. "Brad has kept a photo album of all the men he knew who have died from

AIDS since it started. His friends, his first boyfriend, work associates. I was over at his house one night, we had just started dating—and he sat next to me on the sofa and opened his album. That night, he gave me the—I'm not going to say pleasure, but the lesson of going through the pages, face by face. He told me about them. Who they were. Showed me several hundred obituaries he had clipped from the *B.A.R.* and other magazines. He sat with me for like four hours just looking at hundreds upon hundreds upon hundreds of these people who died because of this disease . . . the same way I'm talking to you, I'm flipping through the pictures of my mind of these people's faces. He went through and circled all the people he knew with a yellow marker. And there were literally, literally, I stopped counting after like two hundred people that he knew, he personally knew two hundred people who died. And that just freaks me out." His lip is quivering now.

"Brad told me this was his life, but it didn't have to be mine. You know, that I have a choice. His generation of friends didn't. I don't want people to know me as someone who died from AIDS. That just does something to me. He did it because he knew I would keep those as images in my head. I picture those names and it is kind of scary. That was his way of taking care of me, of giving me a way to hold on to what this really meant. Whether I was with him or with other guys. And that is what I keep in my head because I'm not going to be a statistic, because of this disease. I'm not. And I'm not going to make anybody else one."

Different men, different worlds, same echo the same concern. Oscar, a teacher in Providence, recalls his feelings when his neighbor got bad news from his HIV test. "He didn't have a circle of friends who were doing what mine do in saying: 'You should be careful.' I wish I had, you know, just taken five minutes to talk to him. Maybe he would have listened to what I had to say." Jack spent most of the plague years in San Francisco: "I try to, when I meet young people and stuff, to sit them down and talk to them about well, how are you handling it, what are you doing with safe sex. Because no one talked to me. I stumbled through this with my . . . I found out the hard way. I didn't have anybody to talk to. I kind of look back like, you should pass it on. I'm a survivor and I think I could educate or talk to other people. . . . You try to pass on your experiences and your education to other people. I try to."

Research conducted through the Center for AIDS Prevention Studies undertook a series of personal interviews about gay men's values of protection. They found that 94 percent of their sample of gay men described consciously playing roles to support others' sexual safety. The men described their roles in many different words: Rich, thirty-four, is HIV-

positive and believes "somebody has got to be the objector, being responsible about condoms. A lot of people aren't responsible, and so it is up to
me to be the responsible one." Mike, an HIV-negative man in Fort Lauderdale, views his role as leadership: "I don't mind being a leader in that
sense because if you're having unsafe sex with me you've probably had it
with someone else. I think that if you pass information on to someone, it
kind of helps them, then they pass it on to the next person. That is
important for me. You can pass on HIV, or you can pass on being safe
about it." Mohammed, an HIV-positive African-American man, lives in
Brooklyn: "In our group, I'm a safety boy, hell, it's my thing. I don't
know what I would be labeled, maybe just the kid that cares." Desmond,
HIV-negative at nineteen, describes moments where "BAM, I'm a
preacher of safe sex." In Oakland, Barry is fifty-one and HIV-negative: "I
guess it is my ministry in a way." Larry, twenty-eight and recently HIV-
positive, says: "If someone wants to have sex with me, and wants it now,
then they're going to get educated by me whether they want to or not.
I'm doing it more for me than I am for them. I get a sense of relief."

"Relief" is a word you use when you care about something. Or someone. Implied or explicit in the words of these men, and in this stack of
studies, are deep and robust patterns of sexual caretaking. They manifest
as condom use and safety, partner choice, disclosure, and prevention
activism. All this we do, in some measure at least, to spare the guy on the
other end of our willy from harm. What we don't do so easily is recognize it.

*Homosexual behavior among nonhuman primates appears to increase the
likelihood that the animals involved will provide assistance to their unrelated sexual partners.*
  —Frank Muscarella[74]

*It's my job to educate the people that I'm with. Because I'm with that person
at that moment in time. As I have been educated and somebody took the time
to educate me, I feel that it would be wrong for me to not say something to
somebody.*
  —Jack, 49, HIV-positive, Hollywood

The evidence has already brought us a far distance from Killer Dick. But
this question of altruism is actually worth noodling on. One may balk at
using altruism to describe any aspects of condom use by infected men. Is
it far-fetched to glorify as altruistic an act that is simply doing the right

thing? Does it even help to anchor this discussion in altruism, when as the evidence we have seen shows, the behavior is a majority practice in a group?

To get some clarity on this, we are joined in the studio tonight by a panel of distinguished thinkers on altruism. Dr. Aronfreed (OK, so he wrote it in 1970) offers a most narrow definition of altruistic behavior as "controlled by anticipation of its consequences for another individual." To his left, another theorist, Dr. Zahn-Waxler, defines altruism to involve "regard for, or devotion to, the interests or welfare of others . . . seen in behavioral acts of helping, sharing, sympathy, cooperation, rescue and protecting/defending."[75] More recently, altruism scholars Batson and Shaw define it to include acts "directed toward the ultimate goal of benefiting the other."[76]

Using these classic definitions—derived mostly from the animal behavior literature—does covering up one's lovestick really qualify? Well, like any good animal behaviorist, let's take the clearest example, that of a knowingly HIV-positive top deciding to use latex. ("Top," for the homosexually impaired reader, is the fella who does the inserting. The pitcher, not the catcher. The one some of you think is playing the role of the "real" man. May we proceed?)

What happens if we apply these classic behavioral definitions to what gay men do in bed (and in alleys, parks, and airplane lavatories)? True, safer sex by an HIV-positive man *does* involve engaging in specific behavioral acts of protection, *does* benefit the other, and *does* increase a partner's welfare in the context of anticipating otherwise negative consequences for that partner. It most definitely benefits the individual "receiving the behavior." (Especially if you use lots of lube. But I digress.)

Now hold on. It's not like condom use merits canonization. Besides, doesn't safer sex protect both parties at the party? So how can using or promulgating latex qualify as an "altruistic" act? Even though research does show that gay men are reducing risk at rates many multiples of heterosexual men, isn't that just a matter of, well, reciprocal responsibility?

Precisely.

Some argue for an even more stringent definition of the "A" word. For behavior to qualify as in any meaningful way altruistic, they say, it must include self-sacrifice. Defined by evolutionary biologist, David Seaborg, altruism is "behavior that has a cost to the individual performing it . . . while benefiting the individual receiving the behavior."[77] Hmmmm. Ever used rubbers, matey? Anyone who has knows that they can carry significant, real costs. The sacrifice of sexual pleasure and sensation, perceived intimacy or spontaneity, the loss of favorite sex acts, embarrassment, losing one's hard-on, the potential or implied disclosure of your HIV status. Even disclosure, for positive men, increases the chance that one's playmate *du jour* will bolt from the room, shrieking that you're a diseased pariah. All are a part of the safe sex levy, and it's no trivial tax. Face it: If there weren't big costs, we wouldn't be having this whole condom discussion at all.

So let's see. "Benefiting the other"? Check. "Interest in the welfare of the other"? Check. "At a personal cost"? Check. If this doesn't start to look like classic definitions of altruism, it's hard to know just what else to call this particular animal behavior. How about . . . sexual caretaking?

You put a condom on because you care about this person.
   —Roberto, 22, HIV-negative, Oakland

By whatever name, it's clear that our team does it differently. It was gay men who first mated the word "safe" with "sex." Still and all, we remain the group of men who maintain the single most adherent, robust, and elaborated safer sex culture on the planet. (What do I mean by elaborated and robust? Quick test: Try explaining a j/o party to your brother-in-law. Or better, just invite him along to Blow Buddies. I rest my case.) For all the ways we don't measure up to our standards, one can find no other group of men so adherent, none who consistently take such care, none who have made larger behavioral changes across the board, none who have worked harder not only to invent the complex social patterns of intimate safety and protection, but have raised the practices of communal protection to such an exuberant art. It is not that the killer dick is more apparent than real, but that our habits of care are vastly less so.

These facts raise profound ethical questions. Why were most of the men in these studies safe most of the time? So why *do* positive gay men tend to be safer with uninfected men? Why do HIV-positive men select positive partners at all? Why do they disclose? Why do any of us talk with tricks about their staying safe? Why, when we aren't safe, aren't we? Why do prevention volunteers spend Friday nights handing out condoms and answering hotlines to save lives? Why should they care, any of them?

Sexual safety is, at root, a decision in large part about values. As such, it is only a part of a broader ethical code of public and private conduct that queer men have been developing. No matter what you call it— altruism, caretaking, self-interest, or some blend of all three—we know that for a decade and a half, no other group of men has behaved as we have. After twenty years of AIDS, it may turn out that there was another

"A-word" in this epidemic all along, a love we never dared speak. Only this one rhymes with "jism."

As with violence and communal caretaking, the single most glaring fact in this evidence is how rarely we hear of it. Despite the sheer volume of research findings, the many ways queer men, of all colors, styles, and ethnicities, take care of each other is somehow Big News. The facts are at dramatic variance with the received gay wisdom that all of us—and others—transmit. Again, we face the question: What are these stories we tell ourselves, where do we get them, and why? Who do they serve?

In part, they reflect what we are told by the larger culture. Research dollars follow controversy, politics inflame it, media incite it. But we ourselves are complicit. We could not weave this particular fable without our own uncritical acceptance of the worst part of our story as truth. We reflect it to each other when we wear the T-shirt that reads: "Gay men are dogs. Train me" or run a personal ad proclaiming "sex pig." At first we do it laughingly, a bravura embrace of our liberation, a step out from the darkness of hypocrisy into the light of spirit and flesh. But if we aren't careful, at some point the joke shades into something else. It subtly infects our own narrative and our expectations, leaching into our hearts and actions. The fable encourages us first to tell it, then to become it. In the end, as with any other set of rules and codes, we come to enact what we proclaim.

It is fair to ask why we silence our most interesting ethics even as we enact them. The facts reveal private behaviors at remarkable variance from the dogma of gay-men-as-dogs. But because we allow these ethics such scant place in our discourse, we dilute and extinguish them. That gay men save each other's lives every night of the week has become our best-kept secret. Instead, we find a striking gap between folk wisdom about how "gay men" generally behave and these very same men's descriptions of their own personal values and experiences. In one set of qualitative interviews conducted on both coasts in 1996, one in five of the gay men interviewed recount anecdotes or concerns about positive men carelessly infecting others. However, in describing their own values and experiences, virtually all the positive men (and 80 percent of the negative men) talk about their own roles *helping protect* other men. In that sample, almost half (47 percent) cited a shared belief that other gay men are uncaring about HIV risk. Yet when asked to speak from their own experience, only half as many—fewer than a quarter of the sample—could cite a concrete personal experience of a sex partner disregarding their safety. A much larger proportion, more than a third of the group, described personal instances of gay men as caring for each other in terms of HIV safety. Yet how rarely we make room for that part of their stories.

There is no better example of this bias than the searing polemics around barebacking. That discussion seems consistently to overlook two key facts. First, that barebacking—defined as "the mindful and intentional pursuit of consensual unprotected sex"—is principally (depending on whom you read, overwhelmingly) a phenomenon among men of like HIV status. One "barebacks" on purpose. That very intentionality and consensuality is exactly what separates barebacking from the garden variety slip-ups, omissions, half-truths, magical thinking, substance effects, and errors that comprise the foggy provinces of the merely unsafe. Even its name connotes. By the time a subculture coins a media-genic name to describe a mutual choice, and has elaborated chat rooms, discussion groups, internet listserves, and sex parties to facilitate it, it starts to look more like marketing than murder.

At a contentious public meeting to discuss barebacking in New York in 1999, an interesting statement came from a man who described himself as the manager of the nation's largest moderated bareback computer list. He stated almost in passing that the list was "about 98 percent poz guys." In fact, it was reported that the list expressly barred from participation people who identified themselves as "bug chasers" or "gift seekers"—negative men expressly seeking to be infected. Several barebacking pundits have noted this. This very debate was convened by *POZ* magazine the month its magazine cover ran their first major barebacking story. The fact that barebacking should cluster at all by HIV status—that it is so much more prevalent among HIV-positive men—is in fact a telling disproof to the doctrine of the depraved dicks. If infected men didn't care at all, you'd expect to see four times more negative men than positive men doing it, in rough proportion to their numbers in the population. But it doesn't seem to cluster that way, nowhere close. It's hard to be a callous, wanton, uncaring Typhoid Mary when you are choosing to do it with other Marys who are choosing to do it with you. And when you've all agreed on a catchy name for it.

As I watched that evening, a second, subtler truth took shape in that crowded room. The standing-room attendance, speaker after speaker rising to malign barebacking, debate and deride it, question the morality and sanity of its practitioners, blast its advocates or oppose its existence—that was the real story here. Listening to the speakers' voices rise with anguish and anger, anxiety and worry, panic and hurt, their tone conveyed more eloquently than their words could one clear idea: *These people really, truly cared*. If they didn't, the discussion would not inflame such passions. It offended their sense of the right thing to do. *It was a sin against a shared ethic.*

What was unrolling in that steamy room in the gay center was not so far different from what happened in the *agora* of classical Athens. A people had gathered in the public square to refine their shared values. To even confront the bareback bogeyman meant we had convened to set our culture's boundaries. This was a high-stakes contest to decree what is permissible and what not. That barebacking was so hugely controversial suggests precisely how deeply it offends an existing—if often unnamed— common standard. The stridency of the barebacking discussion reflected the ferocity of a wish to reassert an ethic of sexual care.

Or maybe this wasn't a room of Athenians at all. Perhaps these Villagers, with their eyebrow rings and tribal tattoos, had gathered in this queer space like so many medieval villagers would have once congregated before a town bonfire. There we were, milling and fearful, armed with clubs and spades and torches, come to drive a monster from our moral midst.

There is a terrible disconnect here. In a culture where looking out for number one is the approved mode, a lifeboat mentality is self-fulfilling. Without language and stories to name or honor our altruistic impulses and values, we trust them less. When what you name is self-interest, it's all you can see, then soon all you can name. Without claiming this chamber of our hearts, we inhabit it less often. We come to feel more alone, to value each other less, which leads to taking more risks.

The result of this delusion rings chillingly in the words of an HIV-positive bisexual man interviewed in New York: "With gay men, a lot of sex is recreational sex, like a sport. With a lot of women it's not a recreation, it's an emotional kind of attachment. I didn't feel like I wanted to take the risk of contaminating a woman, whereas I would take the risk of contaminating a man. Because I figure, we are all dogs anyway." The consequences of the "gay men are dogs" dogma are very real and hugely pernicious. By believing the worst about ourselves, we create it. *We enact what we expect. We become our worst fears with each other.* The interviewer who conducted the interview sent this in an E-mail with the question: "How do you promote altruism and community care among a people who have been taught to hate their own?" How, indeed?

———

As we have seen here, the weight of evidence frames a powerful paradox. The domain of sex, by far the most heavily researched, may have been among the most profoundly misconstrued. One of the ways that interpersonal altruism may play out most dramatically among us is the very place we most ferociously deny that it exists. The patterns thriving in our sexual relationships may be the parts of us *where we know ourselves least well.*

To tell the history of the epidemic as one of sexual callousness or uncaring profligacy is to distort its essential soul. As with violence and service, a large body of facts speaks eloquently. The image of gay men as uncaring sexual predators appears gravely off base. Modern urban gay folklore has it that gay men are insanely risky. If, as some fear, risk is indeed rising, we have all the more reason to look to a deeper truth in the values underlying our actions.

We could just as well believe that heedless acts of infection, when they occur, provoke us so deeply precisely because they so transgress the dominant moral and behavioral ethic. In effect, each becomes a small morality play dressed up as an epidemiological account. The supposed prevalence of uncaring, wanton infectors may be the gay folklore equivalent of the dybbuk, the monster in the dark, the bogeyman loose in the gay erotic.

Look at the social forms and rituals that we have evolved, the acts we commit, the rules many of us live by daily. From safer sex to disclosure to partner protection, we are working to take care of each other in a myriad of ways, subtle and overt. We do not always succeed, but we do more sexual caretaking than any other social strata of men. Ironic, isn't it? Once again, a century later, it is our love—with and for each other—that dare not speak its name.

5 | ALIVE AND WELL IN SEXUAL MADAGASCAR

Our beautiful sexuality is the gateway to spirit. It's different from how all the other religions feel, they need a separation between carnality and spirituality. We see it all as one big ball of wax. Sex and spirit are all one big picture, and that infuses human life. It pushes life into you. Whenever you make love with another man you are exercising spirit.
—Harry Hay

For many years, a day didn't go by when, if I looked for it, I couldn't go have sex with a totally hot guy I really liked within, oh, say, thirty minutes.
—Terry, 39, Hayward, California.

The percentage of gay-identified men who are celibate is twice that of the heterosexual men in our sample.
—Diane Binson

If there's one part of the gay story that many Americans imagine they know best, it is the sex part. Most of us—like most of America—readily embrace the familiar images of us as sexual satyrs. Whether we view us as deviant sluts or exemplary studs, whether we envy, condemn, or just titter at such habits, most of us partake of the endless recycling discussions of muscle, steroids, and sex parties, exclusion and A lists, hot men, body fascism, and testosterone. With all that attention below the belt, you'd think we would understand this part of our cultural habits and practices. Yet it is here we may have most missed the real story.

The scrim of conventional gay sex wisdom, reflected in gay media, from *Cruising* to *Queer as Folk*, from *Tales of the City* to *Will and Grace*, serves actually to obscure the far deeper, more powerful, and transformational cultural aspects embedded in our erotic innovations. It is easy to be distracted by the surface of beefcake and boytoys, especially when gay habits stand in such relief to the *mores* of the dominant culture. But just beneath that shimmering sea of skin swirl powerful submarine currents. The tides of gay sexual cultures are re-forming the continents of how our society understands social and sexual life. We are reshaping the topography of intimacy.

When the blue-green orb of Earth was young, the ink still wet on nature's creation, a vast island landmass split off from the continent that would one day become Africa. Over eons of time it drifted away to mid-ocean, forming the landmass now known as Madagascar. Over numberless generations, that isolated environment evolved its own rich ecosystems and biology, sprouting novel species, varieties, relationships, and hybrids seen nowhere else. This distinctive island continent is today prized by biologists as a place unique on the planet, a living laboratory of nature's craft. Madagascar displays Nature's endless capacity for ingenious self-invention, a living reminder that the most interesting things evolve on islands.

On the socio-sexual globe, gay world is Madagascar. The very concept of a public gay culture—what we oversimplify as "the gay community"—began to take shape and substance in the social crucible of the 1950s to the 1960s. The sixties were an era of huge social and sexual exploration for America. Burning bras, liberated women, the Pill, miniskirts, open marriage, *Our Bodies, Ourselves,* free love, sex toys. From Gay Is Good to the summer of love, it was a heady time. Literally.

It was also immensely terrifying to those rooted firmly in the sexual values of another time. As the walls of the old sexual order came tumbling down, forces within the larger culture moved to defend the ramparts. They tried to discredit, sabotage, and dismantle the collective erotic exploration America was beginning. They fought ferociously against these innovations, to roll the clock back and stamp out erotic innovation. They fought abortion, birth control, family planning, pornography, and Internet chat rooms, railed at free love and drug use and condoms and premarital sex. War was declared on STDs as herpes, HIV, hepatitis were branded onto the popular mind.

Over the next three decades, they reeled the discourse back from hash orgies to herpes scares, from sex ed to abstinence ed, from *The Joy of Sex* to

The Joy of Monogamy. The mission: to bury the sexual changes of the 1960s and make the world safe for their kind. Theirs was a holy crusade to pacify the erotic kingdom. The goal was to teach America to Just Say No.

But somewhere while the larger society was fighting itself bloody in the sex wars, one legion of men slipped from the battlefield and sued for a separate peace. That team was equally busy evolving its own separate sexual ecosystem, just at different hours of the day. The cultural continents began to drift apart. As America pedaled down the alley called abstinence, gay men quietly commandeered the Streetcar Named Desire. As the permissible sexual discourse within the dominant society was denatured to Just Say No, we were the rowdies in the back row, growling "Yeah, baby!" Among us, the communal sexual explorations of the 1960s, so aggressively extinguished in the larger culture, continued, deepened, matured, took new forms.

Today, not only have gay cultural sexual values diverged sharply from the puritanical historical roots of American sexuality, but we have significantly resisted the icy winds of sexual repression that have swept across the American landscape. Taking for granted the sexual privilege of men, informed by our status as erotic outlaws, we have conspired in a lusty, unapologetic embrace of sex and its myriad pleasures. Rather than collude in a cultural narrative rendering HIV as a modern morality play, it was our communities that launched a radical countermeasure. We were the ones who wrapped up our communal ethics of care in latex technology, called it safer sex, and implemented it more thoroughly, with more bawdy bravura, than any other population on earth.

Let the skirmishes rage in the larger society. Our Fantasy Island was just isolated enough from the mainstream so that a vast profusion of sexual variants could evolve. Far up in the hidden canyons of gay world, an astonishing range of diverse sexual species began to flourish. We developed our own erotic Madagascar, a largely unseen erotic ecosystem. In that libidinal landscape blooms a profuse flora and fauna of fantasy, fucking, and fun.

> *I told him my age—twenty—*
> *and he expressed wild wonder*
> *at all the sex ahead of me. . . .*
>   —Wayne Koestenbaum, poet, 1979

Unsheath your pencils, guys. Time for a pop quiz. Compare and contrast what all the following have in common:

aroma
backrooms
ball stretchers
barebacking
bathhouses
bear cubs
Black Party
Blow Buddies
Body Electric
bondage clubs
butch bottoms
boytoys
carnal carnivals
chat rooms
Chestmen
chubby chasers
cigar scenes
circuit slut
c/b t
cockrings
condom demos
Colt models
cottaging
cruising
cum patrols
daddies
docking
fetish fests

fisting
flagging
frat games
fuck buddies
glory holes
hanky code
harnesses
guiche
IML
Inferno
j/o parties
jock sniffing
leather bars
Leather University
lube guns
masters
meatrack
milking
mummification
nipple rings
not-very-butch
   bottoms
numbers
orgy rooms
Path of the Beloved
   Disciple
phone sex
piercing

playdates
Prince Albert
public sex
S/M runs
safe words
safer sex
sacred intimates
scrotum totems
sex pals
slave training
sleaze parties
slings
studmuffins
tearooms
Tom of Finland
tops
trick cards
tricking
underwear parties
vanilla
versatility
water sports
wrestling buddies
_____
_____
_____

(Feel free to list your
own favorites here.)

Kee-rect! If you noticed that these are just a few of the socio-sexual innovations present on Planet Gay, score ten points. Welcome to the great gay erotic imaginary. All of these are erotic innovations we have invented, adopted, championed, led, reinvigorated, or promulgated. Of course, this is just my list. You could no doubt make one of your own, probably much longer, and certainly more, um, personally relevant.

Three things are worth noting. The first is many of us know much of what's on this list. It represents a widely shared pool of cultural knowledge. Second, most other folks don't share it, or even much care to. There's no better way to grasp its queer-culture flavor than, say, to try explaining the hanky code to your mother, the nuances of tops and bottoms to your father or uncle, or the joys of fisting to your brother-in-law.

These habits, opportunities, rituals, conventions, and language flourish *entre nous.* Many remain largely unknown, even inconceivable, outside our clan. Not all, of course; obviously, straight folks have play parties and sex dates, use safe words, slings, and phone lines. Word has it, there are even a few AOL chat rooms that *don't* begin with "m4m". Lord knows, straight men have certainly borrowed a few things from our team. If only you'd invested in Nair and nipple rings when you had the chance.

What is key here is that in gay lives so many of these practices are accepted and known. They have a wholly different cultural centrality. In gay lives these acts and customs are not only conceivable, but common. Obviously, not all of them are universal or monolithic among us. We don't all check down the list like merit badges. I, for one, have never worn a Prince Albert and do not intend to start. But our culture permits us to access such possibilities if we wish. The point is not that any of us are individually randier or more highly sexed. (A paper, for example, directly comparing sexual sensation seeking found gay and straight subjects essentially the same.[1] One of the largest recent national samples of gay men found 24 percent of us are celibate—more than twice the level of comparable straight guys.[2] So much for the myth of the rapacious sexual predator, the wanton wandering dick.)

Rather, the difference is a communal one. In an essay, "Culture, History, and Life Course of Gay Men," anthropologist Gilbert Herdt wrote: "Eroticism is not only easier in the gay culture, it is more a part of gay men's view of human nature. Freud's 'polymorphous perverse' idea of the erotic has found a congenial home in gay culture."[3] He captures a truth, for where the larger society works to circumscribe its citizens' sexual options, our cultures work to broaden them. When you write your own rules, you can write the ones you want.

That tendency has brought us to a unique juncture. We have arguably elaborated the most complex, flourishing, nuanced sexual culture the planet has known. No other population alive today enjoys a sexual milieu so elaborated and robust, so richly creative, as ours. Look at the range of sexual options and customs available to queer men in even a mid-size American city and ask yourself what other public subculture affords so many options to its members' members. Where else is the domain of the erotic so exuberant and exploratory, so democratic and permissive, and (sometimes) just plain fun? Over history, it is hard to cite any example of a culture that enjoyed as comparably rich a set of rituals, conventions, language, icons, images, and technologies of sex as we do. Nor one that has so thoroughly elevated and celebrated sexual power and glory as ours.

So now, let's step ashore on this Madagascar of males. Leave the ortho-doxies of conventional wisdom in the boat. We have beached here to explore several of the natives' most interesting sexual innovations. Accept that the outward forms and practices here reflect profoundly dif-ferent cultural values around sex, pleasure, intimacy, and erotic comrade-ship. Keep your eyes peeled for what is most interesting in this landscape of libido, for while one is easily distracted by the titillating topography, the most radical and interesting flowers are not always the brightest ones. As we explore, keep in mind the key question of every true explorer: What treasures may we find here to enrich the larger society we came from?

The first, most provocative sexual innovation involves the gay rescript-ing of monogamy, and its centrality to emotionally committed couple-dom. It is late on a Saturday afternoon and more than one hundred men are crowded into a meeting room in a downtown Pittsburgh hotel. It is among the best-attended sessions of Creating Change, the annual confer-ence of the National Gay and Lesbian Task Force. Some are couples, sin-gles, and more than one stable three- or foursome. But they all share one bond in common. They have come to discuss how to create, sustain, and nurture their relationships. All are in open relationships, that is, non-monogamous. The crowd is barely seated before they begin to talk, offer-ing tips, experiences, war stories.

Within moments, the room takes on the air of a revival tent, crackling with excitement. The men are testifying like mad: "We only do it in three-ways." "It's OK if neither of you knows the person." "Just on our designated 'boys'-night-out.'" "Only when we travel." "Never with someone in our town." "Yes, but fucking is reserved for just us." "So long as we never kiss." "We're vanilla at home, but he gets kink outside."

Like a roomful of rabbis, these men offer an endlessly inventive series of interpretations on their erotic Talmud. For one, the nuptial bedroom is off-limits. Another forbids "emotional entanglements." Permissible so long as you don't know the person's name. Never in our house. Accept-able as a one-time event. No staying overnight. The room bursts into laughter at the strategy offered by a fresh-faced couple from San Jose: Extracurriculars are divulged within twenty-four hours and the straying one buys his mate a nice dinner—or pays him twenty dollars. "It's worked for five years," they giggle. In this conference room, a hundred Emily Posts are sharing the etiquette of how it's done in polite (gay) soci-ety so nobody gets hurt.

One could imagine oneself in a room of priests or cardinals each arguing for his heartfelt and scrupulously observed interpretation of canon law. Like a lavender Leviticus, some rules spring directly from health concerns: "We always play safe outside. We always use protection with each other." Others see the relationship as the one place where latex never intrudes.

The strategy least discussed here is the most common one: "Don't ask, don't tell." The very mention of it underscores a sweet paradox. Surely, "don't ask, don't tell" is a common strategy in gay coupledom, but the difference is that among us it often has an affectional valence. We use it as a delicate consensual system of spared feelings and sustained intimacies. When the military brass imposed it, one wonders if they appreciated the irony that they were borrowing a habit gay men had perfected to humanely manage our rich web of erotic and affectional bonds. The boys at the Pentagon no doubt imagine that the "don't ask, don't tell" dogma was their idea. In fact, they are borrowing a social custom used by millions of fags to maintain our intimate relationships. But in the armed forces, the policy is used to reinstated shame and secrecy, and has become the most tortured of military doctrines, in the process twisting the military brass into a political and PR pretzel. The military in a clumsy institutional way aped a social practice gay men have long elaborated and refined, the better to be in affectional relation with each other.

Still, the men in this room today are hardly your basic "don't ask, don't tell" kinda crowd. Forgoing sessions about street activism or campus organizing, they have voted with their feet (or other organs) to come here to give the lowdown about what's real in their lives. And talk they do. Some men prefer to know nothing; others wish not to be told ahead; others insist on disclosure afterward. Some prefer to know it happened, without details; others prefer a who-did-what-to-whom instant replay, no gory details spared. Each explicates his own systems and rules, an endless flow of nuance and interpretation.

Similar discussions have ignited in every corner of gay male life. The topic takes over AOL chat rooms (m4mtakenbutlooking), smolders in HIV prevention conferences, echoes at Café Flore in San Francisco, on gay swim teams and at Palm Springs poolsides, at Radical Faeries encampments and Pocono leather runs. The last two Gay Men's National Health Summits have each had workshops on open relationships. The topic has been moderated at each of the National Gay and Lesbian Task Force's annual Creating Change conferences for the past several years.

Most striking in these discussions is their huge sensitivity and care.

An extraordinary inventiveness and imagination underlie the complex etiquette they are discussing. Under these fluorescent lights, these men are doing what clans of men have forever done as they gather around flickering campfires. They are handing down lore, passing along the wisdom of the tribe. Rooms like this are a place we go to learn what works and doesn't. Try this, don't eat those other berries, they're trouble. In a powerful and sweet cultural moment, we are participating in collective self-definition, teaching each other about how to behave with each other. In this living oral tradition, we are writing the manual on ourselves, scribing the next page of our own erotic etiquette. With each line, we define one of our most significant affectional and ethical innovations.

In addition to these men's testimonies, much evidence now demonstrates that non-monogamy is a robust and established cultural practice among us. Precise numbers are hard to pin down, but it is estimated that between 40 and 50 percent of gay men are in committed couples at any given time. Among those men, however, the shape of things is extremely well established. A stack of research confirms that about three-quarters of gay men in stable, long-term relationships are consensually non-monogamous, without it necessarily threatening the viability of the couple. A 1977 German paper claimed "most homosexual males renounce sexual fidelity."[4] In 1979, Harry and Lovely found a majority to be open in their sample of gay couples.[5] The same finding came the next year in a book subtitled *A New Look at Gay Couples*.[6] The following year, Peplau and Cochran found more than 70 percent of the couples they surveyed were open.[7]

Similar findings have been reported by a variety of researchers, in many locales, over the two decades since: among 320 Dutch gay couples[8] among committed gay male Christian couples in Nottingham, England ("the majority of couples were expectationally and behaviorally nonexclusive")[9] A University of California team found 57 percent of gay men studied were non-monogamous.[10] Others sampled both before and after the onset of the HIV epidemic, and found seven in ten long-term male couples were open. A decade later, in a New York sample, two-thirds of the men were open.[11] In the landmark book, *The Male Couple*, McWhirter and Mattison reported that virtually *all* of their sample of long-term stable gay men's relationships moved to be open.[12] The same finding arises in several large national studies in this country, among them the *Sex in America* book.[13]

The weight of evidence makes clear that monogamy occupies a radically different niche in the ecosystem of committed gay relationships than in the larger society. Statistics on heterosexual nonmonogamy are notoriously variable, with enormous political stakes, and have ranged from 10 percent to about 25 percent of married couples. In round numbers, it's fairly clear that approximately the same percent of gay men aren't monogamous in long-term couples as heterosexual men are. But look beyond the numbers and statistics, to consider the lesson in these numbers. Are we just hopeless pigs, and this just one more confirmatory example for the gay-men-are-dogs brigade? Or might something else— something far deeper—be going on?

Most men in our sample had devoted a good deal of thought to the issue of sexual exclusivity.
    —David Blasband

Any such practice that is majoritarian in a subculture, as is non-monogamy in gay life, suggests an underlying cultural difference. Were we a native people somewhere, "polyandry" is the term anthropologists would use for having so many bonded male sexual mates. Indeed, the next time you stroll the sidewalks of Castro, Montrose, or Fort Lauderdale, consider that you walk the tribal homeland of America's only openly polyandric tribe. (A cheeky anthropologist might even note that the varieties of queer polyandric sexual culture bear a striking resemblance to one other uniquely American subpopulation. Like us, that group celebrated males having diverse sexual and marital mates. They also proclaimed it as part of their spiritual and cultural creed. You might think it odd that our closest living socio-sexual relatives, the once-polygamist Mormons, are so vexed by us. Joseph Smith, meet Walt Whitman. Talk amongst yourselves. Maybe Salt Lake City isn't quite as far from San Francisco as it looks on the map. We are, you might say, kissing cousins.)

Clearly, any behavior whose prevalence approaches three in four assumes cultural dimensions. It is not that millions of gay men were absent the day they taught the rules, or know the rules and simply cannot abide them, or are simply flouting them. To interpret non-monogamy as infidelity or cheating is to miss the point in a most stunning way. When a clear majority of stable, successful long-term gay couples redraw the rules to include outside sex, and still about a quarter don't, it says that we *have clearly elaborated a parallel set of acceptable cultural norms*. It seems that the natives of these lavender provinces are not so much cheating as choosing.

The interesting thing here is not that we fuck and philander, but that we don't box it up in that way. Gay male culture—in some ways like European straight male culture—offers permission, language, rituals, and support for this exploration. Listen carefully to the men in chat rooms, read the studies, and you hear an elaborated politesse of practice and protection—emotional and physical—underlying the statistics. One would be hard-pressed to cite any other Western culture which has invented such a nuanced emotional erotic etiquette, one that functions to spare feelings, maintain bonds, and respect boundaries. In writing such radically different rules, we have given ourselves a wider, accepted, more elaborated permission.

Of course, nobody is required to sleep around, but if you both choose to, you need not lie to your mate, your peers, or yourself. As one author researching gay open couples noted: "Lacking a cultural model to which they can relate, lesbians and gays attempt to form new models of behavior unique to lesbian and gay relationships."[14] Gay psychologist Larry Kurdek at Wright State University has studied gay couples for a decade, and has found great strengths in gay relationships. One of those is that unlike heterosexual couples, we "come into relationships with very few pre-defined roles. We basically have to construct those roles." As a result, he says, "researchers often describe our relationships as being built on a general ethic of equality." It makes sense, really. After all, in a society where we cannot marry, by definition *all* of our relationships are extra-marital. We just do them after our own fashion.

Nonmonogamy? There's a lot of good stuff to be said about it, and a lot of bad to be said about it. It's just . . . the bad stuff has mostly been said.
—Eric B, Cleveland

Researchers of sexual jealousy consistently find that it is notably "lower for men in homosexual couples," that "men in heterosexual couples have higher levels of sexual jealousy than men in homosexual couples" and that "sexual jealousy was inversely correlated with what the researchers called a 'self-actualization personality.' "[15] Others have found that gay men "indicated lower levels of experiencing and expressing sexual jealousy, less exclusive relationships, and higher levels of extradyadic sexual relations by their partners" than comparable straight men.[16] Other researchers have found much the same.[17]

Experts now suggest that such differences aren't individual, but cultural. "The homosexual group generally experience relationships in which partner's sexual exclusivity is not expected."[18] A 1992 British research team found 72 percent of gay male couples were nonmonogamous after five years, recognized it as a culture norm, and suggested that open relationships be better incorporated into public health programs.[19] Similar approaches have been recommended by AIDS public health authorities researchers in Australia.[20]

Even the research language provides a subtle but telling recognition of this cultural difference. Look at the index in a recent landmark national sex book, *Sex in America*. It indexes the heterosexual findings under "infidelity," but the gay male sections under the term "nonmonogamy."[21] In such subtle ways do our innovations seep into the larger culture. In the words of another researcher: "The results strongly implicate culture . . . in the development of sexual jealousy. The finding that men in homosexual relationships have lower levels of sexual jealousy than men in heterosexual relationships . . . suggest that culture is also involved in the development of a sexually jealous attitude . . . Sexual jealousy, viewed as an attitude, is mediated by culture and personality."[22]

They are recognizing what gay men have long known: Here at the gay café, our menu lets you choose from column A or column B. We have laid ourselves a different smorgasbord, and by all accounts, many of us find it tasty. But how tasty is it, really? How well does this Brave New Amorous World really work? In a paper, "Sexual Exclusivity Versus Openness in Gay Male Couples," the authors state: "No significant differences were found in the quality of open vs. closed relationships in terms of love and liking for the partner, satisfaction, or commitment." Those men "in open relationships emphasized the benefits of sexual variety and personal independence, whereas subjects in closed relationships stressed their desire to avoid jealousy." From the Netherlands, a paper in the *Archives of Sexual Behavior* noted "both partners' attitudes that sexual encounters are positive for relationship functioning."[23] A similar work, "Relationship Quality of Gay Men in Closed or Open Relationships," examined several measures of relationship health and stated: "Partners in both types of relationships were more similar than different."[24]

At the height of British gay liberation, one of their manifestos proposed: "Our heterosexual detractors betray their limited vision by their mistaken assumption that promiscuity is incompatible with lasting relationships." We may, it suggests, "be in the happy position of being able to enjoy both at once."[25] A quarter century of accumulated numerical evidence appears to indeed suggest that this utopian assertion was not far off the mark. The majority of long-term gay male couples have indeed opted for such arrangements. They have voted with their, um, feet, suggesting that it is a happy alternative for many. According to gay couple gurus McWhirter and Mattison, "We believe that the single most important factor that keeps couples together past the ten-year mark is the lack of possessiveness they feel. Many couples learn that ownership of each other sexually can become the greatest internal threat to their staying together."[26]

Jeff and his lover, Kent, see it that way. Jeff starts: "We opened up things in year five—seven years ago. Kent had always had an interest in doing things I didn't want to, and it got to where I could see he wasn't happy. We were arguing about it, and our eyes were straying." "OOOhhh, yeah," grins Kent. "We knew something had to give. And the more we thought about it, we know we really love each other, love our lives." At that point, Jeff chimes in: "Plus, over time, we got to be not, well, you know, not entirely each other's type." They both laugh. "For us, being open seemed to us a way to keep together, and both get what we wanted. Then we come home and snuggle."

Alden and Raul, who have made Memphis home for nine years, have made a completely different choice. "We're the jealous types," Raul explains. "It just wouldn't work for us, and we both know it. Three-ways are OK—because we're both there, you know, having fun together. It's something we do with each other as much as with a third. That we do a lot." "We call them 'snacks.'" Alden grins. "As in, you know, wanna get on-line tonight and order in a snack?"

From snuggles to snacks, for better and worse, richer and poorer, it seems that three in four long-term gay couples have opted to add a new rider (literally) to the gay marriage contract. One can choose outside sex as a standard option in the till-death-do-us-part policy, without it threatening the sanctity of a committed relationship.

The sheer numbers of happily open queer couples is a matter of epidemiological fact. But far more interesting are the cultural and ethical implications they pose. Most primarily, what is radical is how openly it is acknowledged. Among partners, friends, and social circles, in language ("Roger and I started closed, but opened our relationship in year four"), in the protocols the men in the campfire gatherings describe, in chat room profiles ("Committed but open, no lying," "Taken, permission to play," "Collared, but not caged"), in our fiction and film, woven throughout gay communal expectations and habits, we recognize openly that

sexual compacts can be part of successful relationships when both participants so choose.

Open relationships require couples to make far subtler distinctions
between emotional and sexual fidelity, as many researchers have noted
among gay men. More than twenty-five years ago, a German psychologist noted "the ability to distinguish between affection and sexuality"
among the gay couples he studied.[27] A British sociologist interviewed
thirty gay male couples in "Gay Male Christian Couples and Sexual
Exclusivity." The men, devout Christians all, "embraced the theology of
friendship that emphasizes inclusiveness rather than monogamy." As had
several previous studies, the researcher found that open couples "did not
demonstrate significant differences in terms of their level of relationship
satisfaction and commitment."[28] Rather, they "thought about open relationships on the grounds of sexual variety, prevention of possessiveness,
promotion of freedom and egalitarianism."[29] Others have noted that
"gay relationships are distinct from heterosexual relationships in that
they are frequently based on expectations of equality, reciprocity, and
autonomy."[30] Such findings echo, almost word for word, the utopian
vision of the first gay liberation manifesto, written fifteen years before:
"Gay is a process of attaining mutual and equal social and sexual relationships among all human beings, which is realized only in the free
dynamic expression of love among peoples of the same sex."

A straight counterpart, psychologist John Gottman, compared gay
and straight couples, and found that "unique strengths may be rooted in
the fact that there are fewer external reasons—marriage licenses, children, family pressure—pressuring gay partners to stay together. As a
result, 'process' is much more important for gays in their relationships,"[31] and part of that process is the negotiating around what sexual
rules the couple prefers.

Such relationship openness bears a profound implication on that most
central of ethical issues: the telling of truth. The only researcher to inves-
tigate it directly found gay couples were significantly less likely to lie to
their partners than matched straight couples.[32] The article, "Deception
in Intimate Relationships: A Comparison of Heterosexuals and Homo-
sexual/ Bisexuals," interviewed 159 members of couples, and found a statistically significant difference: "Heterosexual men and women
responded deceptively more often than did gay men and lesbian
women." Gay men were the most honest, and straight women were
found to be "significantly more truthful" than were heterosexual men in
their sample. It bluntly concludes: "Heterosexuals engage in deceptive

behavior more than homosexuals/ bisexuals." Perhaps, the author posits, because "the less normative nature of homosexual/bisexual intimate relationships" affects how "individuals are willing to accept responsibility for their behavior." Without doubt, says one author writing on new marriage patterns, such arrangements, "which combine commitment to the group with multiple pair-bonding among members, are the most complex form of marriage."[33]

Complex, indeed. Responsibility, ethics, truth, the theology of friendship, egalitarianism. Such big words wind far above the ungenerous gutter wisdom that says fags just can't keep it zipped. They ask us to confront the possibility that behind the simplistic "gay-men-as-pigs" narrative lies a far subtler ethical subtext. This amorous clan is consciously, collectively, culturally, and carefully redrafting the convenants we make with each other around fidelity, intimacy, and commitment. We are decoupling notions of shame and guilt, defusing the imperatives of deceit and betrayal which have traditionally welded the seams of committed coupledom.

Obviously, being open is not monolithic—one in four long-term gay male couples are, after all, sexually exclusive. Nor is it uncontested. The magazine *HERO,* for example, promulgated, among other things, "hot monogamy" by, for, and aimed squarely at gay men. What is clear, however, is that the cultural norms operating in our social milieu allow committed couples an option that most couples in the dominant culture don't have.

That makes us Big Trouble. Not only do we pursue these options consciously, we do it conspicuously. We surface our amorous heresies into dominant culture. We do it when the largest-circulation gay magazine, *The Advocate,* devotes its June 1998 cover to a shirtless male couple snuggled in the sheets with their white Shih-Tzu pooch, with MONOGAMY shrieking in sixty-point type over their heads. (Ironically, that month's *Time* magazine cover featured "Everything Your Kids Already Know About Sex.")

We do it again with every sassy innuendo on *Will and Grace,* each suggesting that domestic sexuality may at times be a gang affair. Or when a respected San Francisco clergy leader speaks in public about the four men with whom he has been in a committed relationship for several years, or the Indianapolis lawyer shares that he has been involved in a three-way lovership for the better part of a decade. We do it in another key in the twenty-plus articles that have appeared in sober journals from psychology to public health to social work. Under subversive titles like "Monogamy and Gay Men—Aspects for the Clinician," "Relationship

Quality of Gay Men in Closed or Open Relationships," "Gay Male Christian Couples and Sexual Exclusivity," or "Sexual Exclusivity Versus Openness in Gay Male Couples," such articles acknowledge this common cultural practice, which cannot be ignored, denied, or erased. It has its unique cultural patterns and protocols, recognized in distinct names and nuances. These conventions and commitments demand understanding as a matter of professional competence.[34]

We do it when a holiday card from the Midwestern mom in Madison, Wisconsin, comes addressed to her son and the two men who share his life, home, and bed in Albany. We do it when the twelve-year-old neighbor of a sprawling ranch compound in a northwest Oregon neighborhood refers to it simply as "Ken, Andy, Ward, and Bobby's place—they're married." Or when the fifty-seven-year-old married woman in Jupiter, Florida, calls her brother and asks after not only his lover, David, but also Bryan, whom he terms "his other significant."

What will happen as we more openly share our amorous connections with our straight friends, in our media and discourse, over Thanksgiving dinner, in phone talks with our relatives? Every day that we define this as a permissible exploration, we send off ripples far beyond the pond called queer. Our very candor opens a Pandora's box of radical questions that the larger culture would all too eagerly keep nailed shut.

The problem is that this queer territory, our male Madagascar, turns out to be an island of spreading sexual innovation. And did I mention? Tourism to Madagascar has been on the upswing.

The impact of gay liberation ideology on gay male relationships may be considered a model of predicted changes in heterosexual mate selection patterns.
—John Lee, "Forbidden Colors of Love"

As with gay cultural innovations in caretaking, volunteerism, service, and violence, this cultural innovation holds huge portent for the larger society. In queer non-monogamy, we have issued the most sweeping cultural challenge to marriage since Brigham Young rocked the wagons on the trip to Utah. Along with the growing band of those who term themselves "polyamorous," our most queer habits pose all manner of sticky questions.

What might this gay cultural innovation portend for larger society, as gay men openly share our habits with our biological families, married friends, straight coworkers? Might this queer re-mapping offer transformational possibility to the iron rule of marital law? What will that mean for the one in four heterosexual couples in America who themselves have had extramarital relations?

What if married couples felt less stigma about naming what statistics tell us that so many of them already do? Might we one day erase the words "cheating" and "betrayal" from the matrimonial script? Indeed, might the very concepts slowly evaporate from a more humane marital vocabulary? Could terms like "straying" and "philandering" come to look as quaint as "cuckold" does today? If stable committed partners explored sexual pleasures elsewhere, might they feel less trapped in an angry, resentful, or explosive near-celibacy? Would we see less of the common social pattern of male mid-life crisis, or hear less of married women's frustrated search for a meaningful intimacy?

Might husbands and wives not feel the same social pressure to divorce after episodes of sexual adventure by one partner? Might such arrangements avoid shattering of what may otherwise be a fulfilling and companionate marital relationship? What changes could occur in divorce statutes and church sermons, as the notion of "faithful" acquires new shades of nuance? Would we count fewer breakups, reduced divorces citing "irreconcilable differences," fewer guilt-wracked husbands moaning how their wives don't understand them? One paper even describes the model for intimate separations gay men commonly enact: "Separation of intimates is not expected to be a bitter divorce, but a friendly disagreement in which the partners can continue to relate to each other. . . ."[35]

Our innovations would bring changes at a public health level, as well. Perhaps honestly open couples would adopt safer sexual practices in an atmosphere of consent, reducing the numbers of women surprised at contracting HIV from a mate they believed was faithful. Perhaps we would see less domestic violence than that now inflamed by sexual frustration, jealousy, possessiveness, or shame. One provocative paper directly addressed the cultural ramifications of gay non-monogamy: "Sexual jealousy, viewed as an attitude, is mediated by culture and personality . . . the elimination of sexual jealousy is a realistic goal for those who wish it."[36]

Now there's a bona fide Big Idea. Sexual jealousy has elements of cultural choice, rather than an inevitable, innate response. The notion is not that queer men's cultures say you can't feel jealous, but simply that *you don't have to*. We won't indoctrinate jealousy in the same way, nor inculcate the grim meanings the wider culture has been taught to attach to non-exclusivity. It may turn out that sexual jealousy—all the ways we have been coached to feel, brought up to react—is far more malleable than we have yet seen.

When it comes to emotions, we think that these Gay couples may operate on very different principles than straight couples. Straight couples may have a lot to learn from gay and lesbian relationships.
—Dr. John Gottman, Gottman Institute

There are larger, culture-changing implications here. We can't predict what might happen if more committed straight couples came to recognize, as so many gay men do, a more nuanced pallet between emotional fidelity and sexual exclusivity, if they drew new lines between trust, truth, and sex. Could a franker set of permissions lessen the sexual chasm between men and women, offer stable couples new domains in which to practice intimacy? Might it actually increase truth-telling among married couples? Could they find, as many gay men report, that it can actually reduce tensions and enhance the intimacy that successful long-term partners need with each other? Could it even help redefine the idea of a committed couple, not as a domain where cheating is winked at, joked at, gossiped about, shrugged at, or expected, but as the forum where intimate partners take the risks to tell the real truth of themselves and their desires? Of course, such changes have one grim implication, enough to keep one awake nights. If there comes a day when "cheating" boyfriends, "lying hearts" and "other" women pass into obsolescence, of course, country music lyrics will never be the same. But then again, neither will the country.

A FREE AND GRACIOUS PUBLIC LIFE

Our public opinion, our literature, our customs, our laws, are saturated with the notion of the uncleanliness of Sex. Till this dirty and dismal sentiment with regard to the human body is removed there can be little hope of anything like a free and gracious public life. The sex-relation must be divested of the sentiment of uncleanness which surrounds it, and rehabilitated again with a sense of almost religious consecration. And this means . . . a free people, proud in the mastery and the divinity of their own lives, and in the beauty and openness of their own bodies.
—Edward Carpenter, British social philosopher

After non-monogamy, perhaps our most radical sex culture innovation involves how we explode accepted notions of public and private throughout our erotic lives. On Planet Queer, what we are allowed to know and discuss, to experience and celebrate, to teach and study; the places and ways sex occurs and the personnel involved; what we know of each other's lives, tastes, and practices—all are wholly, dramatically, sweepingly reconstructed. We have enlarged the public turf, and restricted the ground of the private, and with it, challenged the controlling power of those ideas. Three examples serve to make the point. The first is public sex.

The gay male has the advantage of a supporting subculture with relatively diversified facilities for various styles of loving and various patterns of encounter.
—John Lee, "Forbidden Colors of Love"

Call it The Jungle, though that is not its actual name. It is in an unmarked warehouse in an industrial section on the rough outskirts of a well-known southern city. Gangs roam the nearby blocks. You step from your car and notice what seems to be a large metal utility shed ringed in razor wire and sagging chain-link fence. Broken glass litters the gravel lot as you approach the metal door of a worn-out building. To get here, you have to know about it from someone. The Jungle does not advertise, has no listed phone, and depends strictly on word of mouth. It is now 1:30 A.M., and you are met at the door by a not particularly friendly man who inquires what you are looking for in a tone that suggests you better have a good answer. If you do, and if your answer passes muster, you are patted down and allowed in.

Step behind the sheet-metal warehouse façade, and you find yourself plunged into a gloomy jungle path, thick with hanging plants and vines. The air is steamy and heavy. Your eyes adjust to the wan light which seems to come from nowhere. You feel a pulsing techno music and hear a waterfall. A few steps further on, and you come to a circular raised cushion bed, ringed with plants. Men are fucking on it. A few steps down the path, the jungle transforms into a public park in any city. To one side, several men lean against the ten-foot-high wrought-iron fence. A slight breeze stirs from somewhere. What seems to be a giant elm tree lofts twenty-five feet, branching into a dark sky. Next to the flowing water is what seems to be . . . grass? Strategically placed park benches and chairs shelter trysts and provide a convenient place to get amorous. Men sit singly and in pairs, getting blown, stroking, hanging out. To your right, among bushes and tended shrubbery, a boulder rises; so does the man sitting naked on it. Proceed down the grass-lined path complete with landscaping and live plants, past some stones, and you find yourself in a graveled construction site. There is a flatbed pickup truck, its hood raised. Dark silhouettes lean against a chain-link fence, which ends at a brick wall scrawled with graffiti, as yellow lights flash from a construction sawhorse. To your right, a doorway of six-inch-wide hanging leather strips marks the entry to a small leather-walled alcove, where a sling hangs from chains and the walls sport a variety of hooks and eyebolts in strategic places, the better to hold someone there till you're done with him.

Turn left at the truck, through another park-like area that has several padded sawhorses. Next comes a maze of walls cross-jutting at angles, with different size glory holes cut in them. Through the maze, you pass by an open van where some men are in the back having sex, others seated in the front seat getting serviced, a macho lovers' lane fantasy come to life. Next comes a darkly sensual room, very crowded, draped in a range of soft textured fabrics. That opens onto a large room, with several large fish tanks and a half dozen couches where men splay out, some talking quietly, a couple sleeping cuddled, piles of male bodies sprawled on top of each other, in varied stages of erotic embrace. Wander from there through a serpentine maze of psychedelic neon, bright-pulsing tubes of electric color, black light paint, glass walls and mirrors, and trippy music into the buffet areas, where a large table has fruit juices and piles of fruit and snacks. From a side room comes the sound of vigorous rhythmic slaps. Its walls are covered in black leather; a hardcore S/M video plays.

If MGM Studios made nothing but raunchy porno, The Jungle would be its studio backlot. What sets The Jungle apart is its exquisite attention to detail. None of the rooms are foreboding, none of the men disrespectful, throbbing sexy music is playing throughout. But one could find similar settings in any of several large cities. San Francisco had one with a Roman orgy room—with fountain, mock marble columns, complete with a mural of centurions. For years, Man's Country in New York offered several open beds of actual trucks installed in the space, evoking the sleazy *je ne sais quoi* of the city's dangerous docksides, but with all the comforts of home (towels and lube). The Mineshaft's tubs, slings, and accouterments have passed into the realm of the mythic. Near Atlanta you can find yourself in a fantasy Army barracks, complete with bunks, standard-issue furniture, olive drab walls. On a given weekend, several men in fatigues are, um, encouraging a recruit to do pushups. Not far from Palm Springs, you'll find a jail cell, with bunks, bare bulbs, and horny inmates. One place may have a locker room setting, complete with sports posters, an athletic cup hanging on the wall, benches, and a bank of lockers; another might boast a fully equipped fraternity room. Amsterdam's legendary Black Tulip hotel equips every one of its guest rooms with an amenity of S/M play; you select your room by your preference for stocks, racks, or just a simple, tasteful sling. Each such place is like a small depraved Disney World, a Magic Kingdom of men. Just as in the real one, visitors come to see their fantasies become true, for the price of admission. With a wink, a grope, and lots of set dressing, they raise to fantasy the reality of the queer male erotic landscape.

No other subculture has colonized, developed, and adopted the public landscape for consensual sex as thoroughly as gay men have. Every city and town has its nook: libraries, train stations, bathrooms, coffee shops, roadsides, canyons, promenades, parks, alleys, bridges, back rooms, baths, subway platforms, beaches, sports fields, museums, rooftops, lakesides, darkrooms, truck stops, sex clubs. The Fens in Boston, New York City's piers or Central Park's Rambles, Griffith Park in L.A., Buena Vista Park in San Francisco, the Tuileries in Paris and Hampstead Heath in London, Colorado's Dream Canyon, Sunset Park in Las Vegas, Hippy Hollow in Austin, Texas, and basically everywhere in South Beach (just kidding). This land is your land, this land is my land, from the redwood forests of Russian River to the gulf stream waters of the Meatrack (Fire Island) or Dick Dock (P-town). Your land, my land, man's land.

You may have found this book on the shelf next to the perennial gay guide that lists the best sex spots in every city (editions available for every continent), complete with its own legend about the clientele, danger, types, police activity, and preferences found there. Websites are devoted to this (www.cruisingforsex.com). Dozens of gay organizations publish pamphlets about how to have public sex safely and many have gone so far as to hang trees with bags of free condoms and lube, as well as tidy disposal sacks, to accommodate sex *alfresco*. (In a wooded area off London's Hampstead Heath, the condom and lube dispensers on the trees were thoughtfully designed to glow in the dark.) Again, it's not that straight folks don't enjoy public sex—there's that lovely beach scene in *From Here to Eternity*. But let's face it: If straight folks pursued public sex with the avidity and ardor some of our kind bring to it, you couldn't get to a cash machine without a machete.

Now, hold on. Can one dignify this as culturally significant? Isn't this just more of the can't-keep-it-zipped abandon we're known for? Well, no. It may as well be understood as part of a larger project where queer male worlds have radically de-centered accepted notions of private and public. Recognizing this, scores of academic thinkers have explored the role of public sex in gay life. Understanding them, said one researcher, is an "understanding of a gay ecology and to the development of the concept of a community."[37] Papers have chronicled it in contemporary Sweden[38] and in 1920s New York,[39] from Paris[40] to Holland,[41] from Queensland, Australia (in an article, "Poofs in the Park")[42] to Portland and Seattle.[43] Articles on the cultural import of public sex have appeared in august journals from *Journal of Homosexuality* to *Sexual and Marital Therapy.*

One researcher describes how "men negotiate the 'interaction membrane' which enables sex to occur in public places."[44] Another addresses gay use of public space in early modern Nordic culture,[45] and notes: "Most of this outdoor space was invisible to those other than the participants. It had its own differentiation of, and meanings for, 'public' and 'private.'" Reviewing three decades of such findings, one author concluded that: "Men are not publicly engaging in sex more than they did twenty or thirty years ago, but rather . . . engagement with men's sexuality is far more public."

Our innovations have begun to perfuse into and shape the larger culture. It happens through the official language of social science journals and the inquiries of academics. In the 1990s, national public health authorities coined the acronym "PSE" to describe the public sex environments we patronize, create, maintain, and appreciate. In 2001, the Massachusetts State Police issued two pages of guidelines making it clear that "socializing and expressions of affection" and even "sexual conduct" is only illegal when "a substantial risk" exists that passersby will see it. When the same practice becomes fodder for jokes on prime-time TV, when it echoes in the academic journals and law enforcement training manuals, we see how this queer sexual innovation begins to shape the larger society. All are signs, that is, of a cultural, not individual, change, a collective step to Carpenter's vision of a "free and gracious public life."

Public erotic pursuits are only one piece of the radical redefinition of the private now being undertaken in queer worlds. The second echoes in our very use of language.

With gay sex, nothing is assumed. No "slot A, tab B" shortcut for us— confronted with slot-slot, tab-tab, we've no choice but to talk it out.
   —Dan Keane, *Chicago Tribune* columnist

Spend an evening talking with gay men about sex.
   —Gay Pride banner, STOP AIDS, 1995

And talk we do. Incessantly. A core shared value among us is our frank and elaborated discourse around sex—its pleasures, dangers, and techniques. It is part of our public and personal discourses in ways wholly different from those permitted in American majority culture. If language to some extent reflects cultural emphasis and distinctions— remember the Eskimos' fabled forty-five words for snow?—gay men's erotic language offers a window onto our view of sexuality, and the different ways we use language to position privacy in our lives.

Studies say gay men's language differs in a wide range of situations. Enterprising academics have studied one body of literature, the literature on gay men's bodies—specifically, what our personal ads say that we wish to have done with them. Such ads are a minor cottage industry for academic researchers, who have examined thousands of them over two decades. They are an easy target: Plentiful, free, they don't have to be recruited or plied with refreshments, and they provide hours of titillation for the average research assistant. Studies find gay personals are "more explicitly sexual, less likely to offer financial security, status occupation, or personality characteristics than are heterosexual men or women or transsexuals"[46] and far "more frank . . . and more specific about goals for desired relationships . . . than heterosexual ads." The ads, they surmise, reflect "differences in conceptualizing 'love.' "[47] Similar work in 1976[48] and 1984 found our ads more frankly sexual, suggesting "substantial differences between males and females who choose homosexuality [sic]."[49] (Or, one might argue, those who are genetically driven to write personal ads.) Consistent with our use of language, gay men's dating scripts—that is, each person's expectations of shared gay norms— have been found to be "more sexually oriented" than are straight men's.[50]

It turns out we even talk differently face-to-face (or in whatever position one prefers). We are less apt to use erotic euphemisms—"touch me down there," "do that thing I like"—than we are to bellow the occasional "FuckmeFuckmeFuckMeFuckme!!!" or that charmingly earthy staple, "Suck that dick." (A friend jokes, "Why is it always *that* dick when it's in your face? It makes me want to ask: 'Um, *that* dick? Which one?' ") Dr. John Gottman, researcher at the University of Washington, co-authored the first observational work comparing an equal number of gay and straight couples, looking at relationship patterns. Among the findings were that when a heterosexual couple talks about a sexual problem, "basically you have no idea what they are talking about. You never heard them say, 'I'd prefer it if you would touch my penis or my breast.' They don't talk like that . . . they might as well be talking about painting the barn."

Research suggests that we talk just a whole lot dirtier with spouses and lovers. (Here you thought Jeff Stryker was just fantasy.) We use a more erotic, arousing, blunter vocabulary than do heterosexual males or heterosexual females; employ more Anglo-Saxon, less clinical words for genitals and acts; and are less likely to clean up our four-letter words to polite terms than are straight guys during sexplay.[51] When it comes to erotic talk, being gay shapes it as much as being male does. This may as likely be due to the fact that the talk is between males, so avoids the linguistic changes we have been socialized to do when talk includes females. (For those interested in the field of gay speaking patterns, the Lavender Linguistics conference, held annually, is a rich source for endless cocktail-party tidbits.)

A recent survey released by the Midwest Institute of Sexology in Southfield, Michigan, showed "almost nine in ten heterosexual men in relationships with women reported serious problems articulating their needs and desires." Fully half of their women partners reported some difficulties when talking to male partners about sex. In sharp contrast, seven out of ten gay men in same-sex relationships in this sample said it was easy to discuss sex. The authors described the gay respondents as "dramatically less reluctant to communicate sexual desires than the straight respondents. . . ."

Just as we use language differently in private, our public language is also notably different. Take, for example, the official languages used in formal meetings and gatherings. The following are a list of workshop titles given at the gay health conferences held in the last two years:

Oral Arguments
Science of Sodomy
Lip Service
Follow the Yellow Drip Road (a gonorrhea workshop)
Joy of Queer Sex
Getting Fucked
Know Your Dick
Butt Sex 101

(Am I the only one wondering what the prerequisite for the last workshop is?)

What's notable is not how cute they are, nor that the presenters are often eminent physicians, epidemiologists, social scientists, activists, and academics. It's how totally inconceivable such workshop and paper titles would be at the average public health or professional conference.

We take that same public discourse to the streets when a contingent of twenty men could march in the 1992 San Francisco Gay Pride parade bearing a giant sign reading "DON'T BE A PRICK, COVER YOUR DICK" in four-foot letters. Your first tip-off you aren't at the Kiwanis Club parade anymore. Another year's contingent marched behind a banner with bold letters exhorting passersby to "Please fuck safely." There is an image to deconstruct for days. Not only have these men chosen to march behind a message of safety, not only are they issuing a well-intentioned maxim to their erotic brothers, and not only do they cheerily flaunt the F-word in public. But all this they have done on a large banner, in a stylish sans-serif font, grammatically. And what other group of men would think to ask "please"?

Nor is this frankness confined to our spoken or printed word. In places where we control public space, our own iconography reigns. So for years, men entering the locker room of one of San Francisco's most popular gyms opened the locker room by grasping its distinctive door handle: a three-foot, undulating, chrome sperm. The handle disappeared when the place was bought by a national chain. You can find the same spermatic motif in stained glass windows in a gay men's retreat center in Northern California. Or you could walk to the top of a hill on a farm in rural New England and find yourself facing an unmistakable ten-foot-high stone penis, a four-foot-wide spherical boulder improbably balanced on top. "Signifies precum," offers its owner by way of Yankee explication. Then: "Dug these rocks out from this field." Standing in this man's private Stonehenge, an icy November wind buffeting us, I realize this queer place signifies every bit as much as a bandanna in a hip pocket. This granite-hewn phallus will stand long after all men now on Earth are dust. Ever erect, it is a flinty reminder to all who will work these fields that a fag farmer once tilled here.

In our iconography, our chosen vocabulary, our customs, our melding of "public" and "private" speech, we proclaim, "We're reshaping the rules of what can be said—in print, in sex, in public, at work." The central project of gay talk is to defuse shame, disempower stigma, reclaim eros. Our language and symbols challenge the notion of the private. With every word we utter, we trouble the perimeter of the private.

For me gay sex is about the opportunity to connect on many levels. Sometimes it's just about coming. But sometimes it can be about starting a bond for the rest of your life. And the adventure is everything in between. And I think

the great thing about being gay is the freedom to use sex as a tool for connection. We have that opportunity in a way no other population does.
  —Troy, Madison, Wisconsin

Where we have our sex and how we talk about it are just specific examples of the most powerful way that we recast public and private boundaries. It lies in how we allow ourselves to share sexual society with each other. In ways largely impermissible in straight culture, gay men share an affectionate and ongoing familiarity with the erotic preferences and practices of our friends, as often as not because we have experienced them together. It is common that abiding, lifelong friendships begin, and continue, with sexual dimensions in ways largely inconceivable in straight society. One sociologist notes what he calls "breakdown of the 'incest taboo'" on having sex with friends: "On the contrary, there is now a positive emphasis on sex (one or several encounters) as a legitimate and desirable part of the process of becoming better acquainted."[52]

Because such relationships fall outside America's stated norms for relationships, new social potentials are born within this seamless web of erotic relationships. When the rules of engagement allow for the constant possibility that any casual encounter can turn passionate, even intimate, it shifts the rules of social ties and vulnerabilities, dependency and trust. There is a connection, if only potential; an enmeshment, a stake comes to be understood. One becomes differently and more widely connected and, perhaps, even responsible. In chapter 9, we will see how our open sexual practice can also bring powerful obstacles and distractions that can impede a true communion of the heart, and keep us isolated. But in this context, we can just note that it holds the potential to weave a loose web of affectional bonds that take far different shapes than they do in the outside world.

Here I am madly in love with you
on the verge of killing myself for your love,
    and I don't even know your . . .
Name:
Phone number:
    —Trick card at a bar, Tulsa, Oklahoma

In my twenties I tricked my way through Europe. It was so amazing. I got
an inside look and participated in all these worlds that were different than

mine. It was such an important part of my discovering the world, having come from a WASP-y neighborhood where everybody was the same. Meeting guys that way, hanging for a day or two with someone I felt intimate with, romantically open, I learned about different cultures and customs and ways of living. I got to live in each place through the life of the guy I was with, going home with them, being in their homes, waking up with them, eating their food. Even simple things—meeting his friends for drinks, stopping at the store before we went home—was fascinating. I learned how different it was from my life in America. When I got home, all I had pictures to show were pictures of people I had met. One of my friends laughed; he said, "I'd have pictures of churches and monuments, you bring home pictures of people."
    —Tom, 39, Los Angeles

What I totally love about on-line guys is I meet men I NEVER would meet in my life. Professors, a sanitation worker, a white guy who's married, a pilot, artists. I love going over to their places—I get to see lives that are totally new to me.
    —Dayton, 24, Chicago

In a mad way, perhaps one-night stands are potentially more spiritual, more demanding, more extraordinary than anything else!
    —Christopher Isherwood

In 1973 in his book *Memoirs of an Ancient Activist,* gay liberationist Paul Goodman wrote: "Given the usual coldness and fragmentation of community life at present, my hunch is that homosexual promiscuity enriches life more than it desensitizes." In specific, Goodman noted: "Homosexuality throws together every class and social group more than heterosexuality does." It was a common idea, that our open sexuality also allows lines between class and sexual relationships to cross-cut very differently than in majority culture. But that goes much further back, as far as the Greek ideal of Platonic mentoring sexual relationships. When gay was just a gleam in the culture's eye, Whitman wrote utopian poems about his "dear love of comrades," envisioning a sprawling, rambunctious fraternity of stevedores and poets, sailors and surgeons. Modern social thinkers have long written about the ways professional, class, and sexual relationships get drawn very differently than in the dominant culture. 1970s gay lib manifestos like Goodman's celebrated backroom visions of titans of industry on their knees before humpy office boys, CEOs penetrated by postal workers. Gay iconography from Tom of Finland forward gave us the winking class archetypes of the Village People, our eroticization of class-bending rough trade, and a thousand pornos about construction workers, truck drivers, or the cable TV guy.

Gay culture is far from "marginal," being rather "intersectional," the conduit between unlike beings.
—Judy Grahn, *In Another Voice*

Ideally, our liaisons could hold potential to dislocate barriers of class, profession, and race. Each such interaction—OK, trick—lets players from both sides glimpse different worlds. For a moment, there is the potential that different players hold power, that glimmers of cross-racial and class-cutting relationships are seen, that one becomes differently linked and even implicated in these different lives. Such profound social stakes were described in the theoretical language of philosopher Michel Foucault: "Homosexuality is an historic occasion to re-open affective and relational virtualities . . . diagonal lines he can trace in the social fabric permit him to make these virtualities visible." In 1992 there was a survey of about a thousand people, including women, Jews, blacks, recovering alcoholics, gays, and communists. True to prediction, gay men were "more likely to count some or many friends in all six groups," with our friendships more likely to cross lines of color, gender, religion, and politics far more than general population sample.[53]

In practice, we fall far short of Foucault's ideal of drawing diagonal lines in the social fabric. Stubborn social barriers of race, class, and age persist, and we frequently experience bias by color and race, size and age, class and culture. But in theory, gay cultures support the opening of the doors to such interactions, the shared recognition of eros as a shared force that can vault us over established social barriers. That is why our liaisons are so dangerous.

However imperfectly and infrequently we realize this ideal, our contacts still hold a transcendent potential. In a society where power structures usually cement difference and separation, which thrives on strategies of divide and conquer pitting group against group, where common interests are erased in the name of identity politics, we mix up the pot. Ideally such bonding could recast notions of community and competition, capitalism and culture, pose implications for interracial relationships and class leveling, and even open doors to a communitarian ethics and more inclusive values formation. And here you thought you were just getting your rocks off.

In truth, we know, we often fall far short of this ideal. We fall prey to dynamics of race, ethnicity, age, and class as often as we surmount them. But one thing is clear. Outside our lives, this social potential goes almost wholly unrecognized. Even we who engage in them, we rarely stop to consider the meaning of our erotic bonds. Yet these most intimate connections nibble at us, calling us to ask who we are connected to, and why, and how. They let us glimpse in others the reflection of our own lives, the secret desires shared in our hearts.

In the gay lexicon of libido, the entry just after tricks is fuck buddies. Part mistress, part comrade, part buddy and best friend, they are purely grown-up playmates. They are a venerated, widespread, and revered gay cultural practice, proved far more enduring than, say, caftans or nipple rings. In gay circles they are far more openly accepted, discussed, and richly elaborated and celebrated than in mainstream culture. They carry no taint of the illicit, no furtive shame of "mistress," no shame of something "on the side." The relationship is what it is: a pleasure-based, mutually valued, enduring erotic connection, without the expectations or constraints of romantic attachment. It is a socially valued and approved relationship, even an acceptable way to introduce one pal to another. Whether one calls them fuck buddies, playpals, or sexpals, they can last for years, even decades, and often morph into friends-with-whom-one-has-sex, or once did.

A good fuck buddy is a great thing. It's affectionate, but not complicated, we both know why we're there, what we like. We have a great time, then order barbecue in, catch up, then go at it like mink again. Then if we don't see each other for weeks, months, that's OK.
   —Andy, 28, Memphis

Boone and I have been playpals for almost eleven years. We've both seen boyfriends come and go. What we have will never be that. Truth is, neither of us wants it to. It's just good times with a good pal. We know just what to do, and man, does it work.
   —Aaron, 43, Denver

For me, playing with Jason is like going for a massage. I love the way we touch each other. Just a good time, no drama. Sure beats miniature golf.
   —Kent, 36, Brooklyn

As well, these sexual comrades in arms serve as each other's sexual mentors and teachers. Many of us can name the man who patiently taught us to enjoy anal sex. Or the very evening where we learned the secret of deep throating (thanks, "nycfunhunk"). There is a tutelage involved in learning to use a condom correctly, avoid STDs, use sex drugs safely, tie a knot, or take a finger or fist without injury. Most of us have passed along our best tricks to our best tricks, our pearls of wisdom to partners, boyfriends, lovers. As we do that in bedrooms and back-rooms, we recall tribes from Africa to Papua. In those places, they systematically, responsibly take their pubescent young to the huts or forests to teach them the ways of adult love. That care gives social value to that most sacred part of themselves. It is precisely what this lavender tribe does for each other every night of the week.

I see us as a society of sexual secret Santas, who constantly leave each other these delightful little surprises.
—Don, Ellsworth, Kentucky

I see myself as a sexual surrealist. If I have any message in my work, it is to explore your own—especially your sexual fantasies—because if you stifle them, you stifle some part of your creativity.
—Arlene Sandler, filmmaker

Every second Sunday afternoon, in New York's West Village, a group of some twenty men ring the buzzer at a tidy apartment. They drift in in ones and twos, removing their boots at the front door. The host, an amiable former professor pushing seventy, is the author of several mathematics textbooks. He hands out the syllabus for this course and explains that a small tuition will cover the cost of materials, punch, soda, and cookies. The men will come here for four hours every other week. On most of those days, the students will be nude, tied up, or both.

The course runs nine months. Like any good textbook, the syllabus emphasizes a different subject each week: basic bondage, spanking, flogging, things that pinch (the math professor's clear favorite), hot wax, electrical play, hoods and gags, heat and cold entertainments. Over the course of the year, guest presenters will include people who in their other lives are computer analysts, physicians, a direct mail consultant. Some are gay, others straight, but they have been invited to this room because of their expert knowledge and skill in the intricacies of Japanese bondage, electrical stimulation, or anal safety. Each has been selected for his peerless safety and skill, unswerving devotion to safe, sane, and consensual technique, and invited to pass along a piece of his erotic tradition—its customs, practices, and meanings.

Similar programs exist in Fort Lauderdale, where it's a four-day intensive called Leather University; in Washington, D.C.; through Chicago's Hellfire Club, and to nobody's surprise, in San Francisco's LeatherMen's Discussion Group. Versions of them happen over Memorial Day at Inferno, an annual gathering of thousands of leather men; in January at Mid-Atlantic Leather; and in September at Delta, where several hundred men borrow a dormant Pennsylvania summer camp for a weekend, and transform the arts and crafts auditorium into a teaching dungeon to impart the finer points of consensual torture, all in good fun.

In a very different and gentler key, the gay-founded Body Electric School travels to cities across the country, teaching the sweet arts of sexual massage and breathing, anal and genital pleasure in workshops across the country. In that syllabus, its visionary founder, Joseph Kramer, has catalogued an elaborate lexicon of some two dozen-plus strokes for more effective masturbation. (Hard work, but someone had to do it. The Twist and Shout is a perennial favorite, in case you're ever asked.) The school he founded now offers courses in a dozen cities each year.

If you prefer to do it in the woods, you could attend a Radical Faerie encampment in New Mexico, Tennessee, or Oregon, or any of several dozen gay men's weekends where groups and teachers eagerly share their mastery of the arts of Tantric, genital, or anal massage. You could stop in at scenic Wappinger Falls, New York, for a gay men's workshop that "introduces the physicality, drive, and aliveness of sex to the joy and expansive goodness of spirituality and letting them play together," and teaches men to "bring our deepest sexuality and spirituality into our intimate relationships." If you are truly lucky, you might find yourself shedding your clothes at a collective farm in rural Indiana or Sonoma County, where Dr. Kirk Prine has come to lead one of a series of wondrous weekends to explore the transcendent power of intimate touch.

Each of these groups partakes of a tradition as old as the first time a Neanderthal winked to his brother across a cave and gently guided his furry hand downward. In these rooms are the modern gay practitioners of the lost *ars amatoria*—the art of love. Their ancestors are the courtesan, the erotic temple carvings, the sexually wise elder, the *Kama Sutra,* the sacred ancient temple prostitutes, the geisha, and the erotic cults of Europe. The sex we have, the sex we teach, the sex we celebrate and explore, are woven into our chosen cultural rituals. It is our way to open to each other the doors of our pleasures, and through them, our possibilities. We are each other's older and younger brothers. We are our own Wise Men bearing gifts of great wonder.

Sadly, this noble pedagogy of pleasure—organized, mindful hands-on instruction in the erotic arts—has been ferociously extinguished by the guardians of the larger culture's well-being. It has become rare for public schools to teach anything beyond a stilted abstinence, even though when parents are asked, they consistently say their kids should receive instruction around sexual safety.[54] (In a particularly surreal moment of public-health morals, a recent issue of the daily HIV prevention newsletter from the Centers for Disease Control bore two articles. The first cited several studies showing that abstinence sex ed doesn't really work. The other, entitled "State to Get More Funds to Urge Teen Abstinence," quoted Oklahoma's secretary for health and human services arguing for three million dollars for abstinence programs: "We think the abstinence education program is incredibly important to Oklahoma." Important, no doubt. But to whom, and why?)

Even in the rare places where sex ed remains, it has been reduced to anatomy, pathology, and reproduction, ringed with thorns and shadowed with danger. The Big Parental Sex Talk has passed into the realm of a bad joke. It's no surprise, then, that women moan that men haven't a clue, even as in the other locker room, men grouse that women don't give decent head. A major boom industry of bestsellers and magazines are devoted to How to Be a Better Lover. Unwanted pregnancy and STDs are again rising, with half of new HIV infections now occurring in those under twenty-five. The social costs of sexual ignorance are steep.

Yet even so, the idea of a communal, fraternal sexual mentorship, to intimately and systematically impart the ways and principles of pleasure, bliss, and safety, remains unspeakable, even unimaginable. Our society relegates this task, if anywhere, to its whores. What a powerful innovation, then, that so many men have focused in so many ways on the mindful and intentional passing of erotic lore. And how far it varies from the larger cultural practice.

Maybe America's women might not be much more fulfilled if more American men took a leaf from the how-to book of our pleasures. Maybe a lot more American men would like it if the enterprising gay guy could teach their wives and girlfriends those tricks our tricks taught us. There was certainly no mistaking the wry, wistful tone of voice when a straight friend of mine observed: "Look, I get why you guys have fuck buddies. What I don't get, is why I can't."

When a culture bestows such generous permission to pursue pleasure, it allows its members to open erotic doors for themselves. In few domains is the private more policed than in S/M, its fabled whips and chains the popular proxy for all that is shamed and dark. At first (non) blush, one might expect the kingdom of kink to be where straight and gay are most alike. After all, denizens of a sexual demimonde have already stepped beyond the bounds of cultural convention. Yet several studies demonstrate that queer kinksters have a far better time of it.

Compared to straight men, we "evidence a consistent liberal attitude toward sexual behavior in general."[55] Comparing gay and straight S/M players, several observers have suggested that gay subjects report having more fun in S/M; enjoy more cultural opportunities to pursue it, more frequent and enjoyable play; and are two-thirds less likely to have used prostitutes.[56] Socially, we enjoy richer networks of interested playpals, have more friends involved in the scene, and are more likely to find partners.[57] We seem better adjusted, hold less negative self-image about S/M play, and have higher levels of self-acceptance about our activities than do comparable straights. Among gay men, S/M is more often associated with leadership roles at work and off-hours volunteer activity.[58] Even at the fringes, it seems, gay social practice throws open the portals of The Private more readily.

Sexuality, as we now know it, has become one of the most creative sources of our society and our being. We are witnessing the real creation of new possibilities of pleasure which people had no idea about previously. The possibility of using our bodies as a possible source of very numerous pleasures is something that is very important.
—Michel Foucault, Paris, 1991

These words come from one of the preeminent thinkers of the twentieth century, a man who changed the face of modern philosophy, and was reputed to have spent many happy hours in sex clubs around the world. In public sex, in language, in tricks and fuck buddies and kink, it is utterly clear that our very resistance to traditional lines of privacy literally saves lives. It is no accident that this most sexually open culture was the one to create, promulgate, and adopt standards of sexual safety and STD prevention, and that we achieved what has been described as "the largest behavior change in the history of public health." We did so precisely because of our habits of explicit sexual discourse, practice, and mentorship.

We have seen that many studies suggest involvement in our set of queer sexual communities sustains and empowers safer sexual decisions. Health experts have studied our rituals from j/o parties[59] to negotiated safety, cultural innovations like San Francisco's Blow Buddies (a venue first created to encourage lower risk sex) to our culture's support for condoms, the promulgation of practices like "on me, not in me" and the elaborate cluster of erotic rituals that define safer sex. It turns out that bringing our sexual lives into the light literally keeps us—and our playmates—alive. You can't defend against what you can't discuss— so thus the "private" sabotages protection.

We have already seen how that accepted story of fags as sexual profligates, wantonly endangering each other, does not stand up to the light of objective fact. To the dismay of those who preach danger and threat in gay men's enthusiastic embrace of sexuality, one of the most well-established, best-replicated truths of HIV prevention is that risk occurs far more often in intimate relationships than in casual encounters with strangers.[60] Yet listen and one hears only the monotonous drumbeat that it is our casual sexual culture that kills.

Of course, the Righteous Drum Corps pounds that tired drum for reasons that have little to do with our collective well-being. They see the very real stakes in all this gay perturbation of the private. Bringing the pubic public holds huge political implications. The notion of private is used in many ways: to enforce control, to coerce, police, and shame. Privacy is used to privilege some, disempower others, to define and demarcate what is acceptable for all. Sacrosanct notions of privacy echo in phrases like "within the privacy of family," "behind closed doors," "what you do at home is your business," "a man's home is his castle." That privileging of the private is part of the fabric of social control, echoing Victorian doctrines of home (women's) vs. public (men's) spheres.

Ultimately, these questions of the private both reflect and determine changes in the larger culture. They are reflected in issues ranging from a woman's right to choose to public reaction to the private lives of political leaders (does the name Bill Clinton ring a bell?). It affects the boundaries of private and public space built into cities, cyberspace, laws, schools, culture. Gay cultural recasting of these spheres is a direct challenge to the hegemony of the private, the fulcrum of political and personal control contested by both right and left. When Georgia cops entered Michael Hardwick's private bedroom and arrested him for no crime beyond having gay sex in his own bed, it was an attempt to deprive an entire clan of even those privacy protections. When the Supreme Court upheld that arrest, it was a declaration of war on the privacy of an entire people. These are big stakes at play here, and they lead to the blackest heart of social control. It turns out that dropping trou in the bushes and talking sassy are no small transgressions in the politics of pleasure and power.

> *It may well be that gay liberation's pioneering a new model of intimate relationship on the margins of society, which will eventually resolve the problems of larger society. "The love which has no name" may give new names for love, new love styles to all humanity.*
> —John Lee

> *Gay men pass on a special knowledge and wisdom through sex. There is a whole story we tell through the sex we have. I see it as a physical activity which represents the common consciousness. We came from nothing and we return to nothing, so while you are here you can focus on nothing, or something. So why not focus on love?*
> —Andrew Ramer

We close this exploration as we began it, with its larger significance. For forty years, gay men conceived and defined our primary cultural work to cleave out social space for our erotic selves. In that time, as we have seen, we built what is without question the richest sexual culture the planet has ever seen. Yet the possibility that such innovations may hold anything important, humane, or liberating goes largely unaddressed in majority culture and media. At best, our practices are viewed with studied silence; at worst, media view and dissect our customs with wide-eyed alarm and ferocious distrust.

Obviously, such a monolithic conventional wisdom makes sense only if one believes that our larger culture gained nothing of value whatever from explorations of sex and gender in the 1960s. Or that, even if it did back then, that America has nothing further to learn about sexuality. But if either of those *isn't* true—if we're not in sexual Jerusalem yet—then small wonder gay men's sexuality frightens the culture's horses in such a big way. For we embody a far more subtle and unsettling truth.

Perhaps sexual explorations bring not just costs, but unsuspected collective and individual benefits. At this historical moment, gay men are so troubling precisely as living, breathing proof that a subculture can play by different rules. We bring erotic tidings that many would prefer stay unheard: that humans are blessed with open hearts and willing bodies, the better to enjoy a robust erotic communion with each other. In a larger society that has resolutely held its erotic fantasies and desires at bay, we are a reminder that one could instead invite them in to sup—and have them stay the night. Even more disquieting, that maybe, just maybe, we could all awake in the morning to find our humanity not only intact, but vastly enriched. What then?

We have spent this time on sexuality not because, as we usually think, it is our whole story, but because it is our wholly mis-told story. Our queer sex narrative is less a mere morality play of wanton hedonism than a stunning cultural accomplishment. It presents a systematic cultural elevation and recognition of the power of the erotic, a celebration of collective carnality. At its best, it is bounded by ethics and informed by care, and nurturant of relationships. It can open doors, personal, dyadic, and collective (although as we will soon see, we have work to do to fully realize those promises).

This chapter has stopped on this erotic island *en route* to another idea. As we have seen, millions of gay men have built the planet's most unabashedly sex-affirming culture. We have done it in a few short years, in a nation moving away from erotic pleasure, conflicted about sex, ashamed of bodies, and increasingly vocal about our suppression. Yay for our side. But what if it turns out that sex is just a proxy? We built such unparalleled sexual cultures when we imagined that sex was what made us unique. Our sex and bodies were how the larger society saw to name us as different, and for years, they were how we ourselves grasped our prime difference. So we manifested that into being, big time. But our sex may be just the most visible marker of our cultural invention. The sex is the part the world has most easily seen. But what if it blinded us to something else all these years?

Maybe our key difference doesn't lie in our erotic after all. What if it's just our opening act, a way of learning what we can do together? What if all that sex—that lovely, magnificent, sticky, daring, tender, piggy, bold, sweated sex—is just a dry run for the glorious trouble we can make when we put our will to it? At this millennial moment, our deepest cultural impulses may be less about male bodies than about male hearts. Given our unnamed habits of nonviolence, service, caretaking and altruism, intimacy, the hundred ways that we rewrite the rules on men, sex may turn out to be the least radical of our differences. There are richer imports from this Madagascar to the world, richer than we have yet dreamed.

6 | PERMISSIBLE INTIMACIES

I dreamed in a dream, I saw a city invincible to the attacks
  of the whole of the rest of the earth,
I dreamed that was the new City of Friends,
    Nothing was greater there than the quality of robust love—it led the rest,
It was seen every hour in the actions of the men of that city,
And in all their looks and words.
    —Walt Whitman, "Calamus 34"

The development towards which the problem of homosexuality tends is the
one of friendship.
    —Michel Foucault

It's time to ponder the F-word at the center of gay lives. No, not *that* one. I'm talking about *friendship,* silly. But you went there, didn't you? Of course you did; our sexual exploits usually steal the headlines. Yet when we cast an eye beyond the bedrooms, backrooms, and baths, a far more profound set of gay affectional innovations comes into view. For we are rewriting the rules and habits of intimacy. The very practice of friendship is being reinvented in gay worlds.

In a remarkable essay, "Friendship as a Way of Life," French philosopher Michel Foucault defined friendship as the core philosophical issue at play in queer men's lives: "Affection, tenderness, friendship, fidelity, camaraderie, and companionship. Things which our rather sanitized society can't allow a place for. . . . That's what makes homosexuality so 'disturbing': The homosexual mode of life much more than the sexual act itself. To imagine a sexual act . . . is not what disturbs people. But that individuals are beginning to love one another— there's the problem."[1] He might well have added, as others had before him, that the *ways* we love each another differ significantly from those prevailing in the dominant society. Take Jeff and Chris, for example. They met across a crowded gym in 1979. When I met them in 1982, they were the role model of that Holy Grail of gaydom, a stable couple. In 1986, they moved to California and bought a house together, but within a year, Jeff had become involved with a local gardener, Ken. So he and Chris redrew the lines of what had become a rocky relationship. In the landscape of Jeff's heart, Ken would prove to be a short-blooming annual, not a perennial, but by then Chris had met Andrew and become boyfriends. For three years, Chris and Andrew twined their lives together, living separately and then together, but Jeff and Chris stayed close friends.

By 1991, Jeff lived downstairs with a series of just-roommates: Don, then David, then finally Anna, a straight woman. The married couple down the block had made Jeff the all-but-adopted uncle of their five- and eight-year-old boys. In those years, Chris and Jeff shared a house, upstairs and down, but not a bed or a lovership. In 1994, Chris and Andrew parted ways, and Andrew briefly became boyfriends with both Rick and his lover of eight years, George. But when he fell ill, it was the devoted Chris who remained his primary care partner, took him to the hospital, and had to explain a Do Not Resuscitate order to Andrew's shaken parents. Chris was the one with them at the bedside the night Andrew died at thirty-three.

Chris and Jeff had by then dissolved their shared mortgage, had dinner most weeks, and often celebrated Thanksgivings or birthdays together. When Jeff's father fell ill, it was Chris who paid for the plane ticket to fly Jeff home to his father's deathbed. As Jeff moved in—and out—of his next relationship, Chris settled in with first one, then two, deeply bonded, nonsexual roommates, Joseph and Jaime. For years now, the three have discussed boyfriends, sex, jobs, wallpaper, dreams, and each other. They have cared for mutual friends, cooked holiday meals, shared a car, crawled the bars, walked the dog, and ordered in Chinese to watch *The X-Files* together. At that point, Chris and Jeff's lives had remained intertwined for most of twenty years, a patchwork of romantic history and sexual ties, finances and real estate, two decades of sex, *Sturm und Drang,* emotional memories, and abiding love.

For the prior decade, Chris and Jeff's closest couple friends were Dave and David, a couple together seventeen years. The men joked that they were the Fred and Ethel to each other's Lucy and Ricky, if only they could agree on who was who. Over those years, both Dave and David had had sex with Chris, separately and together. Over several summers, David, Dave, and Chris came to share a beach house with seven other men, some of whom were single, others coupled, others with spouses not sharing the house. Some of the men occasionally enjoyed sex with each other; two housemates briefly dated romantically. All called themselves friends.

Last year, Chris and David—but not his lover, Dave—bought a vacation house together with a third partner, Bryan. At that point, Bryan and David had been emotionally and sexually involved for eighteen months, with the full knowledge and blessing of Dave. For six months, Bryan moved in with Dave and David, joining their domestic household, sharing meals, expenses, dancing, gardening, keeping an ongoing sexual-emotional bond with David and a friendly, nonsexual bond with Dave. Today, Bryan refers to both of them as "friends"; he and Chris call themselves single; Dave and David term each other lovers; and all four recognize Bryan and David's shared history. This summer, Dave, David, Bryan, and Chris will share two bedrooms in their new house, in the company of thirteen other men: three couples, four singles, one whose boyfriend lives in Washington, D.C., and a group of three best friends, two of whom have boyfriends, all of whom share one room with a double bed.

The two dozen men above constellate their relationships in a dozen permutations and hues. They have been by turns each other's acquaintance, housemate, boyfriend, lover, trick, business partner, care partner, roommate, fuck buddy, nonsexual bedmate, tenant, landlord, and friend. In varying combinations, many of them have each other's house keys, have met each other's relatives, and mused over the mythic old fags' home where they could grow old together. Some figure in each other's wills; some are legally designated as each other's medical decision makers. After one recent dinner, several members of this sprawling group sat down to estimate the aggregated years of lives this constellation of men had shared with each other. When the total surpassed two hundred "queer years" of intertwined relationship, they gave up, poured drinks, and toasted one another's mutual good fortune.

To some, this roil of relations may seem confusing, controversial, even catastrophic. But to the men involved, it is none of those. Because whatever one calls this improbable posse of pals, to Chris and Jeff, to Andrew and Jaime and Joseph, to Dave, David, and Bryan, to their dozen housemates and the men who twine in and around their affections and kitchens, such is the texture of life.

I should know. I'm David, and it's my family.

And when they become men . . . [they] naturally do not trouble about marriage and getting a family, but that law and custom compels them; they find it enough themselves to live unmarried together.
—Plato, *Symposium,* 193

When it works right, the gay social contract allows a wider range of permissible intimacies. For most straight men in our culture, intimacy is implemented in a duo. It is usually channeled to one other person, one's spouse, what sociologists term dyadic. If the dominant culture issued its adult men a road map of permissible intimacies, it would consist of two concentric circles. At the bull's-eye middle, one's mate. This one privileged spousal site is where the dominant culture allows straight men to vest intimacy. The couple is where (if anywhere) designated caretaking can occur. To that sacred spousal zone is relegated, even mandated, a trusting emotional intimacy. Only on its consecrated ground may reciprocal adult sexuality and physical affection be pursued.

In the next concentric circle out, in principle, comes one's offspring. Social ideals of nonsexual nurture and intimacy extend to one's children. (Given the legacies of deadbeat dads, abusive and absent fathers, hearing the millions who encounter Dad more readily in their therapy than in their childhoods, one might suspect a promise realized as often in breach as in observance.) Yet when it does happen with one's family, male caregiving, nurture, and intimacy almost invariably stop at that outer perimeter. Where family ends, the wagons get drawn round, the doors and shutters barred. The dominant lesson is that the male heart best not venture beyond the family fence. Like some Old World seafarer's maps, beyond there, the globe shades into abyss. Beyond that point lie dragons. Basically, the refrain chanted from the men's choir is "family, family *über alles,*" outsiders need not apply.

Gay men frequently form strong support systems within their culture, sometimes referred to as "families of choice." These persons take on the roles that are usually performed by biological family members . . . in the lives of gay and bisexual men [they] are a powerful resource. . . .
—P. J. Britton

Gay people . . . enjoy greater fluidity in their relations as they explore a continuum ranging from lust to love to nurture to mentorship to friendship in search of a new kind of family.
—Frank Browning

In many ways, for many reasons, we construct affection differently. Where straight male intimacy tends to the dyadic, ours tends to the diffuse. We develop, maintain, and enjoy wide-ranging forms of highly overlapping communal intimacies. We live our lives awash in complex stews of housemates, friendship networks, care teams, communal houses, and play partners. We enjoy multiple-year relations with roommates, and dance with buddies we see nowhere else; we dish with "sisters," play with fuck buddies and tricks, and interweave with their social circles. We have the potential to bond in dyads, triads, and more-ads. It was in a gay context that social thinkers coined the distinction between biological "families of origin" and "chosen families." The very term "family of choice" was coined by us to capture the social textures of gay men's affectional and social lives.[2]

The men in these. . . . friendships hold and enact different meanings about gender, sexuality, and power. The friends signify and negotiate these meanings in how they spend time together; how they embed their friendship in their lives; how they communicate emotionally; and how they deal with the sexual challenges they face.
—J. L. Price

Queer men can enact and experience our intimacies in uncommon ways and niches. As we pursue intimacy far differently, we have created a set of social innovations as sweeping as they are subtle. At root, we are redefining and reinventing the very institution of friendship. The guru of gay male friendships is Dr. Peter Nardi, who has conducted extensive in-depth studies about the different ways gay men implement intimacy.[3] His landmark book, *Gay Men's Friendships: Invincible Communities,* is must reading for all interested in the subject, combining a decade of his findings with that of many other scholars to map the landscape of our communal affections.

Nardi and other scholars have found many specific, systematic ways that our habits of heart are distinctive:

- Where straight men tend to bond around activities and tasks, we tend to create friendships more around emotional bonds.
- Gay men are statistically far more likely to have close friends, and more of them, than straight men.
- We rate friendships far higher in importance.
- We conduct friendship relationships differently and look to friends for more central needs.
- We engage more deeply and fully with those we call friends—touching more, discussing more intimate and emotional topics.
- We even talk with friends differently than other men do. For example, we are more likely to discuss the nature of our relationships with each other and to deal with each other's emotions than are straight men, who are more likely to talk about instrumental subjects, work, shared tasks, and interests. And yes, we are more likely to chat on the phone more often with our friends.
- Gay men are more likely to remain on friendly terms with ex-partners.

In all these patterns, we are exceptions to what philosopher Marilyn Friedman calls "the pattern of non-communicativeness" that often characterizes men's relationships. It is, of course, a pattern that creates enormous costs to individuals. Not long ago, I received a call from a college chum whom I had not seen in more than fifteen years. Enormously likable, smart, and talented, Randy was one of my old gang who had done extremely well, arcing from one to another ever-more-lauded corporate leadership job, with a lovely wife and two winning daughters. For one semester, twenty years before, we had grown close, and maintained sporadic touch for the first few years. But there had been nothing much for the last fifteen years. Yet here was Randy on the phone that day, his voice breaking as he told me of an impending divorce. He had called, after a silence of almost two decades, simply because he had nobody closer to ask for support. Nobody but his wife. I was honored, humbled, and appalled. You can likely confirm this story yourself with a little experiment. Ask a few married or even single straight men to name their three best friends. One often hears versions of Randy's story.

Nardi cites psychologist Beverly Behr, who bluntly states: "Overall the evidence seems to suggest that men's relationships are less intimate than women's. Men are less intimate in their friendships because they choose to be, even though they may not particularly like it." Says Mark Fisher, a gay architect: "As gay men, we're much luckier; we have real friends."

We do friendship differently enough that it has attracted note in several disciplines. Market researchers note that "the gay market . . . places greater importance on friendship networks than do most Americans."[4] Contemporary marketing of men's clothing, in fact, emphasizes male camaraderie and friendships, as market research shows that a lack of closely bonded friends is a key life concern among heterosexual men. Sociologists examining gay men write of our "large and diverse social networks,"[5] with "gay men and lesbians deriving significantly more support from friends, and heterosexuals deriving more support from family." Family experts suggest gay friendship networks raise "a need to redefine the concept of family to include 'friendship families.'"[6] As the writer Dorothy Allison put it: "My family of friends has kept me alive through lovers who have left, enterprises that have failed, and all too many stories that never got finished. That family has been part of remaking the world for me." In the words of Dr. Judith Stacey, writing on gay families: "This historically novel category of family crystallizes widespread processes of family diversification and change that characterize the postmodern family condition."[7]

"Postmodern? Schmost-modern," says Warren, a sixty-something counselor in the Bay Area. To him, "family" means a sexual-emotional quintet with whom he has been living for the last decade or so. These five men have regarded each other as primary life partners, resided together, sharing intimacy, property, and sexuality in varying combinations. "Lord, my family was never like this. It's not so much that I think of them all as my family. Truth is, 'family' seems like too limiting a word to really describe all of it. It's just the best shorthand people have of understanding how we're connected."

We can accept that shorthand or make up our own categories. "The Love Kibbutz" is the one Mike, Paul, and Rod have coined to describe their unconventional bond. It describes not only their three-way affections but also the loosely woven confederacy of men who circle through their lives, hearts, and bedrooms, in varied permutations, sometimes bonded to one, sometimes to more, at times sexual, at times not.

Gay experiments in diffuse intimacy are no big news to many gay men of color. "That's how a lot of us grew up," says Gary. In his case, it was in an extended Chinese family in Orange County. "Queer family just reflects and borrows from traditions more common in communities of color," notes Tom, an African-American leader. "It's a way better way to live, if you ask me." Robert agrees: "I grew in this big old Filipino family. Everybody took care of everyone's kids. We were raised by older cousins, my *abuela* still lives at home. For me, having this group of like five or six *chicos* to hang out makes it like home." He now calls San Francisco's Mission district home. "We all have three separate apartments, but we watch TV together and all just cuddle together. We look out for each other, too. That's family to me. *Fa-MI-lia!*"

To all of us, "family" is a vessel in search of perpetual refilling. Despite its enforced connotation of Nuclear Dad, Mom, and kids, it remains the best label we have to describe our most deeply intimate ties of affection, responsibility, support, and sex. But we may mean something very different when we use the word. Groupings like Warren's or Robert's raise questions about all of our intimacies. What do such deeply intertwined lives bring these men? How does it change their view of community and caring, responsibility, and reciprocity? What does "family" mean when it gets spread around?

Gay love exists outside the forms and conventions of heterosexual life.
—Dr. Simon LeVay and Elisabeth Nonas

Home is where the heart is, no matter how the heart lives.
—Sally Fingerett

Research and lived experience leaves little doubt that our practices of partnership, our forms and norms of friendship, affection, and sexuality contrast sharply and systematically from those of dominant culture. Not only do gay men tend to maintain more friends, we often maintain them quite differently. For one thing, we often share a fluid and generous sexual community with each other. It is more the rule than the exception for gay men to share an affectionate familiarity with the sexual preferences and practices of our friends, in ways unthinkable in the cultures of our heterosexual siblings. As often as not, we have at some point enjoyed sexual connections together. Three-quarters of the gay men Nardi studied had sex in the past with people who go on to be described as their "closest male friends," fully 60 percent of us have enjoyed sexual intimacy with those we call our best friends, and a similar number have done so with men they now consider casual friends. It is common that abiding, lifelong friendships begin, and continue, with sexual dimensions in ways inconceivable in the straight world. As writer Edmund White observed, "Our friends become lovers, and our lovers, friends." There are two possible interpretations for the fact that we are far more likely to have had sex with people we call friends. One can denigrate gay men as sexual dogs without boundaries, or celebrate the customs of our cultures that help us develop and maintain broader friendships among former (even ongoing) sexual partners.

When shared mores allow for the fluid possibility that any casual encounter can turn intimate, it shifts the entire balance of social ties and vulnerabilities, dependency and trust. We more easily morph from last night's trick to today's friend and tomorrow's boyfriend's or colleague's housemate. This seamless web of romance, friendship, and economic, communal, and professional bonds changes things subtly. Knowing that one's emotional and social actions, one's sexual tastes and affectional habits, are known to the wider circles of one's life builds in a certain social accountability. After all, word gets out, stories travel, reputations trail in one's wake. One ignores this closely woven web at one's social peril, whether in an urban gay gym, a suburban leather club, or a rural Radical Faerie encampment.

Our affectional habits, as we saw in chapter 4, also powerfully inform men's personal interest in a common well-being, our ethics of caretaking, even of shared survival. Researchers in California and New York listened to gay men talk about their values in a series of interviews. As Casey, a twenty-two-year-old African-American grad student, put it: "The only way that AIDS is going to stop infiltrating the gay community is if we practice safe sex. I see it as kind of like a collective responsibility that we need to have as a community to dissipate this virus that is going around and killing a lot of beautiful, wonderful people in our community. And we need to think of self-preservation as a communal phenomenon, which is love, I think. Dissipating the epidemic is thinking of preserving that community. Because if we don't, then there won't *be* a community if everyone has AIDS and we're all going to die in ten, fifteen, twenty years. I mean, we will go extinct."

Many of the men voiced ethical concerns over communal survival that they say help them stay safe sexually. Ken, easily old enough to be Casey's father, is a seen-it-all-been-there-twice designer in New York. He, too, describes a sense of shared stake: "I have some sense of responsibility towards our subculture and towards protecting people and as a responsible adult in the community. A certain amount or level of responsibility goes along with that. I feel some kind of obligation to the community or to myself first, and the community second." Different from both Ken and Casey, Roberto describes himself as "your basic cha-cha Cuban South Beach party boy." But, he says, "a community is very important to me too, and I don't want to see that community disbanded by people dying and leaving. . . . I guess I think of it as this big family or big fraternity of men. And I want to take care of them as my family. . . . I really want to hold on to all of these people. I don't want to see these people die of AIDS, if they can help it through their behavior." Slutdom and survival form a complicated nexus around the shared stakes in gay men's lives.

Such innovations in intimacy—both dyadic and diffuse—are some of the most vital parts of the great gay social experiment. They often begin as soon as we enter gay culture. Among queer teens, it has been found that "Non-family members were found to be more supportive than family members," a pattern which continues in our adult lives.[8] The men in gay spheres structure our elective social time differently, and are involved with, and care for, not just spouses, but friends.[9] Reading between the lines of the most austere AIDS journals, one finds many tales of the deep human ways we interweave.

Common wisdom holds that it was the historical accident of AIDS that created such patterns of intimacy and caretaking, but history shows our habits of diffuse intimacy long predate the epidemic. For decades, gay men have looked to each other for emotional, practical, even financial support, weaving webs of interdependency with those in our loosely confederated circles. Research suggests, in fact, that it is this nonsexualized participation in a common life that makes gay men report feeling satisfied, more than it is their range of sexualized interactions.[10] Chronicles of gay lives of the first half of the twentieth century brim with stories of the ways gay men enacted intimacy in networks, circles, webs. Historians like George Chauncey and John D'Emilio recount how gay men habitually posted bail for each other after hostile police—what contemporary gay code termed "Lilly Law"—raided our bars. It was a part of our ethical code to cover—the term was to "beard"—for each other in our professional lives, create alibis at work, and provide backup when family or cops harassed. Then, as now, new arrivals in gay worlds were often guided by more seasoned veterans (who themselves might have arrived only the year before), learning the rules of comportment, sociality, safety, and discretion. One set of interviews of gay men who had moved to San Francisco in the prior decades found that more than half drew on "a preexisting network, to the extent of receiving shelter on arrival" and "receiving information about jobs and places to live through strong ties."[11] Others have examined the role of teacher, guide, or 'helping hand' among gay men, noting "the often benign and helpful role that older, more experienced homosexual men play with regard to younger homosexuals."[12]

The power of diffuse intimacy became real for me one cold Chicago night in my twenties. I had recently taken the seemingly unlikely position of associate editor at *Playboy* magazine (don't ask) and was taking my first trip to the corporate headquarters in Chicago, affectionately known as Bunny Central. Midair, I fell queasily ill, so by the time I landed I was—well, spare the details—not a pretty sight. I worried that my distress might be due to a recent sexual encounter and wanted nothing less than to find myself in an emergency room explaining Gay Sex 101 to an uninformed or hostile straight intern. But as a stranger to this big Midwestern city in 1983, I felt this was my most likely option. Arriving on my first evening ever into a Chicago single-digit night, feeling sick, lonely, and worried, I placed a call to Roger, a gay doctor I knew only somewhat back in New York. "Let me call a med school pal of mine in Chicago," he clucked. "If anyone can take care of you, Ron will." Two calls were made, and within the hour I found myself at the apartment of a man I had never met, getting a house call, free of charge, no strings attached. The bug turned out to be nothing, but the bond endured. Ron and I ended up ordering in Chinese and swapping stories. I had my first Chicago chum. I felt I now had someone to turn to. When I later told this story to my brother, he said he couldn't imagine feeling connected and being taken care of in a city where he knew nobody. In my world, I realized, I had come to rely on my lavender underground railroad, an invisible web of support.

We may not all have such a dramatic story. For some it might have been just a helpful car ride, an opportune couch for the night, a timely piece of advice, a steady hand on a spinning dance floor. How many of us have had moments of support—in ways large or small—from a man with whom we seemingly share nothing but a sexual category? When *where* you are matters less than *what* you are, that's diffuse intimacy at its best.

Obviously, not all of us consistently participate in such rich and sustaining networks. Plenty of men identify as gay, and may even live in gay mecca zip codes, yet feel isolated and lonely. As we see in chapter 9, we have colluded in a range of cultural bad habits that keep us more isolated from each other than we need—or want—to be. In later pages, we explore the ways that our gay cultures can better fulfill the promise of diffuse intimacy for all of us. This book is part of a larger project of helping transform our cultural practices so that more of us can feel this camaraderie and support more often, as explained in chapter 10.

Right now, the potential of such links is not always realized, but it is potential. Much of the time they lie submerged, available to be called into being in the right circumstances. The moments we do find them serve to remind us that at its best, gayness can function as a pass-card into a society of friends, those we know, and those not yet found. As we will see, there are concrete ways to more fully manifest that with and for each other. The point is to craft cultural customs that encourage us to embrace our most loving, nurturant, and hopeful sides in ways we have not yet seen.

Already, researchers note that gay men rely on each other far more for support than we do on our biological families.[13] When we need help or social support, or are anxious about death, we are "more likely to turn to peers than to family for help in times of need" and "more likely to seek help from peers."[14] Repeatedly, studies report that biological family members are "less likely to be sought and were perceived as least helpful,"[15] and that those most likely to help gay men are other gay men. We look to our families of friends deeply for our support as others look to their nuclear families.[16]

All of which means we are far more likely to pass life's milestones—our commitment ceremonies, holidays, grieving, bedside vigils, anniversaries, births, and deaths—in our created families.[17] We are far more likely to share our deepest, most intimate, and vulnerable moments in care teams for sick friends; we are likely to die among chosen families as often as among biological ones. Such powerful moments—of care and support, vulnerability and stress, hope and humanity—are when we see most clearly what we can be for and with each other. They are precisely the threads that weave that sacred web called family.

We've already seen in the previous chapter how gay male couples often implement intimacy differently. Some points strike one as quirky, like findings showing we have different habits of gift-giving. "Compared to previous research on gift-giving between heterosexual partners," the paper reports, its sample of gay men "devoted more attention to selection or creation of gifts and they were also more concerned about the recipient's appreciation and utilization of the gift. They were less concerned with economic equity in the exchange process,"[18] and, as already noted, less likely to deceive intimate partners.[19] Some differences are not so small. Even in our stable couples, where you'd imagine we most closely resemble traditional families, we are rewriting rules of emotional fidelity in ways that carry implications for the larger American family.[20]

Demographers say that long-established gay couples are more likely to maintain separate domiciles than are their straight-coupled counterparts, where it is quite rare to do so. In Madison, Wisconsin, Jon and Phillip have described themselves as a couple for five years, yet happily keep separate apartments. "And we're not about to change it." Jon smiles. "We spend three nights a week together, give or take, but we both like our own space." Brent and Dennis tell a different story: "We considered ourselves coupled for seven years, and bought a home in the Jersey suburbs—cat, garden, the whole nine yards. But in seven years, I don't think we spent more than three months ever consecutively living under the same roof. We'd have driven each other crazy if we did."

> Only I will establish in the Mannahatta, and in every city
>   of These States, inland and seaboard,
> And in the fields and woods, above every keel little or large,
>   that dents the water,
> Without edifices, or rules, or trustees, or any argument,
> The institution of the dear love of comrades.
>   —Walt Whitman, "Calamus 24"

Whitman was right. To every city of these states, inland and seaboard, we do indeed flock in search of the dear love of our comrades. The lone teen who hops a bus in Wichita bound for the big gay city is our queer Everyman. The tale runs deep in our lore only because it reflects such a common truth. Various population studies reveal gay men are far more likely to be émigrés from a smaller town to a bigger city. Ron King was one of those: "Growing up in Maine, I just knew I had to get out. Age sixteen was all about saving money to buy a bus ticket from my home to somewhere else—in my case, Florida. That's where most of the gay guys from Maine went to. As far away as possible." When he stepped onto that bus, Ron became a queer statistic. Demographers have noted that we cluster first in cities, then in specific neighborhoods within them.[21] It is a utopian impulse, to gather in clans. Like latter-day Shakers or present-day Mormons, we group together to live among own. At first we did it in places that became known as classic queer enclaves, areas like Castro and Chelsea, WeHo and Boystown. Such neighborhoods created their own queer numerology of place: 10014 and 10011, 94707 and 90069. Today, one can scarcely find any major American city without its gay neighborhood. Columbus has its German Village, Los Angeles its Silver Lake; it's Northwest in Portland, Uptown in Minneapolis, Capitol Hill in Seattle, and Center City in Philadelphia. Hail them as spreading centers of urban renewal, or hate them as sites of gay gentrification and elitism; both perspectives overlook the more interesting, if quieter, truth of these streets. What's most compelling here are not the newly painted facades or the manicured street trees, not the rising property values. It is the fact that such places are sites of an evolving intentional community among men.

When Whitman proclaimed a social vision of "cities of friends," he might have been headed to brunch in any constituted gay neighborhood in this country. We are brought to such precincts by hope, seeking like-hearted men. One might as well post signs in these neighborhoods: Send us your sissy boys, your gym rats, your Mad Queens, your huddled masses. We come with dreams of living out our best values and hopes, of crafting new kinds of social, sexual, and moral lives with each other. These are places we come to find, and build, our cities of friends. We have made them our queer cities on the hill, the cauldrons where we brew our ethical principles into social habits.

"Gay" . . . increasingly marks a full spectrum of social life: not only same sex desires, but gay selves, gay neighbors, and gay social practices that are distinctive. . . .
  —Gilbert Herdt

It is not as though gay men have cornered the market on friendship, intimacy, or fraternity. Not all of us share in these practices, even when we call ourselves gay or when we reside in identified gay neighborhoods. Too often, as we will see, our created cultural habits can result in us feeling alone or isolated, disappointed in this thing called community, and ultimately, cynical. As we will see, we have work to do if we are to realize the best promise of our diffuse intimacies.

But what is equally clear is that the ways we have to commit communal intimacy are among our most distinctive social practices. We do it with roommates, housemates, in summer shares and group houses, and in ways far more intentional. Such patterns are long-standing and well-documented. Gay men are far more likely as adults to live in some form of communal life or intentional community than are our straight siblings. The pattern has been noted in cities, suburbs, and rural areas.[22] Examining rural queer communities more than fifteen years ago, one author noted "the diversity of community helping structures that . . . gay men have elaborated."[23] Wherever we settle, we form what writer Kath Weston terms "families we choose."[24]

The sleepy farming town of Ukiah, California, seems an unlikely spot for a mass experiment in gay diffuse intimacy. Nestled in the amber foothills of Mendocino County, it is an agricultural town set in rolling farmland, the sort of place where nobody blinks when someone rides a horse downtown. Ukiah has at least two claims to fame. First, it bears the distinction of America's only town whose name spells "haiku" backward. Second, it is home to the Sweet Williams (not the organization's real name), one of the most genial experiments in gay male communality around. The group began in the 1980s as a network of rural gay men taking care of their neighbors and friends with AIDS and educating others about prevention. "You know, looking in on them, taking meals by, caring for animals," recalls an early member. "Just good old queer neighborliness." That queer "neighborhood" has now grown into a loose network of a thousand-plus men, many from isolated rural towns with names like Sebastopol, Willets, and Weed. Many travel three hours north from the Bay Area to attend gatherings. A few migrate from faraway places like Hawaii, Brooklyn, and London. All have come to be a part of the Sweet Williams mission: "To establish intimacy and community among gay and bisexual men, and to build bridges with supportive communities."

The July Fourth gathering may reach several hundred, with smaller convocations at New Year's, in the spring, and Labor Day, and several monthly potlucks. Whenever Sweet Williams gather, gentle acceptance has been elevated to an art form. As it was explained to me on my first visit by one attendee, "The default mode here is affection and acceptance with each other." The prevailing politesse of the place says that when someone approaches you, known or not, a hug might be a perfectly reasonable place to start. Of course, after a day or two in this friendly space, what seems unreasonable is that anyone any place else would see it differently. "The key attitude here . . . is no attitude," says Grant, a regular attendee. "It's such a welcome relief to the high-tension sexual scene in bars." The core ritual here—there are many—is the heart circle, where up to 150 men sit in a circle, sharing feelings and stories, narrating struggles and victories. As the stories unfold, men lie on the grass, on hay bales, sprawled across each other.

At random intervals, several blissed-out chums may clump into a free-form "puppy pile," a happy mandala of male parts, suffused in smiles and a simmering sensuality. Imagine M. C. Escher meets Norman Rockwell meets Paul Cadmus, and you get the basic idea. In circle, men listen to each other muse on their heart challenges, lost loves, personal griefs and victories, and offer life observations or anecdotes. The man cuddled next to me is rubbing the small of my back—the fact that we haven't met is mutually irrelevant. The man on the other side of me, clad in a flowered sarong, sleeveless lumberjack shirt, and a body that flatters both attires, says simply: "I never miss a heart circle." At the moment, an eighty-seven-year-old man is telling how it was to come out only three years ago, and discussing his impending death. The talking stick passes to the next man, in his twenties, who tells in a small voice that he has just learned he is HIV-positive. The stick passes and the next man offers a favorite Sufi erotic poem.

Over the ten days of gathering, meals are prepared and cleaned up communally. The programs flow from whatever anyone is moved to offer: meditation, a hike, drumming, discussions about leather, sex, gay ecology, holistic remedies for HIV, or just a lot of hanging at the pool or hot tub. Massages—nonsexual, Swedish, shiatsu, Tantric, sexual, clothed, naked, your choice—are offered on outdoor tables under huge oak trees, given and received for free. In the words of the day's kitchen coordinator: "I see men open up here in ways I see no other place in my existence." The Sweet Williams share some features with the profuse network of gay adult camps now being created around the country. They go by names like Camp Camp (Boston), Camp Lifeguard (California), Camp New Hope (Pennsylvania), or just plain Camp (Seattle). By whatever name, all are communal crucibles, where grown men share group lives for a weekend, a week, or longer.

Penobscot Bay, Maine, is about as far from Ukiah as you can go in America without getting your feet wet. Instead of Mendocino foothills, the landscape is Maine birch forests, the locals more taciturn Yankee stock than mellow New Agers, and the county's main cash crop blueberries, not marijuana. But the same spirit burns bright at the Make-It-Beautiful Tribe that meets on Penobscot Bay. The "tribe" is made up of two clans—the Sunrise Clan, from the east side of the bay, and the Sunset Clan, hailing from the west. For seventeen years, several times each year, in time with Maine's migrating seasons, they gather. The invitation reads: "Bring tent, sleeping bag, food for potluck, joy of being with men who love men." "We're here to take care of each other for a weekend," says Ron King, one of its founders. "That means emotionally, physically, socially, sexually, and spiritually." Heart circles and touch exercises, massage and sex, meditation and exploration, not to mention the requisite Is-It-Talent? show. "Guys laugh a lot, and cry some." "And don't forget the sex!" grins Mark, another tribal organizer. "It's about being with each other in whatever ways you want."

If one's tastes run to the less tribal, you can spend Sundays with the Bachelor Farmers Brunch Group, enjoy seasonal retreats of Mainely Men, prowl with a local Bear pack, join groups of Faeries at their solstice parties, or hike with any of several gay outdoor clubs. Northern Maine is so sparsely populated that the government still classifies many counties as "frontier." But when it comes to opportunities for diffuse intimacy, the networks are rich and elaborated.

A few hours' drive brings you from Penobscot to Provincetown, one of those renowned enclaves where homosocial structures and customs have taken root and flourished. Richard has gone to Provincetown every year for almost two decades, always in the last two weeks of August, always with a gaggle of friends. The core group, six strong, has known each other since they lived, worked, and sproradically sexed together in Boston in the early 1980s. Today its members hail from Cambridge, New York, San Francisco, and other points, depending on the year. The group now includes mates and lovers, singles and couples, lesbians and gay men. They have visited P-Town in various combinations for eighteen years, sharing hotel rooms and bathrooms, huddling through thunderstorms, giggling over drinks, lying on the beach. Pretty much any of them can and do share rooms, walks, visits, and meals with any of the others—the exact permutations blur after so many years. For two decades, they have strolled P-Town's sidewalks, shopping, kidding and fighting, connecting, arguing, and doing what old friends do. On its dunes, they have grieved lost lovers and courted new ones. Here is the family that all new boyfriends are brought home to meet; here they recall how deeply they are the witnesses and intimates in each other's lives. Theirs is an annual rite of diffuse intimacy.

P-Town offers a queer milieu embedded in a straight town, with gay, lesbian, bi, and straight walking side by side down Commercial Street. But continue down the coast a few hours, and you reach what may be the purest experiment in gay communal intimacy yet seen. Two hours east of New York City, two clusters of wood-frame houses hug a precarious half-mile-wide sandbar between the bay and the beach. Two vacation enclaves, Cherry Grove and Fire Island Pines, have been here for decades. When J. Edgar Hoover was donning drag in the nation's capital to lead the fight against perverts, Fire Island was already an established beachhead of the very People Your Mother Warned You About. Thirty years later, Cherry Grove retains a genial mix of lesbians, gay men, and more than a smattering of straight-but-not-narrow bohemians. But just fifteen minutes down the beach, things change dramatically.

Remember your fantasy about God waving a hand and making everyone on earth into a gay man? Well, She did. And behold, She called it Fire Island Pines. Hike from Cherry Grove across the patch of dune and forest known as the Meatrack, and you step into the most thoroughly gay-male municipality on planet Earth. It is the site of a vast social improbability. The Pines is a living laboratory, the prototype of intentional society that one group of gay men might create if they could. Because in The Pines they could, and here, for several decades, they have done just that.

One need never actually have set foot on Fire Island to hold strong opinions about it. We know it by repute, that sun-drenched Sodom, a citizenry of the drug-addled and dissolute, full of wealthy, white, steroid-swelled gym muscle. Books and film, magazines and porn render the place as an endless carnal carnival, a bacchanal both delicious and dangerous. It is a mythic place in the gay imaginary, our Shangri-La, Atlantis, or Hades, depending on your perspective. Like any good mythic isle, Fire Island has its Sirens on the rocks, luring unsuspecting males to an untimely fate. Only here they are butch beach gods, Sirens on steroids. Their song is a fierce dance beat calling men to an island paradise of lustful pleasures only to doom them in the rocky shallows of drugs and sex. And as the real estate ads remind, life in paradise doesn't come cheap—it can cost thousands of dollars to take a bed here for the summer.

But spend even a weekend on this narrow isthmus and the myth begins to dissipate like a morning beach mist, as other shapes come into view. The first thing one sees is a charming skew of accustomed male mores. Everywhere men hug and smooch; couples walk, hands entwined or casually draped into the rear of a partner's cutoffs. On the Boulevard—a six-foot-wide plank boardwalk—groups of three and four men clasp hands as they walk. Arms drape over friends' shoulders in line at the Pantry checkout; pals tickle each other in the hardware store and bestow pats on heads and butts in the checkout line at Eddie's butcher counter. Couples make out in boardwalk alcoves, clumps of men sprawl over each other under beach umbrellas, knots of sweaty bodies melt into other sweaty bodies on the dance floor. Everywhere, 24/7, an easy male affection suffuses the air, an utterly naturalized praxis of public touch. For a moment, one almost forgets it isn't like this on every sidewalk, in every small-town grocery store and butcher.

Although this affection is most visible in the public square, the most interesting forms of our diffuse intimacy become visible only when you step behind the weathered wood fences. Tonight, in most of these six-hundred-odd houses, a half dozen or more unrelated men will sit down at table to shared meals they have prepared together. They will clean up, argue over music, share bathrooms, go to sleep, roust each other from disco naps at 1:00 A.M. to dance, and learn to discreetly knock before entering bedrooms (sometimes). Every April to October, thousands of such men come together and twine around each other's lives, trading boyfriend stories (and sometimes boyfriends), romantic dreams, and career woes, recounting life's vicissitudes, swapping drag outfits and Abercrombie shirts, giggling over sexual exploits. They become players in each other's dramas, bond on beach walks, pass nights in friendly charades games or a swirl of dancing, cuddle on couches before fires, or watch sunrise on the beach. Somewhere along the way, they become part of the place, the largest ongoing experiment in gay intentional community yet attempted.

It is easy to deride this place as a preserve for the wealthy and white, the privileged and pumped. Some see here only an isthmus of attitude and rejection, and the place certainly has all of those elements. But the unsung truth here is far more interesting than the body culture, the dancing and drugs, the perception of exclusivity and the wealth. It is the fact that Fire Island is a form of queer *kibbutz*. Where else do groups of men from twenty-five to fifty-five (and up) step beyond the rules of single men and domestic coupledom to blend in a messy communal existence? Where else in American culture can a dozen grown men go week after week, to merge their lives, share space, bedrooms, shaving cream, finances, house laundry, beach afternoons, dance evenings, and lazy Sunday mornings over crossword puzzles? Where else do they enact such intimacies among a menagerie of men they may never have known before this summer?

The People's Republic of Fire Island Pines is what locals call it, their winking homage to just how different the rules are in this place. It is a short mile, and world away, from the manicured lawns and SUVs of suburban Long Island, just across the bay. Not just the rules of intimacy, but all sorts of rules are transformed. Doors are rarely locked here, neat rows of $200 sandals lie untouched all day at the edge of every boardwalk down to the beach, and the local police log doesn't show a violent assault in recent memory. For years, Don, a local (straight) insurance agent, has kept an eye on the insurance claims filed from the Republic of the Pines. "It would be hard to find a place of this size with fewer claims," he observes. "For vandalism and theft, there really isn't much out there, not for years and years." But surely he can recall something? He smiles. "A few years back some fella went home with a guy. I guess he was pretty looped, so while all the housemates slept, he grabbed a can of black spray paint and sprayed what he thought were witty sayings on the white walls. They weren't exactly readable." The only other claim he recalls involved "Some pissed-off guy who broke into the house his ex-boyfriend was staying at. He cut out the crotch of every pair of pants in the poor guy's closet. Only thing was, it was the wrong house. Geez, do you have any idea how expensive some of those pants can be?" A natural disaster, Pines-style, but not exactly the sort of catastrophe they teach you about at claims adjuster school.

The difference in values rarely makes it into the Fire Island myth. Over the years, many have looked over its dunes and seen a blank canvas on which to paint garish landscapes of gay men's world. But it is not sad-eyed clowns nor serene sailboats these social artists sketch. They prefer to traffic in allegories of moral panic and deviance. In the 1980s, they offered a grim gallery of gay plague, charcoal studies of the End of Days in Gay World. In the nineties, they changed brushes to render scenes from Hieronymus Bosch, with ghouls of unsafe public sex, Much Too Much Muscle, open-air dancing, and that old standby, Really Bad Drugs. Which, in this tableau, amounts to pretty much All Drugs. Oh, then they threw in unseemly music and skimpy shorts to complete the horror.

Like the dime-store seascapes sold on street corners, such images usu-ally just reinforce prevailing culture's expectations. Any journeyman doodler can look at all-night dance parties and render familiar landscapes of sin and Sodom by the Sea. But it takes an artist's eye to capture the suffusing affection and support, the values of conviviality and commu-nality, the embrace of sheer bliss and celebration, at play in the place. One could instead choose to celebrate and revere the quiet experiments in diffuse intimacy that have flowered in the Pines for more than three decades. Where are the *pietà*s of strangers helping strangers along dark boardwalks, raising funds for charity, breaking bread, rescuing each other from wobbly evenings and boyfriend disasters, comforting each other on the beach at dawn, trusting each other with leases and secrets, housekeys and roommates, caring for each other through illness, breakups, and K-holes? To convey such images takes a subtler palette of pastels.

Render this island as a sun-drenched Sodom if you must. But see in it also a place where values of mutual support and camaraderie can reign, where a value of basic American neighborliness thrives. Lift the top off these houses and you can find sex parties, cliques, drugs, and attitude. But you can also find a herd of friends weaving common lives, dancing in and out of each other's arms, living rooms, and hearts. It is our choice as to which parts of our story we tell. Do we caricature the perils of party life or honor a communal effort that started on a deck in an attempt to raise money to care for dying friends? Do we train the analytic telescope on the place and revile the revels? Or do we peer through its other end to behold a site of celebration, a sacred healing venue where thousands of men have valiantly resurrected a shared life from ashes of mourning and death? These are contradictions only if we insist on calling them that. Our story is not so easily writ as we think. As Whitman reminded us a century ago, we are vast, we contain multitudes. Places like Fire Island invite one to look harder. Beyond the glare of skin and sex, all that sun and sand, some-thing far more tender and sweet is taking root on these dunes.

Two hours to the west of these weathered houses, another group of queer men come together in a very different kind of house, yet another rich experiment in styles of queer diffuse intimacy. They are the vogueing houses. Each involves a sprawling social clan of up to several dozen young queer folk. These houses provide a social structure where young queers of color—overwhelmingly Latino and African-American—can find support, recognition, and safety.

Mainstream America, with its insatiable appetite for the stirrings of youth gang culture, gave vogueing houses their fifteen minutes of fame through the documentary *Paris Is Burning,* an early Madonna tour, and scores of ads and photo spreads in fashion magazines. But what is happening in them has a far older provenance. Some say houses had their cultural roots in the legendary drag societies in Harlem in the early and mid-century. But by the late eighties and early nineties these institutions had morphed into a network stretching from Philadelphia to Washington, D.C., to New York.

House culture has the exoticism the dominant culture finds irresistible. Houses bear fashion labels like Mizrahi and Prada, Aviance, Xtravaganza, or themes like Infinity or Latex. The central ritual of house culture is the ball, where house members compete in runway competitions of walking and dancing. The average house ball can number several hundred spectators and contestants, although those of some houses—New York's Latex, for example—reach upwards of a thousand. Each category designates the comportment of the particular competition. The nuances between, say, Butch, Fem Queen Runway, Legendary Vogue, Fierceness, and Thug are well understood by those walking, those watching, and those judging. "If you can walk, if you know the moves, know how to throw shade and have the right attitude, you can be a star," says Kevin, who has attended balls since 1987. "It's all about attitude."

Beyond the swish, swashbuckle, and shade, the houses have for years provided something infinitely more precious than any designer label. They are forms of family. Houses, at their best, provide commodities rare indeed in these young men's lives. They offer safety and support, an older adult to lend a helping hand, a community of peers. "In the streets I came from, queer boys got themselves dead, in ugly ways, real fast," says Kiki. "Your house gave you standing, structure. A place to be. You know, friends looking out for you."

In houses, that family structure is made literal. Each has a House Mother and/or Father. Mother may help with advice from fashion to relationships, even sewing costumes before the big ball. More important, they are older role models who set the tone, the rules, and the special stamp of character that gives the house its identity. Xtravaganza, for example, counts its membership primarily among young *Puertoriqueños*. New York's House of Latex was organized to keep members and their consorts sexually safe by fostering safer sex, with condoms one of the essential fashion accessories. It is a world where one lives by flamboyance and fashion, where style is your sword and shield, the prime legal tender. Houses are where you find your friends, camaraderie, and comfort, perhaps a bed or a lead for a job, and a familial stability.

From vogueing houses to vacation houses, our experiments in intimacy take a thousand shapes. Yet read between lines in Rehoboth and Russian River. Pay mind in Penobscot, Provincetown, and Palm Springs. Heed the haiku of Ukiah and walk the runway in Philadelphia. In such spots, something powerful is occurring. These groupings may almost be viewed as an unseen network of monasteries. These men make up a resolutely worldly priesthood. They are brothers bound in *bonhomie*, where delight is the doctrine. In such places, a new order of men is brewing a new order of intimacy, one where they learn to rely not just on themselves but on each other. In so doing, they forge a faith to redeem us all.

We have the potential for affectional relationships carried on outside the normative patterns. These friendships and networks are unforeseen . . . the unknown potential of gay relations.
　—Mark Thompson, *Gay Spirit*

Gay {and lesbian} families represent a new, embattled, visible, and, necessarily, self-conscious genre of kinship. They help to expose the widening gap between the complex reality of contemporary family forms and the dated family ideology that still undergirds most public rhetoric, policy, and law concerning families.
　—Judith Stacey

Not all of us, by any stretch, exist in these affiliative stews, pursue multiple relationships, have rich friendship networks, summer in gay enclaves, or settle in mecca neighborhoods. But for many of us, sex, affection, sociality, and support blend far more easily than they do in dominant culture, yielding forms of connection far more diverse than the

Dad-Mom-kids trinity. The point is not that our lives are monolithically different, nor our sociality necessarily more enriching. It is that our cultural habits offer some different opportunities.

There are significant implications—both pragmatic and philosophical—in the patterns of affection and nurture being pursued in many corners of gay world. These queer experiments in diffuse intimacy may hold important lessons for what America is becoming. At the millennium, the U.S. census reports that fewer than one quarter—24 percent—of our households consist of Dad, Mom, and kids. That fraction has been shriveling for several decades, a detumescing demographic if ever there were one. The three in four American households who don't fit this mythic norm may have something to learn from those men who have such long experience constituting intimacy beyond the dyad. Judith Stacey, a family sociologist, writes, "Nongay families, family scholars, and policymakers alike can learn a great deal from examining the experience, struggles, conflicts, needs, and achievements of contemporary gay and lesbian families."[25] Another researcher writes: "A key aspect of recasting the 'family' in social policy formulation will be to institutionalize varied forms of primary relationships by extending formal legal rights and obligations to persons who are technically unrelated to one another (e.g., gay couples, social agents, close friends). Current demographic patterns, with their accompanying changes in cultural values with regard to interdependencies and definitions of family, suggest that the process of redefinition has begun."[26]

One redefinition is that our life scripts do not presume that we will live and die in dyads. Although many of us live as couples at some point, our diffuse intimacies offer different shapes for our life paths. We have created cultures to reflect that. We support and maintain a rich profusion of social options for the uncoupled. Less yoked to the needs of children, we have crafted public institutions to meet the recreational, social, and affiliative needs and interests of adults. It's not that heterosexuals don't enjoy dance venues, travel and cultural outlets, adult camps, and even sex clubs. Rather, adult family roles, obligations, and family habits often place these into the slowly receding distance of youth. As a friend mused, drink in hand, as he looked out over several thousand men dancing in the sculpted topiary gardens of Miami's White Party: "Isn't it amazing what you concoct when you aren't shuttling between the PTA and soccer matches?"

Sociologists see in gay diffuse intimacy important lessons for an aging population. Today, most of us will look ahead to spending time alone or living with nonrelatives; we have much to learn from these parts of the great gay social experiment. What might seniors—or all of us potential seniors—learn from the communality and mutual caretaking in gay lives? One who looked at gay communal networks in Central and Southern California concluded: "The way in which these friendship families are created and maintained has the potential to benefit all elderly, especially those who have no biological families or whose biological families are unavailable for support."[27] Can we imagine the government task force convened to examine the great gay social experiment, to distill the concrete models we offer for care and nurture networks among America's senior population?

Experiments occurring in many gay men's lives can also offer new models of male intimacy. Our popular culture everywhere reflects the notion that most men neither understand, nor are prepared for, the travails and challenges of intimacy. It has become an unwritten rule of prime-time TV, from *Frazier* to *Friends* to *Roseanne,* that straight men are stereotypically ridiculed as clueless in matters of the heart; one recent series bore the title *Men Behaving Badly*. In real life, straight men in couples are often left to grapple over where to find intimacy and meaning. So America gets *Iron John*, Promise Keepers, and a Million Man March—all constituted to help men find meaning in their roles.

Our lives also offer lessons for the uncoupled. In the dominant culture, straight people who don't marry can be exiled to an emotional limbo, isolated from the main socially approved source of emotional succor. Ponder the institutions, cultural forms, and structures that gay men have gotten to elaborate and enjoy. Might not some of them reflect exactly what a culture of unmarried straight individuals would choose themselves, given greater social latitude to innovate?

Beyond its costs to the individual, restricting intimacy and nurturance to couples exacts a great price on notions of community and the common good. With all that energy turned inward to home, hearth, and hellions, less is left for pursuits of community, voluntary service, cultural sharing, what was once called the common good. Various parties feel and describe this vacuum in various ways. Republicans lament "lax moral values," Democrats decry "shattered communities," and everyone frets over the risks to the endangered family sliding into poverty, the couples earning less, the erosion of that most elusive fiction, Traditional Family Values. In his popular book, *Habits of the Heart*, sociologist Robert Bellah provides an analysis of America's diminishing civic involvement. He sees us as a nation increasingly focused on the needs and goals of the individual, with citizens less engaged in efforts that "carry them beyond private life into public endeavors."[28] Yet we give little voice to the costs that our model of nuclear intimacy poses to notions of a *collective* family, all those messy affiliations in which the majority of us now live.

What does it mean when intimacy grows diffuse? In a nation searching for community, our cultural habits may offer answers. Gay sociologist Herdt writes of what he terms "gay *communitas*." Writing in the peak years of AIDS, he stated that gay men across the country have "crystallized a new moral order of gay prosocial attitudes." In his words, a "personal commitment to a new order of public good now prevails in meccas of the Castro and Greenwich Village."[29]

"Personal commitment" is just the point of our myriad forms of connection. In our dance pals and best friends and sisters, our lovers and housemates and roommates, our exes, our sex buddies and gym buddies, our care teams and birthday parties, sprouts a new affectionate order. As we extend in wider circles the love, affections, and privileges now reserved to "family," we are changing ideas about relatedness and responsibility. These queer lives we lead offer new alternatives as to whom men may care about, whom we care for, how we do it, and why.

GIVING LANGUAGE TO OUR LOVES

They do not love who do not show their love.
—Bill Shakespeare, of indeterminate sexual orientation

Gay social laboratories are synthesizing new social compounds, replenishing an impoverished palette of socially approved forms of communal love. We just don't always know how to name the love we show. When I lead weekends with gay men around the country, in groups of twenty and fifty and a hundred, we spend time exploring our queer vocabulary of affection. We go around the room taking time to name, catalogue, and honor the elaborate lexicon that we have coined to describe the range of our relationships. The chalkboard at the front of the room gets crowded with boyfriend, best friend, fuck buddy, lover, trick, roommate, daddy, sister, buddy, number, partner, auntie, playpal, husband, dance mate, boy, master, girlfriend, spouse. Each conveys its nuance, each its limits. The meanings to most of them are well known to most men in the room. When they aren't, great discussions ensue over just what it means to have a "sister" or the role one's "daddy" plays in one's life.

Naming is a powerful thing, and forms part of our shared culture. We can introduce a lover, refer to a trick or a sister, and know what we mean.

Each conveys a subtle shade of nuance and expectation, relatedness and responsibility. They are our culture's accepted honorifics, much like the several levels of respect in Japanese or Korean. We expect something from tricks, another from sisters, something else from Daddies and dance buddies, and something altogether different from lovers.

Our greatest challenge rests in finding a language, a way of communicating across our subjective, across our difference.
—Marlon Riggs

The exercise grows most interesting when I invite the men to create new language for the unnamed bonds in their lives. What other bonds need inclusion in our nomenclature? *The Queen's Lexicon*, published twenty years ago, defined "future ex-old-man" as "ex-lover who can't be gotten out of the blood," as in: "No, I can't say we really go together anymore, he's my future ex-old-man." How about a word for the man with whom we have had a long-simmering, mutually recognized, but unconsummated, sexual tension (one recent group suggested "tension buddies")? What term denotes that special sexual mentor who gave us a lesson or gift in one night of passion never forgotten or repeated? (One-time wonders?) The "ex" we still have soul-baring dinners with? The trick-become-friend? The gang we came out with (Bill, twenty-something, refers to them as his "queer litter-mates")? Even this rich list only hints at the myriad of ways we splay over each other's affections.

This issue of language played out powerfully among three men we can call Donnie, Darren, and Robert. Donnie and Darren had been lovers for fifteen years when, over the course of a year, they consensually welcomed Robert into their relationship. As they recount it: "There weren't major tensions or jealousies at all. We got along great, lived together, shared meals, affection, sex. There was—and is—good feeling among us." But, Donnie notes, "We had no words to convey what we meant to each other or what we were trying to do. People we met would refer to Robert as a boy toy, or property, an interloper, a slave, a house wrecker, a good friend, a kept boy. Every box they had was wrong, either undermining and cynical, or negative and trivializing." Says Darren, "Robert used the lack of language as a shield. We were 'friends'—his way of avoiding naming this bond as in any way important. That was one way he made it clear he never really intended to join our lives. Language was how he kept it at a distance. So long as vagueness kept us unnamed, he kept his options open." They agree: "It's simplistic to say we didn't work out together because of language. But not having words sure did make it feel less clear, less supported, and way more painful."

Their story conveys a larger truth in our lives. We do well to respect this business of naming. Words help us honor, cherish, and revere our loves. To name a thing is to bring it into being, socially, emotionally, even spiritually. Politically, our tribal struggle has long turned on this issue of naming, coming out, calling oneself gay or queer, reclaiming epithets like pansy, fairy, and fag. But among us, finding a shared language of affection helps us envision, participate in, and navigate what and how we are with each other. As we explore new affectionate paths with each other, we blaze the trail with terms. Through words, we demand others take our lives seriously, yet part of our taking our *own* diverse relationships seriously is to swaddle them with language. We are gardeners of each other's hearts, our words our fertilizer.

The simple exercise of giving language to the loves of our lives tells a truth most of us know, but few of us acknowledge. It is this F-word, not the other one, that most deeply informs and shapes our common lives. The words these men have offered up remind us that all of these labels denote various flavors of friend, yet few are only that. We are finding new ways for men to manifest love with each other, yet unnamed. In gay worlds, "friend" is too small a syllable. Our lives stretch the word at its seams until it has grown threadbare and thin. Like a sheer slipcover draping furniture in a shared summer house, it obscures the contours of the places where we sprawl with each other, hiding the lines of the many shapes in which we furnish these rooms, our lives.

> *It is possible . . . that {gay men} may be destined to form the advance guard of that great movement which will one day transform the common life by substituting the bond of personal affection and compassion for the monetary, legal, and other external ties which now control and confine society.*
> —Edward Carpenter, British social philosopher

In this millennial moment, one group of men is evolving a hundred new variations on a very ancient idea: beloved community. Our customs of diffuse intimacy would not seem queer at all in fifth-century classical Athens when Plato wrote: "The lover is a friend inspired by God." The Greek word *agape* denotes a diffuse social love quite distinct from erotic, romantic, or aesthetic attraction. Centuries later, in Roman civic culture as well, they celebrated a public ethic of *caritas* and *communitas*, both embodying a sense of shared well-being and caretaking beyond one's blood ties. Both ancient ideas find renewed forms and expression in contemporary gay lives. Indeed, a Periclean Greek or a Roman senator transported to 20th Street and Eighth Avenue in New York would likely recognize the ethical habits of our lives far more easily than might, say, a Baptist minister in Baton Rouge.

Gay experiments in affection, the norms and rituals of our intimacies, echo ethics taught by a wide variety of religious traditions. These values are strikingly consonant with Judeo-Christian ethics of communalism and social liberation. They sound a lot like what Jesus preached. The innovations in love and community we are crafting today have previously been seen primarily in religious orders, secular communes, utopian settlements, intentional communities, and fraternal brotherhoods. Our habits of diffuse bonding and support, voluntary caretaking, and service recall practices of the first Christian apostles. They recall values espoused by spiritually constituted brotherhoods from early Christian practice, to medieval monasteries, to modern-day religious orders.

Our experiments in families of friends echo the words of the medieval French poet Eustache Deschamps, who, in the fourteenth century, wrote, "Friends are the family you make yourself." Eighteenth-century France founded a revolution on the ideal of *fraternité*. Religious thinkers like the Quakers (Society of Friends) and Christian advocates of "beloved community" explored novel forms of relationship far beyond the dyadic. Their efforts at intentional community, much like those now arising in gay male worlds, were social experiments in a praxis of applied affection. They held the potential to open doors to new intimacies and rewrite codes of compassion and care. They were, and we are, social alchemists, conducting experiments in love. Our experiments are all the more salient because they issue from this most troubled gender called men.

Edward Carpenter, a nineteenth-century British radical utopian, used the term "Uranian" for what we might now call "gay." (Luckily, Carpenter was a better polemicist than publicist. Had this unfortunate term stuck, we'd all be marching in the Uranus Pride Parade.) He wrote movingly about the potentials of a community of men loving men and saw huge social significance in the affections like those that some gay men today enjoy. Carpenter argued that, sexually and emotionally, socially and economically, such bonds could hold the promise to challenge a social contract built on competition, the individual, and self-interest. That is what utopians have always seen as the most radical potential of diffuse intimacy, straight or gay. It holds a radical transformation in social relationship, and these are the very aspects now common in modern gay men's lives.

At about the same time, across the pond, the American poet Walt Whitman proclaimed a social vision of "cities of friends" where "the dear love of comrades" would beget "new laws to link and intertwine majestic peoples." He quite explicitly evokes a brotherly civic culture of men, the "love to weld and weave comrade to comrade, man to bearded man." His vision is robustly male and erotic, physically strong, deeply affectionate, companionate—and ethical. Were Whitman to stand on that same Chelsea corner in his beloved Mannahatta, he could revel in his vision come to life among "prairie boys with cheeks of tan" strolling to the gym. Had he cruised that corner just twenty years ago, he might have locked eyes with philosopher Michel Foucault, rolling out of an after-hours club, musing that "to be gay is not to identify with the psychological traits and the visible masks of the homosexual, but to try to develop and define a way of life."

Quite a gang now crowds this queer street corner in this city of friends: a Gauloise-smoking French *philosophe,* a bearded American poet, a British dandy who fancies working boys, a couple of rowdy French *sans-culottes,* monks in floor-length robes, bronzed Roman soldiers in leather tunics, and Greeks in togas. It's a gay party if ever there were one, your basic transhistorical Village People. Let them argue over gay ways of life, dearly loved comrades, radical brotherhoods and beloved community, *fraternité, caritas,* and *agape.* By whatever name, they are arguing a queer philosophy, whose core tenets have resonated in varied forms for 2,500 years.

The key issue is what happens when responsibility, caretaking and caregiving, practical and emotional ties, are spread around. What changes when sexual, emotional, and pragmatic intimacy is shared among broad affiliative networks? How do conceptions of connection alter when you are responsible to a collectivity, when others in your larger community are potential housemates, bedmates, boyfriends, or best friends of same? In a world where one's stake transcends one's surname, how does the concept of "family" implode—or improve? At our best, in glimmers, in the promise these communities offer, we glimpse where such visions of beloved community may lead. Yet already it is clear that these families of men have much to teach about the family of Man.

Unlikely Bedfellows:
The Love of Gay Men
and Straight Women

Oppression makes for curious bedfellows.
—Arthur Bell, journalist

If only we could sleep together, he'd be perfect.
—Murphy Brown

The epiphany arrived just as the train did, on a nondescript Wednesday morning. I stood on the downtown platform at Times Square amid the bustle of movers, shakers, and misfits that is Manhattan. On the downtown No. 4 platform, my attention was drawn to a red-faced commuter ranting into a pay phone. He was a portly symphony of self-absorption: loud, gesticulating, sweating through his just-too-tight three-piece suit. He postured and paced, his jowls flushing more florid with each raging tirade. He seemed oblivious to the tightly put-together woman who sat two feet away on a bench. She watched, taking it in quietly, first wary, then appraising. As the train rattled to a halt, he slammed down the phone and, mindless of those around him, lurched for its door. Like a sultan of space, he seemed to assume the human waves would part around his cetacean bulk. The woman continued observing. Then her glance brushed my own, and we lodged in each other's gaze longer than the socially accepted instant. In that moment we passed a semaphore of recognition from her vessel to mine. Our faces resolved into politely faint smiles, which then sprawled into unabashed grins between us. "He is . . . a child," her eyes opined. The Morse code of her eyes managed to telegraph an unmistakable message: "ridiculous, clueless, and primitive," all at once. My eyes shrugged back: "Not one of mine, honey. This one plays on your team. Good luck." The moment broke, Manhattan's human tide engulfed us both, and the train rumbled off. But in that moment we touched the shared power of the compact her people have made with mine in the presence of his, since it all began.

Gay men's experiments in beloved community don't just make us relate differently to each other, but to 51 percent of the human race. Because we inhabit distinct structural, social, affectional, and sexual niches in the social ecology, that affords us a unique perch and perspective in the world. It affects how we choose, seek, and are permitted to relate with women. In the most profound terms, gay men and straight women are inventing new ways to be genders together—an experiment that men like us have been trying for thousands of years.

Sex roles are one of the primary ways we identify ourselves. If you can break out of that, it would be easy to see how you could break out of other restraints, to think there is more to the world than we can see.
—Christopher Isherwood

In a variety of native cultures, there have been classes of gender-variant men who broke the mold of other males. Most of them didn't look like what we would today recognize as gay. But in many traditions, a range of sexually different men have been allowed to encounter women differently. Anthropologists like Will Roscoe, Walter Williams, Malidoma Somé, and Robert Levy have written of such patterns among a range of native peoples, including the Sambians of Melanesia, the Ambo of southern Africa, and the Dagara people of West Africa. The Gay Indian organization has documented references to such roles—called *berdache*—in more than 130 different Native American societies.[1] In New Guinea, such men are known as *mbal*; in India they are *hijra*; Polynesians call them *mahu*. Again and again, in societies where gender roles are clearly defined and highly segregated, one distinct group of men is allowed—even expected—to engage in different ways across the gender divide.

Sometimes such "third gender" or gender-variant men have been permitted to communicate, work, dress, or even live among women in ways that other men can't. In some cases, they filled a role of interpreting between men and women, helping forge a *pax domestica* in gender relations. Sometimes they served as gender intermediaries, bridging lines of communication and social habit between men and women. In the Navajo nation, writes anthropologist Will Roscoe, "mythology tells of a supernatural *berdache* who helps the men and women reunite after a quarrel has led them to live on separate sides of a river."[2] Indian *hijra* have traditionally played a role in sacraments around weddings.

In every time and culture such men look different, the roles they play are constructed vastly differently. There is no simple mapping onto Western modern-day "gay," so don't expect to find *berdache* in Boystown any time soon. But in cultural evolution as in the genetic kind, we may share some branch on the tree, enough to hint at a kinship in social function. Perhaps there is a slim thread that weaves from *hijras* to Hollywood hairdressers, from court eunuchs in ancient times to priests in ours. It may be that certain roles can be enacted by a breed of man who occupies a distinct social relationship to women, to family, and to the norms of other men. It is a role that certain kinds of men have filled in other times and places. In our time and place, it falls to us. How queer is that?

If men are from Mars and women are from Venus, we're the ones who hold dual passports. We are the only ones who can dish over coffee with her, then head to the locker room with him. We understand straight guys like women can't—after all, we're guys. We were socialized by default as straight boys, acculturated with straight men. We all need to be able to function with (and sometimes as) straight men. But we also understand women in ways straight men often don't. They are our pals, neither lovers nor spouses nor conquests. De-linking gender and genital intimacies permits a fresh mapping of affection, trust, and power. Not superior, just different. We meet women on a turf of greater gender, emotional, and erotic parity.

When you relate to women as your girlfriends, but not your girlfriend, different intimacies are permissible and enabled. The novelist Edmund White, in his essay "Straight Women and Gay Men," describes such bonds as "straightforward, amiable, and totally disinterested. In such a friendship, neither person stands to gain anything except companionship, support, and simple fun." Because we don't need the same things from women, our relationships can afford to be less freighted, arguably more honest, and can certainly touch on different aspects. "The thing I am most turned on by in my relations with gay men is the freshness and directness, the honesty and sense of humor," says Barbara, a fifty-three-year-old doctor of social work. "Those things are easier to have with people when you don't have your hormones working." As Charles describes his best friend, Roeesha, "Sexually it is safe, that whole thing is just off the table. We can't have a relationship that is heterosexual, so we have something else that works for both of us."

For many of us, such bonds go way back. "In high school and college, all my best friends were girls," recalls Daniel, now thirty-nine. "They were constantly borrowing my clothes. I was a skinny reed of a boy, and they'd return my sweaters all dented out where their breasts had stretched them." But shared clothes were just the symbol of a shared closeness. "We lived in an intensely religious town in Oregon. During high school I literally escorted ten different girls—all friends—to our local birth control clinic to get abortions. I even loaned some of them money and they paid me back. At first, the nurses looked at me like I was some out-of-control town stud. But I was just the one guy these girls had found to come to for intimate things like that. They knew I was safe."

Susan grew up in New Jersey, and describes herself as knowing "a huge variety of gay guys from different walks and backgrounds. I always find I connect with gay guys on a deeper level, very immediate, and it is completely comfortable for me. It's always been for that way for me, forever, since I was about ten. The connection with gay guys is instant. Within a short period of time, it feels like I have known you for a lot longer than half an hour." Peggy, now fifty-four, had her first gay male friend almost fifty years ago. "I was five and he was seven. He was effeminate and I used to stick up for him on the block against neighborhood kids." She smiles.

As adults, we often continue to stick up for each other. The bonds between us open paths to different intimacies—after all, we have men in common. We often discuss our lives with men—emotional and sexual—with a freedom that can be foreclosed by the sexual tension that exists between a man and woman. Says Anna, who grew up dancing in gay clubs in St. Louis, "With a straight man, often a sexual tension exists. Friendship could be based on the fact they are attracted. It is not as pure. What a pleasure to find someone who I know likes me for me, who doesn't have a sexual agenda." Peggy agrees. "There's no such thing as a platonic straight relationship." She shrugs. "Straight men friends are hard as friends because they always hit on you. My entire life I have always gravitated to male friends more than female friends, as people, as thinking machines. My closest friends have always been gay men, my longest loving experiences have always been with gay men."

Amanda's gay brother, Lenny, "had a tremendous influence on me. He sort of raised me, teaching me things and showing me things of the world I would not have necessarily been shown by my parents. That is how I started to develop friendships with gay men. I found a new family of gay men. That felt very special, because I could communicate with them more. My parents were not very communicative, and they provided for me some of the emotional connection and affection I didn't get as a child."

The writer Seymour Kleinberg once described gay men's friendships with women as "the richest, least infantile, and most moral relationships gay men form. . . . Eroticism is converted into something else, and those emotions adjunct to sexual attraction share in the metamorphosis. These men and women do not compete for the same sexual objects; though both are attracted to men, there is little source of envy."

"You have sex with straight men, but you talk sex with gay men," says Susan. Because our evolved cultural norms allow frank erotic discussion, it makes sense that we extend that to our women pals. Where our society has primarily socialized women to keep their sexuality under wraps, gay men not only assume sexual privilege as their male birthright, but raise it several orders of magnitude. Having gay male friends brings women a generous cultural and personal permission for sex talk that they may not find as often among the men they sleep with. One recent study conducted in Michigan showed that half of women in heterosexual couples surveyed reported difficulties talking to male partners about sex, but described gay respondents as "dramatically less reluctant to communicate sexual desires than the straight respondents. . . ."[3]

"With my gay friends," says Susan, "I can discuss anything, like I am talking to my girlfriend. The stories amaze me. They go into graphic detail about everything. We answer each other's questions, nothing's out of bounds, we can talk about anything—and I mean ANYthing. About sex, what's going on, his boyfriend or mine, there's never the feeling that they are talking about something taboo." Our candor rubs off on the women we chum with. Blake, who lives in Austin, Texas, says: "My friend Mel even asks to me about vibrators and her sex—I think she values having a male ear where she can unpack that." For Barbara, who has had sex with men and women both, "I relish that I can talk about my body and men's bodies with gay men in a way I can't with anyone else. 'He has a hot body, or she does, or I think you do.' Gay guys give a permission and openness to talk about bodies that I don't have with anyone else."

Gay world's sexual openness also means less likelihood of a "good girls don't" male double standard. For example, one study found, "gay men are significantly more liberal than heterosexual subjects regarding the propriety of masturbation, extramarital sexual activities, and the sexual activities of their teenage sisters."[4] Our basic position seems that what's good for the gay gander is likely fun for the goose, as well. Sometimes that gets to be too much, says Gwen, who counts a wide circle of gay male friends. When a recent dinner conversation with four of her men friends turned to anal sex, she wrinkled her nose: "This isn't the part of gay life I like," she proclaimed. "I like the part where you all shriek and tell me how fabulous my hair is." Peggy agrees that, at times, our sexuality can also divide. "In most cases you get treated almost equally. But even more than straight men, they treat it as a private club. You're still a woman and unless you have the membership card—a penis—you don't ever completely get in. Gay or straight, sex is always in the back of men's heads; they can't help it," she concludes.

By far the more profound connections occur above the belt. In a study conducted in 1997, 76 percent of heterosexual women interviewed said their friendships with gay guys were closer than those with straight guys.[5] Anna finds gay men "more able to connect, comfortable with sharing their feelings. It sounds corny, but more in touch with their female energy. A lot of the gay men I have met do have a more sensitive side. Not that straight men don't have it—a lot of them do—but I do find it easier to talk to gay guys. I felt the friendships were more substantial, more accessible emotionally, easier to talk to for that reason."

Research on gender and friendship shows that gay men and women are both more likely to discuss emotional and personal subjects with friends (including each other), and more like to spend time discussing the quality, dynamics, and state of their mutual friendship, than are straight men.[6] Says Susan: "With straight men—any time I try to talk about anything intimate or sex related, it lasts a brief period of time, they get uncomfortable. They reach a limit, don't want to go further, suddenly remember they need to go get a glass of water or something." For her, that bond is reciprocal: "Most male-male relationships are beyond understanding for straight men, even for a lot of women. But my gay friends just know I have a kind ear to the types of dramas they are going through."

Her gay brother, Chip, has worked for a dozen years in the fashion industry, which has brought him a dozen very close relationships with straight women. "For me, straight women are nice, the way they can voice how hurt they are sometimes. With women you get all of the feminine perspective you might want from your gay male friends but don't always, because most gay men are so involved with masculinity. Straight women are feminine but without the sniping bitchy thing some guys carry around." Among his closest friends is Deena. "She talks to me a lot about boyfriends because she knows I won't judge or snap at her. My women friends talk to me about how straight men don't treat women properly."

Dora, an attorney in Hollywood, Florida, enjoys "the sometimes outrageous but always interesting opinionated way that gay guys critique life. A cup of coffee isn't just a cup of coffee, it's about skim or not, the shape of the glass, the server or technique. No matter if it's art or food, a movie or show, there's a level of detail, a discerning critical nature. Some might find it pretentious, but I find it delightful. It elevates whatever you are experiencing, the feelings. You definitely connect better."

Those connections occur across genders, regardless of sexual orientation. "Between gay men and women—whether straight, bi, or lesbian—it's just . . . different," Peggy says. "I can be with gay men in the most intimate of experiences and it's not sexual but certainly not without a sexual attraction. It's not exactly male or exactly female, just a totally different species." Barbara, a lesbian, enjoys how "gay men have a better ability to laugh at themselves than any other group I know. Unlike some women—and feminists even more so—gay guys don't demand such political correctness, which helps them keep a sense of humor about themselves and others. As a woman, I find that really refreshing. You're not always dealing with delicate male ego stuff. The other thing I love about gay men," she warms to the topic, "is how they open me to my outrageous self and give me permission to express it more than any other group. I am likely to get back applause or humor more than criticism, because they are entertained by it. That's a very different experience for a woman." Lucy, a Ph.D. epidemiologist, puts it simply: "The reason I moved to a gay neighborhood like Chelsea was because all the gay guys always seem to be doing fun things. There's a fun energy on the street. I wanted to be around it." Susan, who is married and lives in New Jersey, cherishes this element of fun. "With gay men I can clown around better than I can with my girlfriends, who just don't always get where I'm coming from. Their patterns of thinking are more creative. I connect more with gay men on that level; all I have to do is say something and they get it, whether it's fashion, style, current events, or what's going on at the moment. Gay men pay attention, they can define it in a quick, concise moment. It leads to interesting banter."

Not to mention interesting chemistry, says Peggy. "Look at the roles gay men fill in women's lives. Go to any salon in Northwest Podunk, Iowa, or Madison Avenue. Watch some gay man work his magic on a straight woman, touching her face, stroking her head, caressing her arm. She feels this warm bath of male attention. It's the safest sex she will ever have. The makeup artist, a clothing salesman, a designer, in essence they are servicing women. Most women aren't even aware of the sensuality and sexuality they get and look for without having to give anything back. Especially since AIDS, it's the safest, most fulfilling and selfish thing for a woman—somewhere so deep in their psyche they don't even want to be in tune with it, to know that they can just receive and enjoy."

Sometimes the support we get from each other is quite concrete. An example comes from an unlikely quarter: the words of Tammy Faye Bakker Messner. You know, the one with the eyelashes. "When my husband was in prison and I wasn't getting any Christmas presents, it was the gay community that gathered around me and saw that. They gave me beautiful bathrobes with my initials on; they gave me beautiful leopard hangers and leopard shoe bags. And I had the most awesome Christmas I ever had. . . . I still write all these guys! They cared about me more than the Christians cared about me, and that says something to me right there."[7]

At first glance, the televangelizing Tammy Faye has little in common with Karen Ottobone. Karen is a plainspoken woman who retired from a career in property management to live on a 320-acre ranch outside of rural Booneville, California. But if they sat down for a latté, they might have some similar tales to swap. In December 1999, Karen's rural cabin burned down in a freak winter fire. "I lost everything, all my clothes and supplies, all my family's antiques, all gone in a day." For the prior dozen years or so, Karen had participated in an extended network of gay men from across the sparsely settled counties of far Northern California. "I was often the only woman at their gatherings. It was sometimes several hundred men and me."

The ashes of her home were barely cool before something began to happen. "First, the guys decided to take up a collection. They put out a call in a newsletter, on E-mails, and phone calls. Next the men voted funds from the assistance fund to help me rebuild. Then, at a winter gathering, other guys passed the hat and took up another collection." But what happened next surprised even Karen. "They spearheaded their own campaign for a silent art auction in the community. People began appearing from all over to donate—artists, potters, farmers, woodworkers. There were donations coming from men I didn't even know, just because they knew I had been part of this community. It extended beyond just the guys I knew at the time. For two years, I have had different men come up and introduce themselves, asking how I am doing. The feeling of loving arms all around me from this community, the support I got, was unbelievable."

That support was just the concrete symbol of Karen's abiding bond with this network of rural gay men. "The men in the local area, I really love them so dearly." Karen is a dynamic lesbian who made her life managing and developing real estate. "When I am with straight men, I play the butch and come off tough because I don't want to have to deal with the sexual challenge. I have to put up this distance and so I play with the straight guys on a different level. With gay men I am able to be powerful, they like that. But I am also allowed to be feminine. It sounds silly, but for me it's a safe space to explore my feminine side, that's what I have been able to do with these guys, in a safe space. To allow my feminine side out." Karen's extended clan of local gay men "create such a safe heartfelt space. You don't have to like everyone or agree with them, but it's an unconditional kind of love, an underlying support you always feel." Of course, she says, it brings its own challenges. "The boys haven't given up trying to get me into a dress on stage. The last time I saw them, some of them razzed me about it, so I went up to the two butchest rancher guys, I looked them in the eye and promised them that I'd get in drag the day they did." She winks. "I said, 'We'll do it together, on stage.'"

In ways concrete and physical, emotional and social, our bonds across gender hold the potential to open new windows. They provide a deeper understanding of what the other may seek and get from the men they sleep with, and those with whom they never will. For decades, our cultures have recognized the special nature of some women's bonds with us. In another generation we even gave a special name to the women like Karen, who made their social lives among us: "fag hags" or "fruit flies." "I hate the term *fag hag*," says Chip. "To me it's just a woman who wants male companionship, but doesn't get it from straight guys. She may get abused, or may not fit into the girly look that gets accepted, she doesn't want to deal with all the man-woman BS, but likes male companionship. So she turns to gay friends." But whether one calls them fag hags or fine friends, these special relationships have long been recognized as a cherished aspect of gay lives.

In his book *Alienated Affections*, written some twenty years ago, Seymour Kleinberg states: "One of the least-examined aspects of gay life is the long tradition of friendship between homosexual men and heterosexual women." If in 1980 that was unexamined, the decades since have moved it to cultural center stage and the majority society has begun to awaken to how very different these relationships look. To see the proof, you need only stop in at Nick's Café on every Tuesday night. Nick's is in Hartford, Connecticut, but you could as easily be watching at the Midnight Sun in San Francisco, The Cathode Ray in Fort Lauderdale, or any of a thousand gay video bars in any mid-size American city. It is a few minutes before 9:00 P.M.—two minutes until *Will and Grace*. The room settles down as the men find seats, grab bottles of beer or Naya water, and crowd in with arms draped around each other. At this hour, in scores of bars and living rooms from Seattle to Schenectady, rooms of gay men are converging before flickering television screens. Peering into the funhouse mirror that is prime-time television, we see reflected there a truth about our lives we have long known. We have a certain way with women—it's just a different way.

Will and Grace centers on the lives and loves of a gay man and his woman friend, adults who share an apartment, a life, mutual friends, but not a sexual orientation. The show is a pageant of stereotype. Sidekick Jack is the flaming grand-nephew of Paul Lynde. Each episode winks with bawdy innuendo and barbed repartee; the plots circle around their mutual romantic adventures and identities. *Will and Grace* is just one example of many cultural products that in recent years have reflected a growing popular fascination with these relationships. They have been highlighted in various episodes of *Queer as Folk, Normal, Ohio, Some of My Best Friends,* and a half-dozen other television series. In one *Seinfeld* episode, Jerry comments that "people think I'm gay because I'm single and thin and neat," to which Elaine replies, "Plus, you get along well with women." America is apparently curious enough that for thirty minutes every week, tens of millions of us tune in to watch this social experiment being undertaken across gender—almost as if we cared how it turns out.

The bonds between gay men and straight women have been central in films like *My Best Friend's Wedding, Four Weddings and a Funeral, The Object of My Affection,* Madonna's *Next Best Thing.* They are part of a wider American fascination with changing male roles and presentations. The last few years have given us RuPaul, Dennis Rodman, and Hedwig's angry inch; we have read headlines screaming over President Clinton's *affaire* Lewinsky and Jerry Falwell's Tinky-Winky worries. When the gay gene and Matthew Shepard's murder both make *Time* magazine's cover in the same year, it suggests an intense cultural anxiety and flux around diverse modes of male presentation. *The Village Voice* recently ran an article about the ways that straight men are learning from gay men, citing fashion, grooming, body culture—and our relationships with women. That same week, the gay newsweekly *The Advocate* devoted its cover to "Fierce Mothers," with its cover line "Why our mothers often turn out to be our strongest allies." American pop culture is paying rapt attention to this love affair of straight women and gay men, as the mass mind puzzles over what it all means.

One of the most exciting promises of many younger queer lives is the articulation of an explicitly anti-sexist politic and consciousness. It is hard to imagine a term like "fag hag" being coined today. Instead, we have begun to articulate a set of larger truths in these bonds. "Because of our situation," says Jason Reeves, "God has given us an opportunity to almost transcend our gender, which gives us a vision and sensitivity that other people don't have." The claim is hardly that gay men are free of misogyny or sexism, or that our relations with women are wholly enlightened or unblemished. Says Robert Heasley, at Ithaca College, "I have a bunch of gay male friends who stand with me in the trenches, who are really committed to women's issues, who seem like truly feminist men. Far more than most straight men I know. But in general, it's not clear the gay community itself has really stepped forward to do this as well as it might." Clearly, this business of revamping gender politics remains a work in progress among males, gay and straight.

The larger point here is really about potential. Our different structural relationships with women open inherently different routes across the familiar fault lines of gender. We occupy a unique position to broker a new kind of peace in the gender wars. In the words of writer James Carroll: "Homosexual men and women . . . have been crucial to the process of shaping more humane ideals of the masculine and the feminine." The question is: Do we choose to use that position, and if so, how?

Homophobia is all about extinguishing the feminine and extinguishing the child. Gays have a unique function in registering the cruelty and the craziness of the patriarchy and in working to transcend it.
—Andrew Harvey, *Gay Soul*

Just as we expand possibilities for gender relations in our private lives, we do so in our public lives, creating partnerships both personal and political. Gay men command masculine privilege; straight women command heterosexual privilege. When we link arms to march to the public square, we open possibilities for public and political alliances neither could win alone. When we take our queer bonds into public life, we create glorious trouble for existing structures of power and social order.

Such trouble takes a million shapes and forms. Sometimes it is playful, like the troop of men who appeared in neatly pressed Jackie O drag in downtown Boston to address the topic of . . . women's sexuality. "This is what men think women want," they deadpanned to startled passersby, jiggling frenetically as their boombox buzzed with "Flight of the Bumblebee." "*This* . . . is what *women* say they want"—the chorus of Jackies began undulating to a haunting chorus of whale moans and calls. That a group of men takes it upon itself to dress in pink dresses and pillbox hats to goad other men to attend to female desire—well, that's just the kind of gender trouble we are known for. Sometimes the trouble we make is provocative, like the two gay men who conceived malepregancy.com, the first known public offer by a male to carry a surgically implanted fetus to term. Says artist Ming-Wei Lee, the male behind the offer: "The goal is to elicit serious exploration, raise consciousness, and especially, get women's comments and voices. We wanted to expand the realm of what's possible for men and women both. It's a very real offer."

Where the trouble turns serious is in the potential—far from fully realized—for new shapes of egalitarian and cooperative power relations to flower across gender lines. One notes that several gay men serve as officers—even past president—of the National Association for Men Against Sexism (NOMAS). It is no accident that gay men took such an interest in abortion clinic defense. While to some, safeguarding a woman's right to a safe, legal abortion may not seem an especially gay male issue, to Marty it is. He lives in suburban Virginia and was one of many gay men who have spent their time escorting women safely through lines of birth-control clinic hecklers. "Maybe partly it was that so many women had been there for AIDS, to give back. But mostly, I just knew their enemies were mine. The same people threatening the women at these clinics were threatening gay people's jobs and lives and passing anti-gay laws." He recalls his experiences as a clinic escort. "I guess there was some danger, and I hated getting up incredibly early to get there. *That* was the hard part. But it was important to me, to be in it together." A lot of Martys stood on the lines at a lot of clinics across the nation. At their side, more than a few women noted that gay men seemed disproportionately involved in clinic defense, given what might at first seem a limited personal stake in the abortion wars.

There is no clearer example of our bringing our cross-gender bonds into public action than the links forged between the in-your-face AIDS activists of ACT-UP and women working on breast cancer. What may at first have seem odd bedfellows was in fact a charmed marriage. Gay men seemed to command resources and wealth, were empowered around sexuality, and brought access to levers of power in government, media, and medicine. Women who had for years organized around health access brought skills in nonviolent civil disobedience, group process, tactics, and strategy to gay men unused to thinking about the intricacies of advocacy. This partnership has been the subject of numerous articles, sociology courses, and hundreds of late night chats. By 1996, doctoral dissertations were being published on the mutual influences of AIDS and breast cancer activism,[8] as scholars of social movements began to trace the many tendrils—from counsel to support, to resources, in networks and coalitions—that had grown up between women's health activists and gay men, enabling progress neither might have accomplished alone.

Historian James Saslow once wrote that "People who don't fit neatly into strict social categories like masculine and feminine are assigned a great deal of power by human society."[9] Men like us have carried that mantle of power in different ways across different cultures and epochs. Today, part of our power comes in the ways we challenge the culture's sacrosanct givens of gender. The patterns in our lives give lie to prevailing assumptions of male supremacy, the conventional wisdom of an unbridgeable gender gulf, customs of coercion and violence in men's intimate relationships with women, the myth of a recalcitrant male emotional disability.

We are men crafting new ways to be together with women, offering a radically different ethical code for women and men both. But as we do, we raise a discomfiting possibility: if one group of males can do that, why can't another? Who knows what the world could look like if we forged a more durable truce across gender lines; if men felt more emotional and expressive avenues open to them, with new opportunities for support from women and other men? How would that transform the experiences and fears of women and children? How, indeed, might it broaden the possibilities for all men?

He who knows the masculine and at the same time keeps the feminine, will be the whole world's channel.
    —Lao-tse

8 | A FLAGRANT JOY: OUTLAWS IN SEARCH OF BLISS

Gay people are like blonds: They're fewer of them, but they have more fun.
　—Rita Mae Brown

There's a quality of exultation in our differentness. We just have it and it's part of our nature. There's a kind of flagrant joy that goes very deep and is not available to most people. Something about our capacity to live and let live is uniquely foreign.
　—Paul Monette

If you have gone to a baseball game recently, whether at Yankee Stadium, Wrigley Field, or Fenway Park, at some point you're likely to hear a familiar refrain that brings the crowd to its feet. Like so many thousand delirious cheerleaders, they throw their arms up exultantly in a Y, then swoop downward into a vague approximation of an M, then a quick semicircle curve to the side making a C, and finally, in a point over the head to finish with an A. What's it spell? "YYYYY-M-C-A!" the crowd roars. It has become everyman's acrobatic, a staple of pop-culture competence known to most every American below fifty. Yet these hundreds of thousands of spectators never suspect, as they gyrate in the stadiums of the national sport, that they are executing a queer choreography. The song was first performed as sheer camp by men in macho parody costumes including an American Indian, a construction worker, a motorcycle cop, and a leather Daddy. The words, created by and for gay men, pay winking homage to our public sex cruising culture. ("It's fun to stay at the Y-M-C-A/ They have everything for young men to enjoy/ You can hang out with all the boys." Puh-leeze . . .) The cute cheerleading routine that now enlivens the seventh-inning stretch was born on the gay disco floors twenty years ago. This moment of unadulterated silliness is brought to you from your friends in the gay world. The YMCA dance is one of those duty-free delights, just another export from our province of play, gift-wrapped for the larger culture.

The gay social contract allows a different, more generous, permission to center bliss in our lives. "Bliss" here does not mean simply plastering a beatific smile across one's face. Bliss transcends recreation. It means something more philosophical, akin to what the cultural critic Joseph Campbell meant by his dictum "follow your bliss." It is what Paul Monette described as our "flagrant joy." Call it fun, call it play, call it *eros,* it encompasses a wide gamut of playfulness, pleasure and performance, whimsy and wackiness, silliness and spectacle. By whatever name, there is something markedly different in how our queer customs support the pursuit of happiness. Our bliss is the next page where we color outside the lines laid down by the larger culture. The centrality of bliss and play in our lives has political and social implications, affects our cultural and artistic contributions, and may even shape the well-being of the species. We may be having fun, but we're not just fooling around.

We are in a different dance with bliss from the first moment we step into gay communal life. It begins with coming out, our definitional rite of passage. Born alone, every one of us must first face his fears, vote for bliss, and follow his heart to find his soulmates. This process, wholly personal yet deeply communal, requires us each to honor a private truth in order to join a public community. It is the first step in our archetypal hero's journey, our initiation into a new kind of manhood. It is an act of bliss seeking, collectively and individually. Survey data show that about one in five American men report some sexual attraction to other men, roughly half that number may act on it, and about half of those actually adopt a gay "identity."[1] So, as one survey put it: "The majority of men with homosexual feelings are predominantly heterosexual."[2] Although the exact numbers may vary, this spectrum from desire to behavior to identity has been found in many countries.[3] Those numbers reveal a clue about how bliss fits in our values. After all, some significant numbers of men crave that pleasure but don't act on it; a smaller number act but can't shoulder the burden of a public identity.[4] To act on this impulse, even in one's private sexual life, is to take one baby step to prioritize pleasure over propriety. Yet only one subgroup is so intent on bliss that it will break the rules to endure social hardship for its pleasure. The men who sign on to crew the good ship *Gay* have, by definition, made an exceptional commitment to embrace their bliss.

Among the many reasons for that, one may be that bliss occupies an uncommonly important, if not central, place in those men's values.[5] These individuals are willing to pay the price of prejudice for their pleasures, to endure social stigma, ostracism, loss, and even violence to gain emotional and erotic happiness. We, the legions of out gay men, are those willing to step from the ranks of our fellow men to act on our emotional dictates in our quest for personal fulfillment. No wonder we commonly swap coming-out stories as a shared cultural ritual to bond with new intimates. It is a conversation about the praxis of bliss. To share your story is to say, "This was my path to bliss—how was it for you?" One can't help wonder if our clan may in some way be uncommonly attuned to the pursuit of bliss. But if play and bliss-seeking behavior is a shared trait of our social species, you would expect to see evidence of it throughout our lives.

It is a weekend in February, or maybe June, but it could just as well be November. The setting may be a moonlit topiary garden of a palatial estate in Miami, a sunny beach in Greece, a blossom-strewn dance floor in Washington, D.C., or the Olympic stadium in Montreal. It may be called Pines Party, Twelve Gods, Jubilee, Resurrection, Alchemy, Southern Decadence, Snow Ball, or Mardi Gras. Often, the name simply reflects one of a rainbow of revels: Blue Ball, Red Ball, Black and Blue Ball, White Party, Black Party. The theme dictates whether your costume will be ethereal, outrageous, or hardcore grunge—or some mix of all. Whether your plane ticket reads Atlanta, London, Palm Springs, Chicago, San Francisco, Sydney, New Orleans, or any of a dozen other locales, you know the rituals here. The what-to-wear-you-look-great-in-that discussion; the plans about where your gang will dance; the politesse of "party favors," acquired and shared; the swaying of bodies hugging sweaty bodies; the passing of water bottles and glow sticks; plastic bullets appearing from socks and jocks; beefy arms raised in ecstatic salute, not-so-incidentally showcasing shoulder muscles and armpit hair; the light touch on a shoulder that signals another dancer wants to pass; a camaraderie of bleary smiles passing among strangers. Save the inevitable critiques of DJ, music, and lights for tomorrow; tonight we are all seafarers of the soul. We chart our course by arcs of laser light, our Polaris the disco ball overhead, our sails swelled with thundering music. We have embarked on a voyage to the sublime, a transit from exertion to epiphany, with ports of call at seduction, ecstasy, and reverie. Welcome aboard the fun ship, the S.S. *Circuit Party*.

A distinct new form of communal life, the gay dance "circuit" has reached unprecedented size. These vast mobile dance parties now occur almost every weekend somewhere across the globe. It is estimated that the circuit involves more than 200,000 dancers worldwide, and some individual events exceed 10,000 men. As a cultural phenomenon, these parties have been the subject of documentary films, and have been studied by academics from Harvard to the University of Texas to Australia. The circuit boasts its own magazine, *Circuit Noize*, and even a foundation, Electric Dreams, dedicated to keeping its events safe and healthy.

What makes these events noteworthy is that they grew from experiments in ecstatic communion, and are now being conducted on a planetary scale. Where else can one find vast congregations of men gathering by the thousands in a rapture of movement and flesh? They come together to celebrate a deep communal camaraderie, seeking by the thousands to touch bliss, if only for the night. Many use substances like Ecstasy that alter consciousness to make them crave one another's touch and lower barriers to affection. As Jack, a self-described "proud dance pig since 1978," puts it: "I see straight guys go to hockey games, watch competitive sports, cheer at boxing matches, and go out and make soccer riots. When we get together, we strip down, get all huggy and drippy with sweat, and dance till dawn." True, the lines may not be quite so simply drawn as that, and gay men have no corner on dance culture. Teens have had their raves, and straight dance clubs abound in every major city. Yet the ways we enact and pursue mass dance—whether on the circuit, at a club, or a Pride event—take distinctive shape in our worlds.

Some of those shapes are obvious. As we have seen, our events differ in the far lower levels of violence and assault behaviors, levels unseen in other mass gatherings of males. One woman, Diane, has spent twelve years dancing among gay male crowds: "I go out all night, leave my bag on the banquette for hours, and know nothing in it will be touched. In a big city club, knowing you could be that comfortable made it like a family. People looked after each other, treated each other with respect; there was a sense of family and caring that existed." Straight women often describe other differences: "It's just easier to dance at gay clubs," says Jenna, who at thirty-one has frequented gay clubs for twelve years. "Of course, there's not that heavy pickup vibe—no surprise there. But what I really like is that gay guys just seem more tuned into personal space and body movement. You don't have to worry about being jostled and clobbered, or that some guy will puke on your dress. It's not like they were dancing next to me because they want to take me home later. I could go out and share the music and connect on a higher level, in a more friendly hassle-free zone." Cathy was nineteen when her brother took her to her first gay dancing event—at New York's legendary disco, The Saint. "For a nineteen-year-old sheltered girl from the suburbs, this was a life-changing experience. They felt the same way about the music that I did—it was the most important thing. I never went out to a straight club and saw people so closely connected into the music," she says. Peggy, who describes herself as "a fifty-four-year-old club kid," spends many weekends on a dance floor with thousands of gay men. "Some live to dance, I dance to live. I don't find the same magic in straight places."

Randy agrees. "Dancing here is like a fountain. The aura people bring with them builds what you experience." The difference is, Randy is one of those straight guys Peggy is talking about. Divorced, a father of two boys, he grew up in Illinois where he now manages production of trans-missions for Caterpillar. For several years, he has gone dancing in gay clubs with his gay brother in L.A. "With gay guys, you get just a posi-tive energy, there's no negative source." Ever the engineer, he reaches for an electrical metaphor: "Anywhere else, you get a mix of positive and negative energy in the crowd, so it kind of short-circuits out. Like a bad connection that never illuminates, maybe you see a flicker or feel a little energy, but never enough. But with these guys, it glows all warm. It's enough different you feel goosebumps and chills. You know you are being surrounded by something good."

Randy, like many others, feels that the codes of conduct here are so distinct that they change markedly if many straight men show up: "The straights are coming into the parties and are bringing aggression. They do not know the etiquette of the scene," says a dancer quoted in one paper.[6] Another man said: "I stopped going to straight parties. Too much agro [aggression], too much alcohol . . . straight guys don't know how to handle the drugs." In Sydney, the author concluded, "the social structure of the original gay dance party institution had evolved into a hostile environment for many gay patrons with the infiltration of these hetero-sexual outsiders." (More recently, say many, the most dramatic changes have less to do with sexual orientation than with the changing profile of drug use, specifically the sea change from Ecstasy to stimulants like crys-tal meth as the gay dance drug of choice.)

Other differences in gay dance space happen at a more subtle level. Consider who is dancing here. In mainstream culture, the all-night dancers are likely to be adolescents and young adults. After they have reached age thirty, it's less common to find rooms full of hundreds of straight men regularly devoting sleepless Saturday nights to the messy delights of dance. But in queer dance spaces, the room may skew a good ten years older. It is no rarity to see a twenty-five-year-old dancing next to a forty-year-old dancing next to sixty-five-year-old. That expanded age range suggests that the structures of our lives—notably, fewer children—help us keep contact with cultural practices of celebrating bliss and transcendence. Dave, forty-six, grew up in Chillicothe, Ohio, population 25,000. Although his life has propelled him through Houston, Cambridge, and New York, he returns to Ohio every five years for his high school reunion. "I'm the only out gay man in my class. At our fifth-year reunion, a bunch of the guys trashed the men's room at the Elks Club. They still had a lot of energy. But by the tenth-year reunion, they'd started to put on weight and slow down. By the fifteenth, and the twentieth, I was about the only guy left dancing. While a bunch of women were still going strong, it was pretty much the gals and me on the dance floor."

Larry sees it in his native St. Louis, where he teaches elementary school. "Straight guys just stop by thirty-five. They just go dead. Their life path makes them deadened. If they have a family, suddenly having fun competes with family and work. They settle down and become passive observers—spectators, not participants." Market research says gay men are in fact twice as likely as other men to have gone dancing within the last thirty days.[7] The reasons for this might be personal, cultural, or some combination of both. For example, we are more likely to be childless and single. Less overwhelmingly focused on children, we have built public cultures around a different axis of adult needs and interests. But clearly, our life paths and habits do not so soon age us out of contact with this particular form of rapture.

Yet the most interesting aspects of the gay dance world are the collective ones. The circuit is a sprawling experiment in a virtual community, unbounded by geography. It matters little whether you are dancing in Sydney or Mykonos, Ibiza, Atlanta, Paris, or Palm Springs. The community you socialize in, its culture and range of personal relationships, its norms and connections, transcends place. People who would never otherwise meet become friends or boyfriends, develop a history over repeated events, conduct relationships, meet friends of friends, maintain shared norms. Many dancers meet only at these events, forging bonds that span from party to party. Jerry lives in Portland but carefully schedules work travel to attend parties "all over." He nods to his circle of pals: "Coming here to Atlanta this weekend, I see a whole bunch of guys I see no other time. Bob's from Pittsburgh, Antonio lives in Miami, Mike's from L.A.

Over the year, we met up at Black and Blue, some of us will be at Pines Party this summer, then Southern Decadence."

It is this network of friends that draws back so many regulars. Eric is a gardener in Burbank. "You know, my friends don't all have that much money. But it's really a priority to come for a good time here. These guys are great. Going to a party together means a time to get caught up. We share rooms, do meals and drinks together, party, have a great time. We don't see each other till the next one." Eddie, a lawyer, recalls a recent Pride dance he attended. "At that moment, I looked around and I realized it was all my gay family there, all of our friends were there, their faces alive with light from the setting sun. I just wanted that moment to last forever." "I was having the time of my life with my friends . . . sharing experiences on a whole new level," says Scotty. "For all of us, that weekend was all about getting to know each other all over again." In the words of one Australian dancer: "The parties provide social networks, when you're new to the city with no friends . . . the party scene filled a huge chasm, and the people became my immediate family. They provided the nurturing and affection I needed, they invite you into their space."[8]

> *The dance party is a social structure which acts as a vehicle for expression of group identity . . . and appears to serve a function in permitting expression for psychological coping with the HIV epidemic. . . . A rare opportunity for ritualized celebrations among a large group of people who were in a similar mind set . . .*
> —L. A. Lewis and M. W. Ross[9]

These mobile events also create safety in numbers, offering a powerful experience of being out safely that some may not enjoy in their daily lives at home. By mobilizing capital and thousands of participants, these movable fests create what social theorist Hakim Bey calls "a temporary autonomous zone." Rules, habits, and standard operating procedures of the dominant culture get checked at the door. "I would never walk down the street holding hands with my lover at home in Hayward," says Dale. "But coming here for White Party, we can." Similar attitudes have been found among surveys of gay tourism patterns at southern U.S. beach resorts.[10] For Dale and many others, these events go far deeper than "mere" hedonism. They are places to try on the most deeply held dreams: a feeling of freedom in a homosocial environment, easy availability of sex, ecstasies of substances and of movement, safety in public, being proudly "out," late nights and great music, beautiful men, the chance to live in a different skin away from home. It is an oasis moment of social support, sexual adventure, excitement, and affirmation, a cherished chance to live out fantasies involving a sought-for gay male tribalism. One's personal dreams of flesh, spirit, and joy can potentially be brought to life.

A collective transformation can occur as well. When the party rolls into town, it brings with it legions of like-minded souls. Along with ribbed tank tops and Abercrombie shorts, they bring the mores and behaviors of the communities they sprang from, or aspire to. For the collective, such mobile events create a temporary beachhead of safety, a culture bubble where the habits and norms of an elaborated gay world can flourish even in a place that would not otherwise tolerate them. For the weekend, at least, one steps beyond the constraints of the place. This virtual community becomes like a missionary outpost, a venue modeling new habits. For three days, it becomes safe not only to walk down the street holding hands, but to kiss in a restaurant, doff one's shirt in public, dance all night, meet new friends, stay up till dawn, experiment with substances, explore new facets and dreams, try on another of one's possible selves. There may be changes in the locale itself. So the local drugstore stocks up on condoms and lube, restaurants and bars change their hours, local drug dealers lay in more stock, cops discreetly look the other way, doctors and counselors go on call. This charmed outpost may not endure past Monday, but like any good mission, it leaves its imprint on visitors and locals both. How will that waitress who had so much fun with the guys at table six relate to the next gay person who sits down? Will local merchants stock slightly more fitted T-shirts? Will the police dispatcher note that his patrol squad had an unusually peaceable weekend? Might the Chamber of Commerce reassess the merit of welcoming gay tourists? Might that married taxi driver ask a little more directly about what happens at that all-night party? Or even try to get himself invited to the next one?

There is no more central aspect of queer men's dance culture than its role as communal catharsis. Ricardo lives in Houston, and like most devotees, has his perfect dance moment etched in his memory. "It was at a resort in Huatulco, Mexico, on one of those gay travel weekends. A couple hundred of us were dancing at a late afternoon tea on a big esplanade over the ocean. It was 1993 or so, so the DJ was playing Pet Shop Boys' 'Go West,' all about hope and getting through hard times with each other. As we danced, I looked around and so many guys were dancing, smiling, but with tears on their cheeks, caught in the light of the setting sun. It was so indescribably beautiful. I wept, knowing, without anyone saying anything, how much we were all facing in our lives. Losing friends, being sick, the shock of those years, so much horror and loss. All these hurting boys dancing to a song about coming west, into the open air, together. In that moment, it was our story, physically and metaphorically. Somehow we knew to come find hope and comfort by being with each other. For us to have come there, dancing together, on cliffs over the ocean, felt so valiant, as if by facing death through dancing together, we would get through it somehow."

It is easy to forget that these dances began as the most deeply human experiment in hope and redemption. In his landmark book, *The Golden Bough*, anthropologist James G. Frazer writes that fortifying rituals like dance provide both individual and group a sense of control and order in times of great chaos and stress. Philosopher Jean-Paul Sartre wrote that individuals constantly enmeshed in unrelenting life-threatening experiences seek out others who identify with their experiences and lifestyle to help them cope with escalating anxiety. He observed: "They often dance; that keeps them busy . . . and then the dance mimes secretly, often without their knowing, the refusal they cannot utter (to death)." Anthropologist Gilbert Herdt has noted that "humans engage in ritualized celebrations to enrich their lives by giving meaning to their existence."[11]

These philosophers of dance put in words what thousands of us instinctively know by feel. Dance can be an avenue to healing in lives shadowed by disease and death. Circuit events began, and for many persist, as a communal attempt at healing, a mass redemption of heart and spirit in a time of plague. Says one researcher: "The dance parties afforded many gay men the opportunity to witness, and celebrate, their own survival and that of other members of their own community over the AIDS pandemic. . . ."[12] In fact, many circuit events grew out from a series of individual parties to raise funds and awareness around AIDS. New York's controversial Morning Party, which ceased in 1998 amid furor over drugs and sex, had begun in 1983 on someone's deck, the invention of a group of men raising money to care for dying friends. The same is true of Miami's White Party, Washington, D.C.'s Jubilee, and many others.

Over the years, we have come to view these parties through a dark filter. Our public discussion has often stressed the destructive side of these revels and, by extension, of all who participate in gay dance culture. Without question, some boys dance their way into trouble. A small minority overdose, as they do on the streets of our nation every night. Others have unsafe sex, as do all those committed couples where HIV risk is known to occur far more frequently. Indisputably, attendance at these events is skewed by class. Those plane tickets aren't cheap, nor are the drugs or the D & G pants. The party circuit—like skiing, hang gliding, motorcycle racing, or dog shows—has its cognoscenti who command significant wealth and privilege. But, says Harold, a forty-six-year old native Chicagoan who has attended these for years, "I know as many teachers and hairdressers who save their *sous* to get to these parties as I do doctors and bankers." Others feel excluded by the image of these events as an intimidating display of male physical perfection, a privileged playground for only the beautiful and the buff. Adding to the list of woes is that in recent years, dance veterans have noted a sea change in dance floor ambiance. Between roughly 1980 and the mid-90s, Ecstasy was the dance drug of choice among gay men. More recently, however, crystal methamphetamine (Tina) has come into wide use. "Tina completely changed the vibe for the worse," laments one circuit insider. "People are harder-edged, more brittle, self-contained. It used to be a flesh and love-fest. Now it feels edgy and sharp. My friends and I talk about how dance places feel less connected and sweet but more aggressive."

Given all that, it is no surprise that when the topic comes up in my workshops among gay men, a wary unease often chills the room at first. For these men, as for many of us, the themes of exclusion, sex, drugs, and death are repeated uncritically, often most vocally by those who have never set foot at any such gathering. "Whose side are you on?" the implied challenge crackles through the room. "For or against? Us or them?" But the point in these rooms is not to replay that shrill debate, which has become almost the only mode we know to talk about such events. It is instead to point out how meager and unproductive that line of discourse has become, and how it serves to obscure any wider or more humane understanding of these mass gatherings.

The goal of this discussion is to step back to find a wider truth in these mass bliss events, one more uniquely true to our own lived experience. As the discussion moves, invariably men start reflecting on their own stories of dance and bliss in their own lives. How many of us have put in our time in shirtless abandon on a dance floor at a local bar, disco, or club? For many of us, dance was how we first found each other, first let ourselves be seen, that place where we got to know our friends and, often, ourselves. The room starts to come alive. A man named Louis recalls: "When I was a teenager I wasn't sure being gay was good. This music saved my life . . . I felt I belonged to something, it set me free." As we talk, eyes light in the realization that the circuit, so demonized and distrusted, is just part of a larger story about the ways we permit bliss in our lives. Tom says he started going to dance parties because "I just couldn't stand it any more. I wanted to dance and celebrate life." To Greg, "It's about celebrating survival and being alive." A man named Dean Miner, writing on a webpage, says: "I have discovered ways to release anger and the pains of my body, physically and emotionally." David's eyes grow soft recalling the night his father, 3,000 miles away, died: "My housemates took me dancing. I went to say goodbye to Dad on the dance floor. I went there to feel his death and commune with him wherever he was. We told each other we loved each other, and I invited him to see that his son's life was full and wonderful, so he could go on in peace." Salvatore, a dance floor devotee, puts it: "After eight or ten hours of dancing, I am physically wiped out. But I feel so spiritually alive and purged. I know the physical exhaustion will pass in two days—but the spirit I touch there is like nothing else in my life."

Circuit for me means uplifting, celebrating, being aware of something larger than yourself, bridging the gap between myself and the rest of humanity.
—Scotty VanTussenbrook

When the sociologist Emile Durkheim witnessed the lives of Australian Aborigines, he described dance as a "collective effervescence" which he came to believe was the emotional basis of all religions. If he visited today's natives on the dance circuit, or even observe a good Saturday night at a gay dance club, Durkheim might well recognize it as a place where our tribe performs our rites of collective effervescing. As one researcher notes: "The dance parties . . . fill an important role in melding both the sacred and the profane and not experiencing them as dichotomous aspects of life."[13] No wonder so many gay men discuss the experience in spiritual terms. As Phil put it: "For me, the circuit is an opportunity to let my spirit find its place in life . . . it is one of the places where I get to create who I am." "Bliss is all about safety," says Chip, a dance party veteran. "You have to feel safe to open yourself to it. On the dance floor, with smiling faces around you, it's a safe environment to let joy find you and let yourself come out to play." "As an artist," says Chris, "I have appreciation for the artistry of the place. You had philosophical conversations on the side of the dance floor, talking about reincarnation and God. I got completely hooked. I had never known such spirit. To share this experience with these people, knowing they understand this special thing I understand, made the friendships grow out of that."

Many observers have seen parallels between dance and shamanic practices. Anthropologists note that "shamans (healers) in pre-literate societies used similar stimuli (drums, dance, colored objects, smoke) to facilitate altered states of consciousness among their adepts."[14] Gay men tell their own stories. Dean Miner, writing on his own dance experiences, put it: "The angels appear when we start to remember all our friends, the music reminds us of our times together. I looked around the second floor balcony . . . old friends appeared from memories that had long gone. These spirits had returned to watch the new generation celebrate. Choirs of dance tunes painted this night . . . the anthems carried them home." As Chris recalls, "When I started dancing in gay space, you'd see people playing instruments, fanning, twirling with fabric and cloth, African drums. It seemed like everyone brought something to make the party, stepped up to the plate. It was a real tribal ritual, I get goosebumps thinking about people having these experiences with music and connecting with each other. You contributed something to it, you became part of the experience, not a mere spectator." To that list can now be added lasers, black lights, strobes, phased array lighting, room-rocking amplification, glow sticks and, of course, the definitional totem of gay dance space, the disco ball. They are tools in service of transcendence, all.

When I dance, I feel the music, lifting me up, rising all through me.
I feel its joy and passion, power and energy, throughout my body.
—Bryan Mathison

Our easy abstraction of "the circuit" obscures the truth that gay mass dance in all its forms—whether in circuit parties, at one's local disco, a sunset tea dance, or Gay Pride street fair—is just the most recent facet of a broad connection between queer men and the bliss practices of dance. Studies tracing the role of gay men in the world of professional dance find some interesting patterns. One recent paper reported "aggregate sample estimates that 58 percent of professional dancers are gay men," and concluded: "It does not seem possible to argue with the basic conclusion that gay men are massively over-represented among professional male dancers."[15] Some evidence suggests this attraction runs deep. Anthropologists cite links between ecstatic dance and gender-variant men in several cultures[16] and note that gender-variant men are common in areas of traditional dance like Hawaiian hula.[17] One fascinating study interviewed its sample of professional male dancers and asked why they became dancers. Six of ten straight male dancers, and only 13 percent of gay men, report starting dance due to parents' encouragement. But among those who reported feeling a more personal, intrinsic attraction to dance, the pattern reverses: Only 19 percent of straight men, but 50 percent of gay men, describe their interest in those terms.[18]

The best research is simply to come here, let loose and dance. Let yourself see the undulating sea of smiling faces, experience the camaraderie of sex and spirit which routinely occur, and one senses that something potentially culture-changing is happening here. Afloat in these tides of swaying, smiling men are radical reformations of heart and body. The crowds enjoy a Dionysian mysticism of ecstasy and trance, great physical affection, profound experiments in a sweet community and sociality, all wrapped in a virtual communalism that transcends place. There is something sacred and moving, much transcendent and powerful, in these gatherings of tribe. To read in such events just a seamy plot of danger and disgust suggests a dim and stunted perspective. One has only to hear these men's heartfelt words for their richness to grow clear. No, our clubs and circuit are not flawless and, yes, they have their dangers. But neither are they trivial, empty, or easily dismissed. To see in them just another occasion to replay familiar tales of drugs and death, steroids and unsafe sex, exclusivity and attitude, is to miss their point in a big way. One could as well describe a transcendent High Church Mass as an event where finger food and wine get served, decorated with some guy in a loincloth on a cross, where they pass a collection plate. All objectively true, yet quite missing the grand magic of it all.

When we uncritically accept the "dance-bad" critique of these celebratory cultures as our received wisdom, we commit a reverse alchemy of the soul. We transmute the gold of our lived experience into a morality play of dull lead. That interpretation urges us to ignore the ways we ourselves may have touched our own Divine through dance. It dismisses the power we have found in hours of rhythmic movement, distances us from the rich personal experiences of friendship and camaraderie, incites us to forget the discovery and bliss, the rapture we have known in those charmed hours between midnight and dawn. When that critique becomes our sole rendering of the experience, it helps us forget that these rites, at their best, open a powerful portal where we can touch something beyond ourselves. If we let that tribal forgetting be complete, the alchemy will have done its job. We will, once again, have rewritten a truth we know from our own lives, accepted the least kind framing that has been provided us, and colluded in calling it truth. In so doing, we risk severing our souls from the radical power that is to be found in those realms.

We could as aptly see in such events the echo of ancient cultures like the Mayans and Mesopotamians, where groups of men created temples where they could step away from the world, went away to conduct rituals of ecstatic dance, substance, and mysticism. We could as well see reflections of the Sufi all-male trance-dance of the Dervishes, inspired by the love of the mystic Rumi for his beloved male soul mate, Shams. In many times and places, such men have been called priests, their practices revered. Their male participants have often been honored as emissaries, charged to look over the horizon and bring something back from what lay beyond. What if, instead of deriding the excesses of the circuit and its devotees, we let ourselves conceive a very different possibility? Perhaps human cultures need to elaborate such a role—the dancers, the touchers of bliss, those who open channels to other realms through rite and movement. Perhaps both in our professional and personal lives, we are among those who play that role in this moment in history.

I spend my time on the Circuit spreading positive energy,
a smile and a kind word are the tools of my trade,
I harvest the positive energy that comes back to me
from all that I meet on the dance floor.
Returning to my job, people sense my love of life—
it's contagious, and it's a disease I love to spread.
—Steve Kammon

We haven't talked about our capacity for joy.
Joy is a prime frequency of the universe.
Our journey as embodied spirits is to become the receivers/transmitters of
this energy.
—Andrew Ramer, *Gay Spirit*

It is worth a moment to ponder what it means that, over a growing swath of the planet, hundreds of thousands of men step from their mundane daily routine to participate in rites of bliss and transcendence. Is there a social function here? Having moments where they touch bliss, do these men return to the world differently? We already have seen census figures that suggest that gay households are statistically more likely to hold jobs in service, caretaking, and artistic professions. For such souls, what gets nourished here, what recharged? Do inspirations flow in these transcendent revels? When rooms of such men spend nights in rapture, it may bring something to their daily practices, elements that carry over into their work in the world. When legions of flight attendants and bank tellers, insurance dealers and sales clerks, touch bliss on a magical Saturday night, what subtle afterglow illuminates the workplaces and lives they return to on Monday morning? Might modern circuit boys have more in common with those ancient shamans than we guessed?

We have examined dance at such length because it is among our most controversial bliss practices. But it is far from our only one, so now it is time to cast the net more broadly. In the popular imagination, we are the males who have been ceded mastery of the domain of performance, spectacle, and flamboyance. We are fabled to be gifted in decorative and performing arts, recognized for leadership in fashion, arts, and theater. Tubs of ink have been spilled over the possibility of a gay aesthetic, our supposed "gay sensibility," our celebrated penchant for beautifying the world. A hundred years ago, Sigmund Freud noted that " 'inverts' included some of the most creative contributors to society throughout history."[19] The idea recurs repeatedly in gay archetypes, career stereotypes, popular culture, media, myth, and academic studies.[20] Together they have populated a menagerie of males—the drama coach and choir director, the florist and artist, the dancer and actor, the interior decorator and graphic designer— that raise this image of us to the level of a social truism.

> *Let's face it. If you took all the homosexual influence out of American culture, all we'd be left with is* Let's Make a Deal.
> —Fran Lebowitz

> *Do you want to protect your children from gay influence? Very well. Destroy the* Mona Lisa *and the* Last Supper, *silence* Messiah *and* Swan Lake, *and burn* Moby-Dick *and* The Portrait of a Lady. *Gay culture is all around you and it belongs to everybody.*
> —Bruce Bawer

As we saw in chapter 3, U.S. census figures on gay-partnered households suggest that gay men are "greatly over-represented" in such artistic and creative fields, and in human service professions. The gay men in that sample were twenty times more likely to earn a living in personal grooming jobs like cosmetics or hair, about seven times more likely to be a designer, two and a half times more apt to work in decorative landscaping or wallpaper hanging.[21] Of course, such patterns may have as much to do with accessibility and acceptance in those career paths and, as with all census data, are limited by the questions Uncle Sam will ask. But some interpret these differences as reflective of deeper personality traits. They point to evidence that cohorts of gay men have been shown more likely to have cognitive profiles of better verbal than nonverbal ability, which some say is "associated with excellence in the humanities and the arts."[22] Other research finds that "compared to heterosexual men, gay men's interests were . . . more Artistic and Social . . . less traditional for men."[23] In the 1990s, a comprehensive review of the literature concluded that despite "a popular perception that gay men are artistic," we have "little scientific data addressing this subject."[24]

So far, the evidence we do have supports the common wisdom. Until more facts are in, we cannot know just if these links will prove true. Still, one thing is clear. The domains we are believed to cluster in—theater, music, design, fashion, performance, decoration, arts, even personal care—embody elements of play, spectacle, and beautification. They reflect what one study terms our "ongoing search for a link between playfulness and seriousness in everyday life."[25] In the view of modern Western cultures, at least, our clan's life work is deeply tied to the invention and production of opportunities for bliss, in the broadest sense. It is a prime gift we bring the societies where we live.

Sex roles are one of the primary ways we identify ourselves. If you can break out of that, it would be easy to see how you could break out of other restraints—to think there is more to the world than we can see.
—Christopher Isherwood

Really, darling. The whole point of drag queens is about joy, being silly. From my special vantage point between six-inch heels and a two-foot beehive, I can't help seeing things in a fun and playful way.
—Lucinda Navy

The next example comes when we toss gender into the crucible of gay play and brew up drag. Men dressing as women, more or less, is a form of play that tweaks the rules of sex roles and binary gender. For some gay men, drag is a romp in the fields of camp and entertainment; for others, a lifestyle. Some prefer its close cousin, genderfuck, where men don women's clothes yet keep markers of masculinity like facial and body hair, the better to trouble the accustomed markers and assumptions of maledom. For others, it is a form of political and social exploration, a way to play in the fields of social habit and meaning. Mario Mieli, the Italian social theorist and father of that nation's gay liberation movement, wrote: "There is more to be learned by wearing a dress for a day than there is from wearing a suit for life." (By "drag" here is meant something quite distinct from cross-dressing—what was once termed transvestitism—or "passing" or transsexualism, all of which involve a deep core of one's sexual, social, and psychic identity.)

Whether one throws on a wig for the evening, or spend tens of thousands of dollars to scale the summit of the Imperial Court, such recreational drag is an invitation to play. It jumbles the categories, explodes expectations, distorts the cultural map of gender, tickles our habits of body and speech, fulfills fantasy, and yes, even lets us dabble with hair, gowns, and makeup. Historian James Saslow sees drag as "a way of laying claim to all the possible archetypes of the universe." It is also a chance for fun, exaggeration, and spectacle, he argues. "Gay men do not generally dress up as housewives from Peoria. If you're going to do this, you tend to dress up as somebody larger than life. If you're going to live outside of normal social rules and regulations, you might as well upgrade."[26]

Lucinda Holliday (a.k.a. "Tucson's Queen of Comedy, larger than life and just the right size") would agree. "Life is supposed to be enjoyed and fun," she says. Behind her boa, Lucinda is Larry Moore, the producer of Miss Gay Arizona, a statewide drag pageant. "People enjoy female impersonating for its entertainment value," he explains. This contest includes contestants, a panel of judges, and $2,500 of prize money ("And tiaras, don't forget the tiaras" he stresses). Every spring, it rents a downtown hotel where some seventy contestants match wigs and wits for the crown of Miss Gay Arizona. The audience—a thousand of them—range in age from fourteen to seventy-five. A quarter of them are straight. "The pageant system is a way for young men to express themselves as female impersonators in a pageant form. It makes a well-rounded entertainer, with poise, beauty, how well they conform to a certain standard of doing things." Those "things" include Male Interview—"business attire, like you're applying for a job"—Creative Costume, Evening Gown, Talent, and finally, the On-stage Interview. The Arizona pageant is one of the thirty-five pageants nationally that feed into Miss Gay USA, which, over its thirty-year history, has involved more than a hundred thousand participants. That, in turn, is just one of the four largest networks of professional gay drag pageants now in existence.

"I do it because I love to make people smile," admits its *zaftig* impresario. "If I can make one person smile every day, I have done my job." His was not the average job description in the farming town of Alexander, Iowa, population 250, where Larry grew up. "My family loves me for who I am. My grandmother is eighty-five and she just loves it. Both my parents are retired, and they enjoy me being an actor. Last March they visited and saw their first show. They liked it so much, they stayed for an extra week to catch the second one."

Even if one never competes, the play of drag takes a thousand shapes in gay lives. Some, like the Sisters of Perpetual Indulgence, have grown legendary. The most hirsute order of nuns yet discovered, each novice takes vows "to promulgate universal joy and expiate stigmatic guilt" in "a shared ministry . . . of public manifestation and habitual perpetration." Only then do they receive the holy names of their order: Sr. Bea Attitude, Sr. Nicene Easy, Sr. Teresa Stigmata, Sr. Which Hazel, Sr. Mary O'Stop, Sr. Hellena Handbasket, Sr. Lazy Susan, and Sr. Mae B. Hostel. From their roots in San Francisco in 1979, the Sisters have grown to include local "abbeys" in more than a dozen cities, including such far-flung places as Angers, France; Manchester, England; and Sydney, Australia. But if the Sisters are an obvious example, one might be less quick to name Waco, Texas; Missoula, Montana; Ogden, Utah; or Fresno, California as hot spots of high drag. However, these are just three of almost sixty localities that host chapters of the International Imperial Court system, a confederation of drag societies reaching from Mexico to the United Kingdom, and which has been in existence since 1965.

From coast to chiffon coast, in less formal ways, drag is among the most accessible and ubiquitous of our cultural personas. It shows up in every outrageous costume and four-foot wig on the floats of Pride parades from Palm Beach to Palm Springs. It happens in New York's Wigstock Festival, which now numbers some ten thousand participants (in 2001, Chicago hosted its first Wigstock event). Drag pitches its tents at Radical Faerie gatherings—"why do you think we call them 'en-*camp*-ments'?" grins a twenty-something Faerie—in Arizona, in the Tennessee mountains, in Oregon and Vermont. If you live in Philly, you might witness it on Wednesday drag nights at Twelfth Air Command bar, but it also happens at any of a thousand gay bar drag nights in almost any city across America. You see it at the meetings of Miss Vera's Finishing School for Boys Who Want to be Girls in Greenwich Village. You see it in the Kinsey Sicks ("America's favorite dragapella beautyshop quartet"), a trashy camp vocal quartet of Trixie, Winnie, Rachel, and Trampolina (a.k.a. Maurice, Irwin, Ben, and Chris). You see it in the Invasion of the Pines, an annual rite where a ferryboat full of hundreds of drag queens lands dockside to re-enact a bouffant version of a lunch-counter sit-in, to the delight of local residents and the reward of a lot of free drinks. You see it in that ever-evolving pantheon of princesses with such lovely, if improbable, names as Lady Bunny, Sister Boom Boom, RuPaul, Hedda Lettuce, Gina Tonic, Anita Blowjob, Sandy Knees, Orangina, Rollerina, Miss Carriage, Miss Understood, and the hands-down favorite, Chlamydia Burns.

Drag is among the most well-worn gowns in our cultural wardrobe. It seeps into the larger culture through *Wigstock, the Movie* ("A celebration of life, liberty, and the pursuit of big hair"), and in films like *Torch Song Trilogy, Mrs. Doubtfire,* or *Priscilla, Queen of the Desert.* It gets brought up on the public stage in *Nunsense* and *La Cage aux Folles.* It ricochets around society when an HBO special follows Varla Jean Merman on a tour of five cities, or when Cashetta hosts *Star Search.* You meet it in the two men built like professional wrestlers who are earnestly selecting makeup at a Wilshire Boulevard Clinique makeup counter. Whole books have been devoted to the rich complexities of drag and cross-dressing, and it exceeds our present scope to give drag the full attention it deserves. For now, we note that drag is yet another facet of play, pure and simple, a mischief at once silly and whimsical, provocative and pretty, liberating and transforming. This particular flavor of play reminds us that the steely binaries of gender can bend under a weight no heavier than a feather boa.

It was inevitable that outrageousness exploded with the beginnings of gay liberation. Hooray for sassy risk and silly experiment and anarchic joy!
—James Broughton

Even when we hang up our heels, the twin sprites of bliss and play lie in ambush around every corner in gay world. They happen in moments like the holiday tableau at a recent Christmas, in a suburban duplex in a Las Vegas tract. One enters the unprepossessing living room to find a charming full-size Christmas tree. The conifer fills the room, exuding its fresh-cut scent, a pile of lavishly wrapped presents heaped generously at its base. The tree drips with enough garlands, lights, and ornaments to make Martha Stewart blush. The image comes straight from the pages of a *Redbook* reverie, but for one small detail: The tree is hanging upside down from the ceiling. Each branch droops straight upward, defying gravity. Each ornate ornament "dangles" heavenward on stiff strings ("Hairspray," confides Markey, the creator, a six-foot-two fullback of a man, a former drag performer whom his friends describe as "a total Mad

Queen's queen"). The angel ornament on Markey's tree's peak aims straight down ("Straight to hell"; Markey smiles); the presents so carefully arrayed beneath it are lovingly glue-gunned to the ceiling, every bow starched to stand straight up. This is one man's topsy-turvy parody of holiday domesticity run amok, a sort of scene guaranteed to convince Santa he's having a bad acid flashback. Norman Rockwell meets Norman Bates. That there would be your basic gay sensibility.

That fabled sensibility, as Supreme Court Justice Potter Stewart famously described pornography, is one of those things that "you know it when you see it." We all see it in our own favorite moments. "For me, it was last Pride Day," recalls Lou. "The street was bursting, so many gay people they had to close off the whole street. Cars were trapped, so rather than fight it, people just got out of their cars and started dancing with everyone, in the moment. At one house, a guy had massive six-foot speakers in the two front bay windows blasting Sister Sledge: 'We are famil-EE, I got all my sisters and ME!' in a dance mix version that went on for about twenty minutes. On the ledge between them, barely two feet wide, was this huge muscle guy, a total linebacker type, wearing nothing but women's black panties and fishnet stockings with a garter belt and spiked heels. Crazed beefcake in drag, you know the sort—very *Rocky Horror*. At one point the guy went in and reappeared with giant six-foot angel wings on. Somebody else from the crowd tossed up pompoms to this huge football player guy who was now wearing a G-string and angel wings, stiletto heels, waving pompoms, dancing to 'We Are Family,' shaking the block. The whole street went crazy, dancing, screaming, laughing. In that instant, I thought: 'How could you ever really explain this moment to anybody outside it?'"

> *There is more fun in art, and more art in fun, than many of us will even allow.*
>
> —J. Babuscio, *Camp and the Gay Sensibility*

We indulge our whimsy in a million ways. We don't just create dance clubs; instead, mad New York theater queens knew that what was *really* needed was a domed ceiling that slid back, a planetarium projector to throw the starry heavens onto the dome—and, *voilà*, our legend The Saint was born. Sadly, history may never record the first gay club where someone got the inspired idea to fill up the room chest-high with foam and have several hundred men dance in it. "I had a skin reaction everywhere for a week," recalls one dancer, wincing. "I mean, *everywhere*. My boyfriend was five-foot-five, and he nearly drowned." OK, OK, so foam dancing never caught on. But who else would come up with it? Or visit the small bar in a nondescript brick building in Des Moines where you pass through the bar area to a small unmarked staircase at the back, descend through some hanging car-wash-type rubber strips, and find yourself in a room where it is . . . raining. "Cool, huh?" smiles a drenched patron, Carl. "They got this great idea!" In this case, to make warm showers of artificial rain cascade down from the ceiling, *inside.* It wasn't enough that men had a room to go play; they decided we needed to do it under a waterfall of rainwater. Accompanied, of course, by "It's Raining Men."

A few hours' drive away is Chicago, home of the International Mr. Leather competition. Tim, a forty-three-year-old producer of industrial videos, sees IML as an eddy of pure play in his life: "It's incredibly great. Whether you want a circuit party, sex in the hotel, a convention, a dance event, a Chicago tourist weekend, or a theme party or a conference, it's all there. Everything rolled into one. It's incredibly friendly, there's a great feeling, the guys are just open and warm. You see friends from all over, and everyone's up for a good time." Harold and Matt have attended IML, separately and together, for years. "You can't imagine a more wild gay scene. Every conceivable kink and fetish is milling around the lobby, in the elevators and hallways of this hotel, like some twisted Fellini film. Guys in buttless chaps, full leather and harnesses, just in G-strings and jockstraps, with tattoos, piercings, even basically nude. Roaming around in this ordinary Midwest hotel. Through it all, the hotel staff is floating around working in these perky little uniforms. Here's an old Polish lady cleaning the ashtrays, or somebody's granddad sweeping the lobby as some big leather daddy walks by with a nearly nude boy leashed, gagged, and on all fours. They don't bat an eye, like we were some hotel convention of Omaha seed salesmen. You know this is a freak show to them, totally out of their experience. But our guys are so friendly and accepting, and really respectful of the staff, so the whole attitude helps the others see it for what it is—a moment of fun, nothing to worry about. The weekend totally puts in relief the different way we do things."

This spirit of play extends even to more earnest pursuits, like our volunteerism and service. Let your dad keep his Kiwanis and his Rotary; we have the Imperial Court, whose charitable mission reads: "To hold functions and fund raisers to benefit those communities and help those in our community who are in need of our assistance." Mainstream male service clubs like the Lions and Elks seem downright domesticated next to, say,

the Sisters. "Work in the community was central," recalls Sr. Mary Hys-
terectoria, one of the fifteen founding Sisters. "Collectively the focus was
spirituality with fun." For behind the wimples and whiskers, these
troops of men were carrying out a wide variety of service work, even as
they went by names like Sr. Florence Nightmare and Sr. Dana Van Iniq-
uity. "We never spent money on ourselves. From the beginning, we made
postcards and sold them, and always gave away the money to other
causes, like benefits for the Gay Men's Chorus and for early AIDS work,
or for Cuban refugees." The Sisters view the street as their sanctuary,
appearing on random corners handing out whistles, recruiting for anti-
violence patrols in front of a local church or, as on this particular Saturday, swooping into a local hardware store to bless the customers with an
impromptu HIV education sermon. "Make holiness a habit," winks one,
who sports a carefully coiffed goatee. Then, with a quick pinch of a passing muscle boy's nipple and a clatter of Rollerblades, they spirit off to
their next divinely inspired brush with the unconverted.

In keeping with vows to "support to our fellow sisters toward our personal and collective enlightenment," the Sisters often marry silly with
somber. "We brought ritual to places where people had been attacked or
murdered. In the early eighties, a man was stabbed in a cruising area at
Buena Vista Park. People were scared to go up there; they were feeling
endangered. One night, totally spontaneously, several of us put on our
habits to go cast a circle to reclaim the space and take away their fear.
Another time, a group of Christian bullies were coming into the Castro,
bothering everybody, preaching about sin, singing all these songs at people as they came home from work. We decided to fight song with song.
Several Sisters got dressed at the Haight-Ashbury 'convent' and grabbed
disco blasters. Everyone showed up, dressed, and piled into an old VW
bus. Then we popped out, dancing with our boomboxes. This group of
dancing nuns with beards freaked them out, as we circled dancing to *our*
disco blaster, singing *our* songs. The idea was to meet them with laughter. In faerie tradition, instead of anger, you make something frivolous. It
was wonderful and silly, but we were serious about it."

If this Sisterly vision of volunteering weren't enough to give your
average candy striper hives, you might check out the TTCA in Seattle.
Many other organizations might describe themselves as "a nonprofit
membership organization that provides financial support for other nonprofit agencies and organizations," and claim that their volunteers "build
bridges between communities through activities that bring people
together to work for a common goal." But there is only one that calls
itself the Tacky Tourist Clubs of America, Seattle Chapter. Their mission

statement reads: "We seek to elevate social and civic consciousness with humor and good-natured satire." TTCA, Seattle chapter (the only recorded chapter, it seems), "produces flights of the fancy and guided tours to realms of the imagination" and produces, by its own admission, "the most fabulous parties in gay Seattle." They preach a fiercely fun-loving philosophy: "We are tourist-class passengers on the luxury liner of life, dedicated to the proposition that, without chemicals, polyester itself would not be possible. We seek to milk the Sacred Cow of Taste to create a Cheeselog of Love, making the world a gay place in which to live. Charity goes further at group rates. Go around the world with us." Yet there is method behind the mad merriment. The group has provided a quarter million dollars to support organizations that provide direct-to-client social services, safeguard human rights and civil liberties, promote civic improvement, the visual arts, performing arts, or athletics. Charity beneficiaries include AIDS housing, Friends of the Earth, support to homeless families, Seattle Rape Relief, the Washington Toxics Coalition, the Seattle Municipal Elections Committee and, of course, the ROTC (that's the Righteously Outrageous Twirling Corps. Were you maybe thinking something else?).

Likewise, a thousand miles away, in Tucson, Arizona, one could find several organizations that work with at-risk adolescents. But only one—called Drag 101—gives the teens a chance to learn the finer points of cross-gender impersonation. "It's a mentoring system; it starts off young, people from about thirteen, who know they want to be female impersonators. Oh, and drag kings, too." It loosely involves several dozen teens. "We try to keep the kids off the streets and out of trouble, give them a good role model and good mentoring," says its adult leader, a long-time local drag queen. "It's about learning to take responsibility for yourself. That means life responsibility, not using drugs and alcohol, staying in school. Because, as we all know," she intones gravely, "beauty brings responsibilities."

Paris is about as far from Tucson as you get, but this same spirit showed when the International Gay Swim Team competition convened there in 2000. Like any world-class amateur athletic event, the events showcased three days of superb athleticism and tough competition. But how many other sports events have a famed Pink Flamingo competition? The event, which began as your basic aquatic drag swim relay, has now grown into a camp Esther Williams extravaganza. It is hard to imagine the basic heterosexual water polo team making an entrance like the West Hollywood Aquatic team (a.k.a. WH2O), whose twenty-five members paraded in dressed as pink poodles in puff skirts, floppy dog-ear hats, balloon tails, painted noses, and fishnet stockings like so many camp cancan dancers. Along the way, their two "trainers" stripped down from lavish hats and dresses to fishnet outfits and poodle underwear (don't ask) before dogs and all ended up in the pool for an acrobatic water routine. They beat, by a wet nose, the rival New York Aquatics gay swim team, who had counted on their pink flamingo finery to carry the day. It's a dog-eat-dog world out there; these competitors are world-class, in silliness as in swimming.

Back on dry land, that same silly spirit enlivens Guerrilla Queer Bar, a moveable-party-zap phenomenon that began in queer San Francisco and now pops up in places like North Carolina; Austin, Texas; and Heidelberg, Germany (where it is known as "Queer Guerillo"). The group delights in transgressing boundaries around "what types of people" belong in neighborhoods and bars. They are known for rattling tourist cages with events like their St. Patricia's Day party ("The patron saint of drunken sexual mistakes"). The group usually descends unannounced on straight bars and nightspots, "collectively bringing with them campy, edgy, and queer sensibilities they might not individually exhibit, especially in non-gay spaces."[27] Translation: Joe Sixpack may suddenly find himself dancing with a boy in a bunny outfit, downing brews with a dyke in leis and luau gear, or watching karaoke performed by someone of indeterminate sexual orientation in a large gorilla suit. One GQB regular describes it as "cacophony, absurdness for its own sake. There are a lot of places I'd never go otherwise." Says Frank, a straight man who manages a local bar: "These novelties are part of our dynamic. People come to the city expecting to have a cosmopolitan experience and expect this sort of thing."[28] He puts his finger on a truth we know: that to live in a gay world is to savor a million such silly moments. Of course, no rule says straight guys can't do this. They could, as well, address each other as "Girlina" and wear hats with lots of tropical fruit on them. It's just that they usually . . . don't.

In city after city, gay men are purveyors of a splendid civic silliness. In Boston, a city not famed for frivolity, a wacky streetcorner theatricality is brought to you by Abe Rybeck and his gleefully absurd Theater Offensive. The group materializes all over the city with a quirky combination of savvy commentary, smart skits, and mad costumes. When serious business calls, we have always kept absurdity in our arsenal. Thirty years ago, it was Jose Saria at the Black Cat in San Francisco, leading choruses of "God Save the Nellie Queens" as the police pushed bar patrons into paddy wagons. Then came those legendary brawling drag queens blockading the cops in the Stonewall Bar. We were the ones in North

Carolina to drape Jesse Helms's house with a thirty-foot condom, the ones in Washington to storm the National Institutes of Health headquarters with pennants trailing twenty-foot plumes of red and green smoke, and on Wall Street to dress in corporate drag, infiltrate the New York Stock Exchange, and unfurl embarrassing "Sell Wellcome" banners from the balcony to shame them for price-gouging HIV drugs. And who but a SWAT team of sisters would penetrate the CBS studio to carry our point to a stunned Dan Rather live before America on the evening news? And what more quintessentially queer moment was there than the night thousands of us marched into midtown Manhattan to protest Matthew Shepard's death? With traffic snarled for blocks, the crowd roared "Whose streets? Our streets!" until one observant marcher saw among the stalled cars an SUV containing . . . Martha Stewart. An electric frisson spread through the crowd, whispers and glances were exchanged, and within moments, the chant morphed into a friendly "Whose sheets? Martha's sheets!" There is a reason *gay terrorist* is an oxymoron.

As Jedi masters of play, we use our gifts in many ways with each other. Sometimes there is even a quiet Zen to our zaniness. "Not long before our friend George died, he had moved into a new house," recalls David, a house painter in Providence. "Nobody had to say anything; we all knew it would be his last Halloween. So it became intensely important to go over and play with George. That Halloween night, eight of us came over for a drag slumber party. Two outfits required. One guy was a six-foot-something blond Midwestern corn-fed Adonis, who came as a country-western singer with red polka-dot dress, giant boobs, crepe hair in gingham ribbons hanging down all over his hairy chest. Eight of us spent the night on the same bed, all twined around each other, keeping George company, laughing and being silly with him." The line between silliness and sacrament can be thin, indeed.

We center pleasure in our lives differently, recognizing, redefining, and reinventing it in diverse forms. But the play that gets the most attention in our lives is, of course, sex. For many, to utter "gay men" and "play" in the same sentence by definition, is to move the discussion below the belt. Consider the sign over the bar at an Arizona leather hangout. It looks like one of those official highway construction signs, a yellow diamond with authoritative black letters that reads: "CAUTION." But something's odd about the graphic. Look close and you see a stylized male figure bent over, another man standing close behind him, hands grasping the first man's hips, in a graphic pose that no highway department ever sanctioned. Then you read the text below: "Men at Play." We acknowledge this role of play in our common language of "sex play," tell friends that we "went home to play," or make "playdates" with "playmates."

As we have seen, gay cultures have evolved unparalleled opportunity for sexual, sensual, erotic, and physical play. We enjoy unparalleled networks of opportunity, create rich structures to find partners, to communicate and magnify desire, and to realize fantasies. With our enormous cultural support and latitude for sexual expression, exploration, camaraderie, and discovery, comes a generous sharing of techniques, lore, language, and technologies. We even share partners and spaces. Yet we easily lose sight of the fact that this rich erotic horny-copia is actually part of a larger and more subtle constellation of play in our lives. Each of our thousand robust and exuberant forms of sexualities are in fact open possibilities for bliss (in principle if not always in practice).

Sex is but the most obvious thread in the rich tapestry of play we weave through our lives. In the ecstasies of the dance floor as in the intimacies of tantric touch weekends, at the talent shows at gay weekends and the sex shows of backrooms, in the pageantry of drag parades, the silliness of guerrilla theater, in massage exchanges and leather runs, in feather boas and leather chaps, we explore a galaxy of opportunities for play. We play with each other and with ourselves, with our social and communal relations and bonds, with our bodies, our fantasies, our desires, our minds, dreams and spirit. These abundant forms of bliss and play add up to an ineffable gay sensibility, the *je ne sais queer* that transforms the humdrum into the fabulous. It happens each time you think: "That is *so gay*," each moment you smile "I can't believe I'm doing this," and in those "I never thought I'd be here" moments. It sneaks up in glimpses around a dance floor or a sex party, as you laugh at a float in a Pride parade or smile across a dinner table of friends. Such moments distill to an essence that defies easy description yet constantly reminds that Kansas is a planet far, far away. That very idea—that there is a cultural Kansas, and we're not in it—speaks volumes. That such a notion has gained enough currency to emblazon our T-shirts and enliven our conversations suggests that we know our lives take a slightly different shape. It is a way that we celebrate our tendency to bend the rules. When a clan devotes such uncommon energy and imagination to this plethora of play and pleasure, we need to ask why. Could there be anything bigger than hedonism going on here? Is there any method to our merriment, any larger meaning in our madness?

Gay people insist on ecstasy, which is outlawed because it helps one to see beyond society's limitations.
—James Saslow, historian

Whatever the public blames you for, cultivate it: It is yourself.
—Jean Cocteau

Like so much of what we do, our bending the rules to find bliss holds implications for the wider culture. Our larger society devalues play, and readily dismisses its implications. In our time and social moment, play and bliss-seeking are dismissed as "mere hedonism," mindless indulgence, as shameful, disreputable, immature, or just plain wrong. But look deeper, and you see that this revaluing of play has a potent magic. Historically, gay men have been excluded from full enfranchisement in the citizenry of men. When we emigrated to a queer new world in our quest for bliss, we became outlaws before the institutions of family, work, church, government, and military. Our quest for bliss placed us outside society's pillars of power. Viewed as something less than "real" men, we were not permitted the benefits of society's version of "true manhood," as fathers or husbands, as soldiers or priests, as leaders or presidents. As we were denied those benefits, we were also freed of some burdens of masculinity's iron yoke. Being exiled to the margins gives one more latitude to frolic, indulge frivolity, and savor silliness. That is, to play.

In that play we prod and poke at accepted truths, which makes it an inherently political act. Our very collective existence reflects a political tension with the structures of authoritarian social control. Simply by being, we suggest that bliss is pursuable, at times even attainable. We embody the principle that all citizens have a potential to trust their hearts, recast the rules, sass the system, and seek their bliss—and that things may turn out happily. As such, we become living, breathing reminders that rules are negotiable. That makes us both envied and feared by a larger society that demands its citizenry color within the lines.

What we must work on, it seems to me, is not so much to liberate our desires, but to make ourselves infinitely more susceptible to pleasure.
—Michel Foucault, "Friendship as a Way of Life"

This queer penchant for play and our willingness to transgress places such men in a queer conjunction with American mythos. We embody a thread of character—what social philosophers term "expressive individu-

alism"—that weaves deep in the American psyche. In American literature and film, from Whitman and Thoreau, to Gary Cooper, Arnold
Schwarzenegger, and Bruce Willis; from the Lone Ranger to Rambo to
Batman, our heroes are individuals who define their own values. Pitted
against the corporation, the Machine, the power structure, the stubborn
individual following his bliss, is the cherished American myth.

When gay men lead open lives, we do precisely that. Coming out is
our quintessential act of authenticity and hope, the formative bliss-seeking act that makes us, in the truest sense, a community of faith. Our faith
was that the power of our hearts and love would lead us truly and well. To
gain admission here, one had to say no at least once to the Big Rules.
That requires a hero's spirit, a little contrary and a lot courageous. It also
creates no small irony. We, the patriots in this principality of pals, are
guilty of no more basic American act than taking to heart the founding
fathers' creed of life, liberty, and the pursuit of happiness. But it turns out
that embrace all three with equal fervor, and you get called un-American.

What use to us are laws of right and wrong?
    —Charles Baudelaire, poet

What happens when a subculture's members have assumed outlaw
status at least once in their lives? Having stepped outside the lines once,
do we any more easily question other cultural givens, challenge other
rules? Interestingly, one study of personality types noted that their gay
sample was, in fact, "less submissive to authority and more unconventional."[29] Tom, who grew up in heartland Dayton, saw this link play out
in his own life. "The first time I had real sex with someone I cared for,
the waves just rolled off my shoulders. It felt so right, so good, and so
pure, nobody could tell me anything wasn't good about it. It meant I
knew there could be love in my life, all the things they said couldn't be,
really could. My anxiety just melted away, there was just no question it
was so totally right. In that moment I knew all that stuff that had been
told to me, drilled into me, was just wrong. So, if they were wrong about
that, that enforced that I had to go explore the world, have my own experiences to find out the truth about other stuff. Because what they are
telling me wasn't necessarily true. I had to go and take risks to know.
Gay sex gave me permission, not just about gay and sex, but it forces you
to discover truth for yourself. That's a big undertaking, to take chances,
put yourself out there, to see what is true."

What might it teach to have even once voted with one's heart against society's rules? Todd, a straight man in Madison, Wisconsin, thinks a lot about this because he has a gay brother. "Because you're gay, you've been able to accept something that's unacceptable, something about yourself that has made you open to the more untalked-about, unthought-about feelings. If you were conditioned to a way of life, regardless of what you may really think, it restricts you from free thinking. Gay people don't confine themselves to that process of thinking. They evolved into who they are because they are able to accept it. So they think free, and go from there." In the words of writer Rictor Norton: "We have amongst our own ranks—in our culture—a wealth and variety of collectively liberating experience undreamt of by merely mortal heterosexuals."

Many have suggested that experience underlies our seeming uncommon presence in the arts and creative sectors. A generation ago, gay writer Christopher Isherwood said that gay men embody "the archetype of fool, trickster, one who turns situations inside out, laughs at power, transforms cultural rules." Last year, writer/producer Clive Barker put it: "Once you survive the experience of being told no or that what comes naturally to you is, by their definition, unnatural—something happens in you that is wonderful. It forces you to work on a new definition of what is natural. And when you start to reassess yourself, you begin to reassess those who tell you, 'Thou shalt not.' And when you do that, you start to reassess the whole fucking culture. And that's a wonderful place to be. William Blake said: 'Make your own laws or be slave to another man's.' If we can stand up for the right to be other—and maybe that means being excluded from a party that isn't very much fun anyway— then we are strong."[30] Our very existence is a rebuff to the rules. We are a society bonded by a shared act of social rebellion, the worst nightmare of the keepers of the rules.

Sometimes, however, the harvest of bliss is thorns. Our attraction to play and bliss-seeking may carry within it the seeds of our shared undoing. We have few models for what happens when any subculture has a swath of individuals who are uncommonly attuned to bliss, some with the material means to indulge it, a culture that creates ample opportunities to magnify it, and whose shared norms afford extraordinary permission to seek it. But if recent history is any guide, it isn't always happy. At least two problems may arise. First, things can get out of hand. In our enthusiastic pursuit of bliss, we sometimes get burned. We can get lost in sex or drugs, occasionally lose ourselves or our bearings, feel depressed, isolated, or unworthy, suffer from addictions. None of these suggest that the impulse toward bliss is not worthy of great reverence. It is precisely because bliss-seeking and play are so deeply powerful and transformative that we can so easily get hurt. When your cultural job is experimenting with the extraordinary, it is an occupational risk that sometimes your experiments blow up on you. It is the shadow side to all that heady sex, drugs, and rockin' and rollin'. Second, less dramatically, the pursuit of bliss can bring illusion. "The real question is why bliss doesn't exist on a more regular basis," notes Chip, thirty-six, an editor in Williamsburg, Brooklyn. "We have bought into the idea that bliss is just one product away. Drugs are the classic case—bliss in a pill. We even *named* it Ecstasy, for God's sake. But the same is true for products, clothes, vacation destinations. They are all marketed as shortcuts to the bliss people truly seek." As we will see in the pages ahead, much of our tribal trauma comes as we try to reconcile the tension between all our hearts would have us be—freely loving, open spirited, nurturant, transgressive—and the society where we live. As we see in chapter 10, we are easily wedged between the ways we might reshape the world—our search for bliss—and the ways that our own habits obstruct us. We all too easily accept the narrative of a majority we could instead transform. Until that changes, gay men will not fully deliver the gifts we might, either to the larger culture or to ourselves.

It is this question of gifts that underlies all this discussion of bliss and play, because it raises a profound possibility. Animal behaviorists have long noted that in most social animal species it is the young animals who introduce innovation. They do it through play behavior. Whether you live in a pack, gaggle, flock, school, or suburb, play is society's way of evolving new social strategies. Play may manifest as new roles or repertoires, new amusements or technologies, as art or changes in customs. Biologist Gerald Heard once wrote that "gay people are those within the human species who best represented the biological concept of neoteny, prolonged youth . . . allowing people to be open, growing and mobile, exploring long after our heterosexual age peers have been forced to settle down into the specialization and stability required of parenthood and so-called maturity. It is because of our neotonous non-specialization that gay people have been able to make such a contribution to culture." Charlotte Bach, a mid-century British social thinker and sexologist, wrote: "The heterosexual majority provides the stable, generally conservative, base necessary for our species' ongoing reproductive survival. On the whole, the sexually ambiguous minority provides for the evolutionarily significant behavior changes that in due course trigger evolutionarily significant anatomical changes."[31]

From this perspective, our playful habits take on new dimensions. To play is to redraft reality. We who have so long created trends and lived at the edge, we the tinkerers with social forms, purveyors of the arts, we are Jedi masters of play. We use these powers to transmute meaning and metaphor, bend gender and power, sexuality and masculinity. Through it we transmit pleasure and understanding, touch bliss and return to tell about it. As Judy Grahn, in her book *Another Mother Tongue*, points out, we test the boundaries of the possible. "Society uses all gay people who participate in gay culture for special purposes. We are closely watched to see what constitutes the limits of a thing: too far out, too much, too low, too bad, too outrageous, too soft, too dangerous, too rough, too cultured, too aggressive, too sexual. We are essential to them knowing who they are."

Our passion for play makes us society's tricksters, change agents to authoritarian structures of church, state, society, convention, and law. It may even have a larger species significance. Perhaps in this social animal as in others, Bliss and her silly sister, Play, are the driving engines of progress, and we are their acknowledged consorts. That may be one reason so many societies seem to have carved out a special place for men like us.

The possible usefulness of "abnormal" types is illustrated from every part of the world.
   —Ruth Benedict, American anthropologist

Placing this mass of modern social findings in larger historical and cultural perspective compels a question: What if we, or someone like us, has passed this way before? The idea that a clan of sexually variant men may have something to teach is as old as civilization. Cultural anthropologists tell us that against all biological odds, over eons of evolution, in scores of cultures, over thousands of years, hundreds of human societies have recognized a different breed of men. They have taken forms as diverse as the Native American *berdache*, the contemporary Indian *hijras* and Polynesian *mahu,* the *galli* of Ancient Mesopotamia. They have appeared from Aleutian Islanders to Ambo West Africans, from troupes of medieval glee-men and bards to Cheyenne Indians to brothers of the Roman Catholic Church. In various permutations, such males have often been seen as sexually and gender-variant, sometimes spiritually transformative. In diverse forms, sexually different males of the sort we might now call gay have played vital, even revered, roles in societies. They have been variously conceived of as "third gender," "third sex," or "two-spirited," and have often been associated with the holy and sacramental. They have filled roles as teachers and caretakers, shamans and priests, artists and performers. They have been viewed as sexually distinct and spiritually potent, whose function it was to walk the boundaries of spirit and flesh, bringing back to their cultures teaching and direction.

All of which, some say, poses a riddle. Gender-variant folk should, by all rights, be an evolutionary dead-end. That might seem to be basic biology—ask Darwin. In the reproductive scheme of things, what more hopeless trait could there be than a non-breeding homosexuality? As the author of *The Moral Animal* argues: "One wouldn't expect natural selection to create people who are disinclined to do the things (for example, heterosexual intercourse) that get their genes transported to the next generation."[32] Some have suggested that without reproducing, such a group should have all died out long before Madonna. So why are we here?

That this is what biologists term a "conserved trait" could be deeply interesting. For such a profound variation to endure—especially one in such seeming contradiction to evolutionary advantage—suggests there may be powerful reasons for it. If Einstein was right, and God does not play dice with the universe, it may be that whatever role such sexually and gender-variant men may play, it is one worth keeping around. That riddle has intrigued many thinkers in evolutionary and population biology, and many have proposed evolutionary theories about the vital social functions homosexuality may play.[33] Scholars have proposed theories ranging from an accidental genetic variant to the possibility that some of us play a necessary role in species caretaking. Some have asked if we may play key roles in the survival of the broader society—if, relieved of procreative responsibility, we take on roles as the communal caretakers, the nurturing uncles who help make the whole tribe work. Biologists term this "avuncular behavior" or "helpers at the nest." Some have even argued that it is as inborn as breathing, something hard-wired in our genes.

There is much to argue with in any strict sociobiological view.[34] But the key point here is not that West Hollywood studmuffins are reincarnated *berdache*, nor that all these forms of gender-variant manhood are the same. We do well to remember that the very notion of "homosexual" is itself a parochial personhood, a culturally bound category that belongs to a specific moment and place. In most other times and places, for example, even our gender-variant ancestors more than likely bred children as well. The more important thing here is the broader cultural pattern. Perhaps today we play certain roles that bear striking similarity to ones that cultures have sustained again and again over their continued evolution.

We may play a role that cultures have an adaptive need to elaborate. Across scores of cultures and eons of time, civilizations have made place for men with some of these traits we share, men situated in a distinct relationship to the sacred and to spectacle, charged with interpreting the divine, males who traffic in cultural innovation and vision. Perhaps there is a deeper social need and function for such a class of beings.

Gay people are not in the habit of thinking of ourselves as leading our civilization, and yet we do.
—Judy Grahn

A hundred years ago, utopian social theorist Edward Carpenter wrote of what he called "the real significance of the homosexual temperament." In his view, "the non-warlike man and the nondomestic woman . . . sought new outlets for their energies . . . different occupations." They became "the initiators of new activities." In this decade, Reverend Peter Gomes, chaplain of Harvard University's Memorial Church and Plummer Professor of Christian Morals, put it: "The place for creative hope that arises out of suffering is most likely now to be found among blacks, women, and homosexuals. These may well be the custodians of those 'thin places' where the visible meets the invisible. They may, in fact, be the watchers at the frontier between what is and what is to be."

We meet this idea again in the final chapter. For now, let us simply note that in many of our social patterns, ethical customs, even in our distinctive rituals of play and exultation, we may be unwittingly enacting a modern version of an ancient sacerdotal tradition of social or spiritual exploration. Perhaps in our tribe's reaching to touch bliss, we are like Prometheus, bringing a fire both playful and sacred back to the rest of the human clan, the better to light our common way.

MIND THE GAP: WHEN PRIVATE HEARTS AND PUBLIC HABITS COLLIDE

What would happen if gay men flew as high and wide as we could? We could make dear love of comrades the law of the land.
—Paul Monette

We have seen our story, half told. Under the shadow of a plague, we have been evolving a set of radical cultural transformations, without even understanding their full import. These pages have parted the scrim of conventional wisdom to reveal complex patterns of male altruism, and uncommon levels of male caregiving, service, and volunteerism. We have uncovered evidence of the least publicly violent culture of men known in modern times and traced deep patterns of sexual protection and nurture. We have shown that in the places where our subcultural practices have been permitted to flourish, we have evolved a strikingly open set of sexual practices and mores, exploring domains of erotic pleasure generally foreclosed to the members of the larger society. We have examined a radical redefinition of intimate relationships, shifting the balance between the dyadic intimacy of couples toward a more diffuse, communal intimacy. We have witnessed a redrawing of boundaries of public and private. We have documented innovations in friendship and affection with broad implications for family and society. We have explored the broad permission for pleasure and play that queer worlds afford, and found new meanings in play and innovation, celebration and spectacle. Finally, we have gazed through the new windows that gay men can open with women, and seen the potential for different kinds of relationships outside usual patterns of gender roles. As many women now recognize, they include less threat of violence or intimidation and offer an alternative of playful coexistence to patterns of gender strife common in the larger society. Call us heroes, outlaws, renegades, or innovators— our lives clearly look different.

Examine the facts, witness the social forms and rituals we have evolved, note our myriad responses to AIDS, map the cultures we have built and the rules we live by daily. You find a pattern that is persistent yet unacknowledged. Virtually all of these values revolve around a central theme of *care*.

These innovations amount to nothing less than a newly evolving public ethic, without clear parallel or precedent. It is remarkable that these wide-ranging developments have evolved in secular communities, without benefit of dogma, monastery, or church, school, state, or family of origin. "What amazes me is that our cultural differences seem to have been evolved, not instructed," observes Lou, who, at thirty-one years old, has lived in the evolving gay worlds in Las Vegas, Chelsea, San Francisco, Austin, and now Brooklyn. "What is different about what we do comes up from the grass roots, not down from a central religious authority." It is noteworthy, too, that these sweeping experiments in care have arisen among this most troubled gender called men. It is rare for males to do such things, and even rarer for communities of men to do them, and unheard of to do them unbidden.

Something powerful is afoot when unprecedented numbers of men in free-living communities are daily following practices espoused by the great spiritual traditions. Were such altruistic patterns observed in any other subculture, it would be remarked on as an event of historic spiritual dimensions. In our case, it has occurred as a community's spontaneous expression of its members' values. The male mores arising in intentional gay worlds resemble nothing so much as a free-living, spontaneously generating experiment in a vast, communal spirituality.

So now we collide head-on with the core paradox of queer lives: Why does so much of the common life we have created with each other do such terrible injury to our hearts? Because, let's face it: Life is far from rosy in the lavender kingdom. You may have read this far and seen in these chapters no gay world you know. Indeed, the discussion may have led you to suspect that I live on some far, dimly lit planet. You may well be asking why, if we embody such rich patterns of love when nobody's looking, do we so often feel loveless? Why do our shared gay cultural habits, in many ways so humane, so often feel so dehumanized and dehumanizing? Evidence says our lives reflect profound ethics of altruism and nurture. But where is this nurture and care in our daily lives? Research may demonstrate that we routinely practice myriad forms of kindness and compassion. Yet how often do dating, socializing, sexual and intimate relations feel hurtful, unkind, and uncaring?

Reflect on your own life. You may find yourself with important dreams yet unmet, engaged in a midlife search for meaning. Or be in your twenties and unsure of where you fit into this thing called "gay community." Maybe you are single and worry that you may stay that way, unsatisfied by the options you find in the scene. You may be in a committed relationship, yet wonder what lies ahead for you as the first generation to live "out" gay lives. You may have recently come out and be wondering what life promises ahead, or you may be getting older and worry what place the gay world will hold for you. Perhaps you are on an evolving spiritual path, are HIV-positive and pondering what really counts in your life, or are in recovery and seeking new, more fulfilling ways to connect to others.

You may reside in a gay mecca neighborhood and have experienced hurt at the hands of the men you meet, never knowing just why. You may live in a rural county and ache for a community of even a few other men like yourself. Perhaps you have been puzzled at the seeming aimlessness of the cultural moment in your gay world, the sense that there is no "there" here, or have been wondering where the center of gravity is. At the core, whatever your story, maybe you simply don't find your values reflected, or your heart fully met, in the communities of men you encounter. Maybe you thought it was just you. It's not. You are not alone. All of us are asking what we can expect from our gay worlds, where the innovations and revolutions our people fought for have led us. Many of us strain to find meaning in the givens and habits long associated with our chosen queer cultures.

All of which makes it hard to believe that gay men are indeed architects of new forms of communal caretaking and intimacy, gentleness and bliss, when so many feel isolated, inadequate, and cynical. In short, if we're such a great group of guys, why are we so often mean to each other? What is *that* about? And whom does it serve? So if you've started to wonder "just what queer planet is he living on, anyway?" you've put your finger on the core quandary of gay male lives. Now we change directions, to lift a few rocks and see what wriggles out. We have no choice but to wrestle this contradiction to the ground if we are to give ourselves the shared lives we most deeply want.

"How can people be so cruel? Better to be kind . . ."
—Gerome Ragni and James Rado, lyric from *Hair*

Gay men may pass our weekdays nurturing best friends through breakups, carrying meal trays or stuffing envelopes, playing peacemaker and sensitive man, favorite uncle and supportive son, undertaking to beautify and heal the world, and caring for comrades. But when Saturday night rolls around, a fair number of us find ourselves in bars, wanting connection and finding only competition; in baths, seeking solace and finding only sex; in clubs, seeking affection and getting only attitude; or standing outside them all, wishing for inclusion, yet feeling excluded. If love stirs our private acts, it sometimes seems too little in evidence in our public institutions, rituals, and customs. For all the evidence that we manifest love in powerful ways in our private lives, our public habits often drip with distance. Look around in the clubs, bars, and baths; our media and advertisements; our recreations and relationships; our institutions and organizations; our politics and activism; our discourse and conversations; our icons and heroes.

Too often, we participate in a set of public practices that, if anything, work to *extinguish* those very values of love, care, compassion, and kindness, that move in our private relations. We collude in norms that say we must compete, that we cannot publicly embrace our most loving natures. Sex, while seemingly abundant, can often feel confusing or empty. Our quest for erotic authenticity has yielded cultural customs that often do violence to authenticity of emotions and tenderness.

As a result, we are often left hungry for intimacy. We too often raise attitude to an artform. When being hot is cool, being loving grows laughable. We feel bereft of tenderness. We learn to guard ourselves from others. We miss the simple touch of affection. We come to distrust other gay men and defend our hearts. Then we project and enact that with each other. That cycle plays out in our confusion in finding relationships, our longings for intimacy, how we handle sex and touch. Eventually, we may despair of ever finding anyone to love. We start grieving the intimacy we fear we'll never find.

So we turn on each other the tools we have long honed to keep a hostile world at bay. We draw lines around age, body, status, color, class, kink. We dismiss the circuit boys and party boys, deride chubby chasers and chicken hawks, dish this one and that one. We attack rather than affirm each other, suspect the worst, and stop even being able to see our best selves. "You know how gay men are," we say. "Dogs," we laugh. "Pigs," we proclaim. Not to be trusted. We elaborate a gay archetype, the Bitchy Queen, all tragic venom and sharp nails. We come to view fellow gay men as dangerous. We adopt behaviors that further sabotage intimacy.

Not surprisingly, we grow to feel betrayed by "community," and cynical about its possibilities. Lonely, alienated, disappointed, we dismiss the very word. Ask a hundred gay men to describe their feelings about "gay community," and you won't likely hear the word "caring." When researchers at the University of California recently did just that, they found that, at best, gay men view "community" as something someone else has. At worst, say men, it feels like a fraud. There is no such thing as "gay community," we say, nor can there be.[1]

Mention "gay community" among men of color and you hear about habits of racism, exclusion, objectification, and invisibility. Do so among young men, and you'll hear about being objectified, preyed upon, and ignored. Twenty-somethings swear there's no such thing; it's yesterday's social construction. Forty-somethings tell of feeling invisible, discarded, devalued. Lovers of kink feel marginalized and shamed. Trannies and sissyfags feel excluded from the tyranny of the butch. And most all of us feel inadequate on the beauty scale.

It is easy to regard the most visible, accessible practices and structures in gay communities—bars and baths, skin rags and substance use, A-lists and relentless body imagery—and feel anything but loved. In truth, there is no more universal wound in the queer male heart than the conviction that you have the wrong kind of body. Think how often that issue comes up in your own life, among your friends. It surfaces in countless HIV research papers and throughout gay oral histories. It arises in health findings that gay men suffer far higher levels of eating disorders than heterosexual men do, and in consumer studies that we are far more committed to "maximizing personal appearance."[2] It is brought up when we gather, often voiced by some of the most physically attractive men there, many of whom are objectively gorgeous, certifiably buff. It echoes in gay characters on TV and in films, plays, and books. The anxiety over beauty inadequacy is a relentless, ubiquitous *leitmotif* of gay male lives. Our customs almost scream: "If you don't feel inadequate, work on it!" It is a stunning way we keep each other, and ourselves, in our place.

This dreary refrain is one we have largely composed for ourselves. Most of us scan any gay magazine and feel anything but embraced. Over lunch recently, an editor friend told of meeting one of the cover boys gracing a recent cover of *HX* magazine, New York's bar rag of record. The cover had featured this white-underwear-clad muscle boy—call him Brandon, which is in fact his name. With ripped abs, killer smile, and youthful panache, Brandon was that week's *HX* heartthrob, lauded for his starring role on the covers of a set of dance-mix CDs. From the reportage, however, one might easily miss the fact that buff boy Brandon spent most of his time pursuing an advanced degree in poetic composition at Columbia University, and held a key policy job at City Hall. That part of him—hence of us—was not seen as worthy of more than a passing mention.

But hold on. Should the local bar rag devote its cover to a bespectacled grad student reading Ezra Pound? Not bloody likely. Yet Brandon's story does pose a larger question worth chewing on as we ponder gay lives. Examine our magazines and their advertisements, the travel posters and life insurance ads we read. Consider the art hanging on our walls, the coffee table books and holiday cards we give each other, the icons we revere, the films and cable shows we watch, our conversations over dinner. Peruse the décor at our stores and boutiques, the images at our watering holes and dance venues. How often we default to stressing only one of our syllables. In what newspapers but ours do dentists, opticians and chiropractors shed their shirts to woo clients? Can one imagine a married insurance broker pumping up in his muscle tee for his photo in the local Rotary Club newsletter? If you doubt the iconic cultural aspect of it all, wander down the gay aisle at your local bookstore. See those shirtless studmuffins entwined on the cover of Frank Browning's *The Culture of Desire*, and the naked buff boys in tasteful sepia luring you into Douglas Sadownick's thoughtful *Sex Between Men*? How about that midnineties gay bestseller whose central thesis was a critique of the supposed gay obsession with bodies, the cover of which displayed the author's pumped biceps in a just-too-tight black short-sleeved Calvin Klein tee? Then there was John Boswell's *Homosexuality, Christianity, and Social Tolerance*, a work breathtaking in its scholarship, written by one of the world's most eminent medievalists, a professor of history at Yale. Yet there, on the rear cover of the paperback edition, the author smiles, all boyish bare chest beneath a bright come-hither smile. A scholar with a fluent command of a dozen ancient languages, his shirt flapping open down to his abs.

Well, why not? Weren't we the ones to rewrite the rules to say you could be a famous classics professor *and* show pecs? Yay for our side! Big ideas and big arms, that's what we fought a revolution for, right? But somewhere along the way, we hardly noticed when this liberating erotic impulse came instead to construct and magnify a relentless mythos, one that suggests that we meet each other first below the belt, and only later elsewhere. We failed to note the nameless day, somewhere along the line, when that mythos morphed into a habit that has left us, well, just where we are.

When we promulgate a public culture that so relentlessly reveres one part of our shared selves—the part between neck and knees, ideally when it's smooth, blond, and under twenty-five—our wider gifts can fall into shadow. Do that often enough, and we fall out of the habit of looking for anything else. Collective amnesia sets in, and we start to forget that those other parts are there for us to know at all.

How easily we stop unwrapping the other gifts we offer others. We start to eclipse the parts of us that could open other ways of knowing, valuing, and being with each other. We lose sight of the other aspects of us to value and honor, to revere and discover. We forget how to access and feature them in ourselves, and how to support, celebrate, encourage them in each other. Who thinks even to ponder past the pecs to question what the Brandons of the world may offer when fully clothed? As we learn the habit of looking right past our poets, we grow deaf to each other's poetry. Adrift in a sea of skin, how easily we lose touch with the many ways we know to touch each other.

BODIES, BEAUTIES, AND BITCHY QUEENS

When gay men sit to discuss, the question often arises just how we came to our current juncture. Why this striking gap between the private values of our hearts and the public practices of our cultures?

We must first sketch some questions about how we got here, before we can follow the signs about where we go next. Let's start with the core topics of sex, beauty, and desire, for they are among the most charged of gay issues and hold a unique resonance in our lives. I will start by laying my own cards on the table. I participate, quite happily and unrepentantly, if inconsistently, in gym culture. Yes, I like working on my body, for all it brings in well-being, personal ease, and sociality, in the sexual economy, in health and strength. So I make no case either for or against any ideal of physical beauty, for or against one's right to embody, enjoy, or pursue it. If such a case needs making, I'm the last guy to do it.

Besides, we've all heard that case a few thousand times before. The turf of beauty and desire is the most-plowed corner of our communal domain. Grousing over the evils of "body culture" and "body fascism" has grown into the modern homo cottage industry. Scores of queer books have sought to dissect it (Frank Browning's *Culture of Desire*), decry it (Michelangelo Signorile's *Life Outside*), or defend it (Tom Bianchi's *In Defense of Beauty*). It is hard to find a view, pro or con, that has not been amply argued to death in magazine articles, workshops, heated meetings, public panels, and late-night chats among pals. Whether you hang with bears or buff boys, gym rats or geezers, your crowd likely shares a sound-bite on the subject of bodies. Your pals may sneer at mindless muscle men who "don't see beyond pecs and dicks" or roll their eyes at the terminal trolls who "don't get off their fat asses to take care of themselves." You may stand outside feeling excluded, inside feeling objectified, or somewhere in between. You may use language of self-esteem or invisibility or pride, feel envious, enraged, excluded, smug, empowered, resentful, anxious, or by turns all of the above.

But no matter where you fall, the topic has become one of the most predictable, even tedious, parts of our cultural performance as gay men. The discussion as currently conducted represents a complete dead end, with remarkably little new of interest being said or surfaced. The camps have been set up in the battlefield, the trenches dug, re-dug, and dug again, until only mud remains. Ask yourself: When was the last time those discussions unearthed something new and interesting for you? When did they last inspire anything beyond complaint, resentment, or pessimism? When have they opened for you a productive or stirring vision for us to embrace with each other?

We have sewn ourselves into a boring body bag, and it's time we clawed our way out. We owe each other better than the muscles-bad/muscles-good blah-blah-blah, the invisibility-objectification-body-fascist focus of the common chatter. Such easy dichotomies mislead and simplify. They are a red herring, simply another invitation to damage and deride each other. We crave some new thinking on how we handle the issue of beauty and bodies in our lives if we are to move beyond this stalemate.

It seems a first principle that diverse standards of beauty and attraction are our birthright. That is what we fought—and still fight—our queer revolution for. Big muscles or none, testostero-man or tranny, we all came to this parade marching under the standard of libido libertarians. The platform of this particular fringe party of libertarians—OK, it's nonexistent, just work with me here—is to defend our right to pursue our happiness, whether affectional, aesthetic, somatic, or erotic. That means we judge each other's attractions at our peril. We skate on thin ice when we create stigma and draw lines around those who are choosing their erotic path. It is risky for us to wag fingers at each other's yearnings, just as it is when Jesse Helms does so, albeit in different ways.

As a corollary, we could agree that we each have an inalienable right to pursue and develop our ideal body, no matter if it looks like Paul Bunyan, Paul Lynde, or RuPaul. Ideally, to inhabit it as best we wish to, to see what that feels like. You get to like who you want, and look how you choose—hold the guilt, nix the PC mandate. In our individual pursuits of happiness, may we get to disport ourselves with that ideal as often as can be, provided we're willing, they're willing, and we all still manage to get the laundry done and the dog walked.

Second, note the ways we ferociously map cultural ideas onto our bodies. You may be a gymrat aspiring to a 44-inch chest and 5 percent bodyfat or a "gainer" looking to reach 300 pounds, or simply sport a tasteful nipple ring. Boytoys and bears both embody a social aesthetic in beauty's name. In that, they are like the African tribespeople with earlobes and lips distended, or Native American infants with their heads bound on flattening boards. But in our case, the natives may have teased, shaved, pumped, Naired, bleached, cut, rippled, waxed, muscled, inked, injected, groomed, pierced, and plucked ourselves into a (pretty) pickle.

Our fierce cultural devotion to mapping beauty onto bodies has made it easy to miss what was being engraved on our hearts. Whether you jump for gym boys or chase chubbies, the beliefs we share about beauty and bodies work to *help us erect barriers between each other*. They have become the single most fertile domain where we enact difference and distance. Looks are the first place we dismiss, devalue, diminish, and disrespect one another. They are the prime site where we damage each other's beings, hopes, and desires. But as we do, we damage our own. Perhaps the more apt cultural comparison is not with those Andeans and African natives, but with foot-bound Asian maidens, the Victorian ladies in their tight corsets and unwieldy bustles, modern women jammed into stiletto heels. As other genders in other generations did, we have clothed ourselves in habits that leave our breathing constricted with each other, wobbly on our feet, bodies unfree. We chafe against our too-tight garments even as we don them.

Body is never just metaphor for culture, yet never not. In our case, we came to this idea of a collective, these worlds of men, in search of something male, warm, and fuzzy. Yet we have built ourselves into men hard and smooth. In body and heart both, the parts of us once supple with each other have become sculpted for each other. Muscle is gay culture's embodied metaphor. But if it is one thing to contour our bodies, it is another to constrain our hearts, and still worse not to grasp the connections. Most important of all is the knowledge that these aren't the only two options.

Body and beauty are powerful drugs for a clan of males suckled on inadequacy, raised on ridicule, and dieted on derogation. Collectively and individually, we have worked to feel different in our skin than once we did. That we can is progress. But how many of us feel vaguely different, as well, from what we might hope to feel with our fellows? In our symbols and our very flesh, the reviled sissy boys we might have been are long gone. Yet how keenly do the men we have become ache to touch the hearts of the boys we once were?

> *Yet each man kills the thing he loves,*
> *By each let this be heard,*
> *Some do it with a bitter look,*
> *Some with a flattering word.*
> —Oscar Wilde

> *These men who think it's high art to channel Oscar Wilde or Bette Davis or some* Melrose Place *diva or any one of the hundreds of icons of bitchiness our culture offers—so many gay men think that in the name of wit, if the result is a laugh, it's o.k. for them to lacerate others with their verbal swords simply because they possess the ability. No! Bitchiness hurts.*
> —Tobias Aldrich, in *Speaking Out*[3]

There is a second, distinctly gay, cultural habit that contributes to distance and wounding. It is one we know intimately, yet note rarely. I refer to that most familiar fag consort, her Majesty the Bitchy Queen. Queer men go way back with this dame. She has been with us since before gay men became a social species. Long before men like us began viewing themselves as a species apart, she was there. Oscar Wilde was channeling Bitchy Queen fifty years before gay meant anything but fun. For a century now, she has haunted queer lives like a vampire, reincarnating in each generation, perpetually undead. She is Oscar Wilde and Noël Coward and Boy George, she stars in *The Boys in the Band, Torch Song Trilogy, In Living Color, La Cage aux Folles, Will and Grace* and *Queer as Folk;* she inhabits Miss Thing and fierce divas, shade and attitude.

At a recent gathering of thirty men in Providence, Rhode Island, we took time to have an intimate encounter with the she-bitch within. First, we listed some of her attributes: mean, cynical, vindictive, superior, asexual, tragic, angry, shaming, malicious, hurtful, defended, oppressing, emasculating, pathetic, damaged, predatory. "Not so fast," some protested. "This character is not so simple as all that." The Bitchy Queen is also powerful, precisely what makes it such a resilient archetype. It protects and defends. "My fierce tongue was all that kept me alive," says Larry, who grew up in Detroit's rougher black neighborhoods. It also tells truths, deflates pomposity. It wields great power, and often defends the ramparts of queer. The Queen can be funny, caustic, worldly, and smart, equal parts camp, catty, and cutthroat.

As we step back to examine this long list of adjectives, a light dawns. We all clearly know this tart-tongued, trash-talking persona very well. Jason, a Wisconsin twenty-two-year-old, pipes up: "You know, even coming out, I definitely knew that was the one thing I needed to know to be a successful gay guy." The point is not that the Bitchy Queen is all we do, nor that we channel this all the time. But that no matter what else we know how to do, however else we know how to perform gay, we know how to enact her. The proof comes when I ask the room to name any other archetype whom we can flesh out so thoroughly. There isn't. It is, apparently, the single most familiar and richly elaborated gay persona we share. Think about that.

I try not to be an evil queen, but sometimes you have to.
—Boy George

What does it mean, here, to "have to"? The Queen is a role written for us to play, one we are taught to perform with each other. If you doubt its link with gay performance, think how inconceivable such a portrayal would be in a pro athlete's locker room interview, a business leader's boardroom, or a politician's stump speech. No, she is the ultimate fag hag, hovering in the background wherever we gather, ready to material-ize among us at a moment's notice. This character is relegated to our cor-ner of masculinity, handed to us, enacted by us, perpetuated by us, inflicted by us on us.

A quick show of hands in the room: Who among us has felt the Bitchy Queen's barbed sting? Every hand lifts. How many of us have *channeled* it? Again, a clear majority. Now the clincher: How many here have ever found ourselves channeling this role reflexively by habit, as "wit"? For that matter, how many have ever winced at what came out, wished we hadn't gone there? An uncomfortable stir as hands rise tentatively. The discussion has moved to deeper water. Although the Bitchy Queen is as much a part of gay male mythos as brunch, the thought dawns that it is no persona of our true heart's devising. It is a default social category bequeathed to us by historical gay habit. It is a part we play by tradition, a vestige of another time. We may still construct, enact, and transmit this archetype. But just who chose this as our mascot, anyway? Do we even ask if its creators are still in the room, or if they left long ago? Today, this Queen is often amplified and reiterated by the dominant straight culture, where she plays the role of an exotic amusement— a minstrel. Yet what is entertainment for them is for us a lived social habit. It is we who enact her, we whose hearts she shreds, and we who take those poisoned arrows in the name of fun.

Regard this ugly dowager up close. Beneath her thick pancake and bravado, she lives in pain and inflicts it. She traffics in hurt, denigration, and mockery. The tools of this one's trade are humiliation cloaked in humor wrapped in ridicule. Is this really what we need now? The next time this apparition appears, we might ask if it serves, or sabotages, our intimacies? Does this performance build trust or shatter it? We are the only men who have reflexively come to reprise a feminine archetype as a cultural habit. What does that convey about our view of us as men? Or about the women we care about?

How easily each queer generation takes this role into its midst anew, largely unexamined, mindless of its dark powers. But whom does it serve? How do we use her? How does she use us? Is this the most useful archetype for you to blindly enact with your friends, unexamined, all in the name of good fun? If not, what would you choose to do with it? It is not clear that the Queen should be laid to her final rest. Dave Abbott, in that room in Providence, put it best: "Sometimes I want to wear the Queen. That can be fun and powerful. But I don't want this to be the only gown I have to put on. I need other gowns in my closet." We are the couturiers of our common culture. Set up the house, garçon: New gowns for all.

THE QUEEN IS DEAD, LONG LIVE THE QUEEN

After a century, this Queen may need a rest. At the very least, she—and we—deserve some more diverse company, a few other equally resonant personalities that we may know as intimately and deeply as we know her. Can we invent other archetypes to open fresh ways of being with and for each other? Surely there are more nurturant, sustaining roles we could find, archetypes more congruent with all that our people have become. New roles will help us put flesh on these queer bones in new ways for a new millennium. Can we invent a persona that less echoes what we once were, and more invites us to what we might be? In the words of Rodney Simard, an English professor: "Bitchiness and wit are not the same. In any case, cultivate the most valuable verbal abilities, appropriate and sincere compliments and apologies."[4]

Tomorrow new generations of men like us will arise. We can bequeath them a new entity, one reflecting habits of affirmation and affection. We can cultivate a persona where generosity reigns, whose dramatic flair flows from inclusion and generosity, and whose sharp wit helps delight, not damage. Who then will we be channeling? We don't even know what such an archetype will look like. All we know is that when it is that bright being who is our consort on Saturday nights, our time together will feel very different. It is our joyous work to create that radiant apparition. Only then can we get down to the far more serious task of deciding what in heaven's name it will wear.

The Bitchy Queen has a cousin once removed, Cynicism. It should be understood here, not simply as being jaded or worldly, but in a broader philosophical sense. It is the deep knowledge that things are not what they seem, so cannot be fully trusted. It plays a similarly special and complex relationship in gay lives and operates in quite distinctive and powerful ways among us.

No people knows cynicism better than we do, because we inherit cynicism as our queer birthright. It gets bred in our bones by the closet. Growing up, every gay boy feels in his soul that uneasy rupture between appearance and reality that is the very core of cynicism. Our very hearts remind us things are not always what they seem. To feel what you can't be, want what you can't name, say what you don't feel—each day we spend closeted provides a daily catechism in cynicism. We learn early on about subtexts and illusions, feints and postures. In our marrow, we feel a schism of hope and heart, a rift between what is felt and what is performed.

At the same time, it keeps us ever on guard. We learn early to hide and keep secrets that protect ourselves and that distance others. Like children of abusive alcoholic parents, we master a great acuity in reading cues. We grow hyper-vigilant for any clue to suggest dissembling or disguise, each premonition of pretense, even a shadow of sham. We have to as a matter of survival, and it is extraordinarily adaptive for us. It helps us sense danger, physical, emotional, and social. Equally important, it lets us find other beings like ourselves, who live in split-level souls. We must read so closely if we are to find our soul mates. Those once canny enough to wear green when the world sees just Thursday; he of the just-vague pronouns and the just-lingering eyes, the one who drives that SUV with the discreet rainbow decal. The closet ensures that cynicism is *the* queer occupational hazard.

How then can we be surprised when it pervades our emotional habits as adults? Think how many chosen queer cultural customs reenact patterns of cynicism. Cynicism as a performance style underlies our fabled arch repartee—the compliment as barb. Nice words aren't what they seem, presto-chango, beware trust. Bearding, passing, the closet, all are exercises in existential cynicism. The tactic of outing shrieks with cynicism, using bigotry's flame to singe souls in the name of liberation. "Being out is so good, it hurts"—there's a cynical appeal. Our celebrated cultural traditions of camp, drag, and genderfuck are cynicism applied to gender and raised to art. Nothing is what it seems. Trust at your own peril.

More dangerously, the Cynic shadows our lives with each other, inflicting damage both subtle and corrosive. Knowing our own hearts aren't what they seem, we wonder if anyone's can be. No wonder it is so easy to distrust, so hard to trust. We replay and induce cynicism throughout many of our cultural practices. It happens when we use phone lines where we cut others off in mid-word with the "#" key, without so much as a goodbye. It occurs when we lie in chat rooms. And in bars, where we hunker inaccessible along the walls. The travails of tricking itself can induce emotional cynicism and guardedness. There's cynicism in that bit of gay socio-sexual politesse that some feel allows them to treat last week's trick as next week's stranger. Most of us have felt the curtain of postcoital awkwardness descend as the morning's veneer clicks back into place over a moment's vulnerability. As a Long Beach bodybuilder was overheard to observe: "One thing gay men do that straight people don't, is we accelerate the whole dating process. It's not about dating, it's about jumping into a relationship, immediate gratification. I'm over it." Cynicism is infused when we lament how "He gave me his number but never phoned," or tell friends, "We were dating, then he dropped me cold, without even a reason." In each, the culturally sanctioned content is: "Act as if you don't care. Nothing is what it seems."

Cynicism is even woven through the quintessential queer custom of cruising. From glances to gaydar, lingering stares to winks, we have put eyes at the center of queer male cruising convention. Our cultures have wrought an unparalleled cultural vocabulary of eye contact. We have given eyes their own powerful language, its rituals and conventions, which we practice on, use with, and teach to each other. While much good comes of it, the habit also brings its unseen effects. We rarely think how using our eyes to open sexual doors can close others. For example, when we don't care to signal sexual interest, we learn to avoid another's eyes, to not send the wrong message. We fall out of the habit of meeting others' eyes in friendship. We crowd our bars, our parties and street corners, with men who don't meet each other's eyes, don't invite one another in, save for one reason. When that becomes our norm, contact and friendliness, openness, and warmth suffer. So we start to experience those spaces as full of attitude, rejection, distance, invisibility. And so the cycle of cynicism begins afresh. It is not surprising that one researcher studying well-being in gay men's lives finds it "significantly higher . . . in individuals with high levels of non-sexualized participation." The findings, he writes, "also suggest [that] sexualized interactions may relate negatively with gay men's sense of wellness."[5]

Who among us has not experienced that convention of queer eye culture when, during a conversation, the man you are speaking with keeps darting his eyes over your shoulder? Again, it is an element in our culture's permitted politesse of pick-ups. Somehow, most of us manage not to do this when talking with our mother, boss, or parish priest. But with each other, we weave distraction into the complex conventions of our cruising culture, for better or worse. Subtly it signifies. It may convey: "I'm not fully here with you." Or "You don't merit my full attention." It may suggest: "You can be replaced, at a moment's notice, by something hotter." Or "I can't help myself. This is how we all are, isn't it?" When even our gaze is unsteady, what does it promise of our hearts?

These examples don't suggest we're bad, shallow, or thoughtless. We're not. They simply call us to mind the countless cultural choices we make together, all of which have quiet consequences. In the ways above, and more, we teach each other lessons of cynicism that none of us came here to learn. The ways we use our bodies, our eyes, our intimacies, comprise a hundred little habits we adopt that work to subtly derail our hearts. They combine to convey a very male moral: Don't open up or invest with each other. "Love is not what it seems." "Guard your heart." So in a hundred ways we offer cynicism a seat among us, and in a hundred ways prepare the very feast that starves us.

Some argue that these habits of distance and divide come with the terrain of maledom, as the inevitable cost of our gender. "Men are like that" is an argument you hear often, but a moment's thought reveals why we shouldn't buy it. To accept this convenient gender essentialism misses the Big Point. We are a group of men who have already rewritten many of the deepest cultural rules of our gender in mighty and powerful ways. We have seen that we break the mold in scores of ways around male violence, male caretaking, male roles with women, male community, male sex and intimacy, male friendship and families. So why would we imagine that our own social patterns are etched immutably in our male chromosomes? Why on earth would our interpersonal modes of interaction be the *one* place we fall back on our gender as an excuse? Why should this be that one wall we cannot scale? Whom does that assumption serve? It ignores the many ways we daily remake maledom, runs counter to fact, and sells us massively short. Most of all, it leaves us stuck in place.

We could instead entertain another possibility. Simply, that we have not devoted enough of our energies to consciously crafting customs of nurture, affirmation, and affection in our shared culture. We can close the gap between our private values and public habits. We can do better with each other, if only we care to.

When we enact customs that reflect cynicism on each other and back on ourselves, we strangle hope. While that might be true for any social group, it has a uniquely toxic effect on us. Because when you think on it, *we only ever got this far through hope*. There is no less cynical, more hopeful, act than the coming out which first brought us to this idea of community. Of all people, gay men should by rights find cynicism the most unnatural of acts. Our very dream of a life together was forged in a furnace of hope. A preposterous hope was your heart's native reply to a society that said you couldn't have happiness, couldn't follow your heart, couldn't enjoy love. Without the unreasonable hope that life could be better, none of us would be here. Only through sheer giddy hope did any of us leave the familiarity of home and family to seek a world of affection among men. It was in hope's green currency that we all paid our dues to get here. Whenever and however it occurred for you, hope fueled all of us to defy the odds, jump the hurdles, hop the bus, and sass the system. Otherwise, Tiger, we'd all still be living married in Duluth.

Yet we have wedged ourselves into a terrible irony. The very community we sought out once in hope teaches instead a killing cynicism. As Franklin, a gay African-American teacher in Chicago, sees it: "The kids come here on the bus from Peoria, and in six months they've got calluses on their hearts." Not only does that hurt our individual hopes, it has a collective cost. To a tribe so *primarily bonded* by hope as ours is, cynicism is a terminal social disease. Its symptoms are alienation, anger, and anomie. We transmit it by our social habits. Cynicism is our smallpox; we infect each other with it, in an act of tribal suicide. By strangling our shared hopes for each other, we will cease to exist. What an irony if it turns out just when we got used to thinking of saving each other's lives as a medical problem, that meaningful emotional and cultural survival may be as much a matter of affection as infection. Perhaps we need to look not just to our virologists to save us, but to our visionaries. Which is to say, to ourselves.

Most guys affect attitude because they think it's attractive. But attitude is never attractive. Get over it.
    —Mitchell Gaynor, gardener

A lot of guys use attitude against overly aggressive types. If you don't like others' attitude, ask yourself how often you have come on so strong that you have made others' attitude go up?
    —Patrick Browne, M.D.

Accept that I might want your friendship, your advice, and your mentorship without wanting you to fuck me. And don't take that as an insult.
    —John Solsberg

Teach me how to set limits and respect boundaries, not how to suck cock.
    —Mark, 21

Remember, when you tear someone to shreds, it hurts. Try to remember the time in history when you didn't fit in.
    —Richard Brendon, counselor for the deaf

Don't treat your trick like a trick.
    —Slugger, retired party boy

As these men's words suggest, we are both the subject and the object of our malaise, as often perpetrators as victims. It is far easier to moan over invisibility, body culture, ageism, racism, and looks-ism than to honestly ask ourselves and each other who it is *we* cruise first at the bar. Who and how do *you* invite, and ignore? Have you ever channeled the Bitch at the cost of a brother's fragile heart? Avoided someone's eyes to scorn their interest? Have you ever ended a relationship badly, failed to communicate, carried sorrow for some way you have treated a gay mate? Of course you have. We all have. We all participate in the very patterns that hurt us.

For the record, the hurt runs both ways on the beauty continuum. For every wallflower wondering if he will ever be loved, there is a muscle god wondering if he can trust the men who seek his body. For every sixty-year-old feeling invisible and discarded, a twenty-year-old feels preyed on and confused. For each of us standing frozen before an unapproachable idol, an idol stands alone, wondering why nobody approaches. Our hearts hurt in a thousand ways in equal and opposite universes, spinning in polar rotations around the axis of desire.

Few of us have clean hands. Most of us collude in customs of body and beauty, distance and dismissal, in ways that sabotage the very things we seek. We readily mine the mother lode of injury and grievance, but rarely take time to pan for the golden nuggets of spirit. It is a cultural habit that most of us can more easily tell how we've been done wrong than ask for what it is we most desire from each other. We far more easily rail how "gay men" are hurtful and unfeeling than gently ask each other how we might do better with and for each other.

Until we get as easy with the second discussion as with the first, things won't change. Our individual lives won't feel better in the ways we wish they would. I doubt there is a gay man alive—from wallflower troll to A-list beauty—for whom this collusion works in the long run. Who among us would not like to reclaim the impulse of love that brought us together to each other, to this ideal of beloved community, in the first place? I know of none who would not prefer to increase his measure of tenderness, if he knew how. Who better to stand up for our nameless, improbable hopes with each other, than each other?

The culture—our own queer one as well as the larger society's—encourages us to quickly dismiss such sentiment as hopelessly naïve. *Of course it does*. Yet look with your own eyes, and you see abundant clues all around us. Consider the Gay Vacation Syndrome. That's when you see the same guy daily on the bus or at the store or bar and pass for years without so much as a grunt, but meet on a mostly straight tour bus in Machu Picchu, and you're sisters for life. Likewise that man you "know" would never give you the time of day back home, greets you with a smile when you bump into him in P-Town or Palm Springs. Even on Fire Island, that reputed ground zero of attitude, one longtime regular named Danny recalls a recent weekend where a storm cut power to the island for a day: "It was amazing. For twenty-four hours, everyone was relaxed, chatty. They ran the disco on a portable generator, with one speaker, one turntable, and one flickering chandelier. But all the guys were having the best time, laughing, all in it together. Anyone you bumped into would swap stories. The distance stuff died with the power supply, but when the juice came back on, so did the attitude."

Carlos tells a similar story about being out on the Castro's streets after a significant earthquake a few years back: "Everyone was out helping each other. Guys who'd never give each other the time of day were all cracking open beer and trading stories together. We ought to have an earthquake every day." We all have stories of when, freed of the constraints of our cultural habits, we default to an easier mode of connection. Each such tale holds a clue about our hearts. They suggest that our distances and defenses are learned habits, something we may perform but may not prefer. Perhaps, like our friend the Queen, they are habits we channel unwittingly.

Or consider the ways we frame the use of drugs in gay lives. We so easily condemn the ways gay men meet over alcohol, dance under drugs, socialize around substances. We all can repeat a vehement, ubiquitous analysis of the culture of clubs, the rates of abuse, the prevalence of problems, the drug scourge *du jour,* the value of recovery. But how rarely we stop to celebrate and nurture the fragile impulse that flickers beneath. The point is not to defend or deride, but to seek the impulse behind the image. A moment's reflection says that when we down drinks to lower barriers with each another, it's because we seek fewer barriers. When we swallow Ecstasy to make it easier to engage each other, it's because we crave that engagement. Snorting chemicals to help us embrace on the dance floor bespeaks the impulse to embrace. The ways we use and abuse substances—to be more open in sex, swing wide jammed emotional doors, feel more included or intimate—can be read, at least in part, as a seeking for openness, emotionality, and inclusion. As one young man put it: "The drugs shortcut the socialization process . . . you drop your social guards, enabling you to approach a total stranger in a loving and caring way."[6] Listen through his words and you hear that camaraderie that is the drug of choice here, chemistry but a means to its end.

So . . . might we not approach it more directly? What if gay party venues devoted as much infrastructure to providing forms of friendliness and fraternity as they do to forms of pharmacology? What if these events came to be widely understood as mass experiments in brotherhood and welcome? What if you were greeted on arrival, supported throughout, and nurtured at the end? Now that would be your basic mind-altering experience. The driving wish here is so plain and sweet: to touch, connect, engage, be open with one's fellows. That is the key moral here about our heart's desires, if we just see it.

We have grown out of the habit of naming that impulse. But once we do, we face a choice. We can adopt the scowling mien of medicine and public health, the finger-wagging of social science and social rule that criticizes and condemns our acts, and by extension, ourselves. Or we can apply our own uncommon and generous gay genius to the topic. We could instead seize this as an opportunity to mobilize our queer capacities of compassion and heart and celebrate the tender impulses that stir our mates' hearts. Why not recognize the wish, revere the impulse, and invent new ways to meet it? In substance, as in sex, as in so much of what we do with each other, if we better saw the heart that beats beneath our habits, we might gently coax out our private wishes into our public practices.

These familiar storylines of substances and of sex are just two of the ways we face an opportunity—to write a plotline of pathology or one of promise. We choose which view we will narrate, and thus magnify in our lives, and which we will embody in our practices with each other. But one script deadens and distances us, makes of us less with each other, while the other opens onto a more nurturant and expansive life together.

Just as there is much we do through our own actions and choices, we need to recognize one central element that pulses all around us, and contributes to our queer conundrum. We need to grapple with the corrosive ways that economic forces conspire with and shape our own cultural habits. Capitalism is completely interwoven in most of the ways gay men now connect. If you seek to attract certain men, you pay a gym or trainer to acquire the body; you pay one salon for the right shade of tan, another for a desirable pattern of body hair; the dentist for the teeth; the optician for the eyewear; the nutrition shop for the supplements; the clothier for the bathing suit and designer T-shirt; the realtor or the cruise line for the right to be among them to begin with.

Likewise, shared fraternity now comes with a fee. If you want to hang with friends, you pay a bar or club. If you want to flirt or cruise, you pay AOL. If you want to have sex, you pay a sex club, bathhouse, or phone line. If you want to do it alone, you pay the video rental or phone line. We have developed a set of cultural customs that levy a toll on touch. If you seek it, you can buy a massage, a touch experience weekend, a healer, or a hustler. You pay to dance at a circuit party or dance venue. In the "market" for a mate, or "shopping for a husband"? Pay a video dating or matchmaking service, or pay a newspaper or website to place a personal ad.

When profit wedges itself between pals, we all pay the toll. The simple act of brother meeting brother has been mercantilized. Scott Perret, a writer and director, captures this dynamic very well: "A person has many layers. In the late twentieth century, we tend to focus on the retail layer. We have all been trained to look at, look for, certain appearances. We test each person's ability to mimic the images advertisers create to inspire longing in us all. We toss aside so many hearts this way. Another J. Crew casualty. It has not stopped at the clothes. Advertisers sell mood, longing, image, so that our very faces and bodies have become subject to retail analysis. Impatiently, we thrash through the piles of people we see, looking for the one that will at once enflame and quell our desires as deftly and exactly as that Calvin Klein underwear print ad."[7]

There is no lack of commentary on this topic. All of us can think personally about the hidden costs *you* notice when your meeting becomes mediated, when mating becomes mercantile, commodities replace communities. Gay men are hardly unique in this. It is, some sigh, the inevitable cost of living as a subculture in a capitalist world. We cannot expect immunity from the results of capitalism, nor expect to dismantle it. As one essay put it: "As soon as the L & G community is 'known,' it becomes a new territory for global capital to exploit. As soon as its codes are cracked, its images are easily appropriated by those with different political agendas."[8]

There are no easy answers here, but two ideas are worth thinking on. First, we shouldn't be shocked when such structures don't meet our hearts' needs. They weren't ever meant to. They were invented to create markets from our lives. They exist to permit third parties to profit by our interactions. When affectionate meeting is mediated by moneymaking third parties, the dictates driving it are theirs, not ours.

Second, we can easily rail about the fact that our communities have become a market niche, an idea you heard so frequently these days that it has entered the realm of proverb. But that is not our only option. We can say no to niche-itude by creating alternatives. Just as we have evolved a thousand other novel social rules, we can craft some other structures and practices with each other, practices that offer alternatives to a steely mercantilism at their core. There is no reason that men, tired of eating dinner alone in restaurants they are hard-pressed to afford, cannot create a dining cooperative where, on a random Tuesday night, you could go and expect to prepare a common meal. Those who don't cook, clean. All enjoy. We could equally well institute a social practice of queer massage cooperatives where we could go and expect to give, receive, and learn touch as a cooperative venture with our fellows—nonsexually or sexually. We could have free and open discussion groups about our values, the ethics we seek to embody with each other. We could craft the same richness of social options, but do so in ways that require a different kind of investment, opening not just wallets but hearts and minds.

Obviously we do that in a lot of ways already. There is no reason, for example, you have to buy touch. Body Electric has spawned sensual massage circles in various cities; many open-air sex venues cost nothing. But these are just the start of the ways we could develop alternatives to the ways we now pay third parties so we can be touched. Can we conceive what a cooperative, secure, and free sex club would even look like? We could sponsor free salons as friendly sexual mentoring venues to teach each other what we know so well. Would you attend an evening, say, of accomplished and experienced tops and bottoms offering best tips on how to fully enjoy anal sex or give the perfect blow job? How about skilled players teaching how to use bondage safely and creatively or divulging the ten simple tips for sublime tit play? Again, some sexual mentoring work occurs now in the world of HIV prevention, gay men's health, and S/M. But far more could exist. All could offer both an opportunity and an emblem of our cooperation and connection.

What if you knew you could stroll down the street in any gay neighborhood and find such cooperative environments as freely available as bars and sex clubs and rainbow flag shops? Might we not decide to create and enact these sorts of practices, to complement the range now available to us through purely commercial structures? It is a powerful thing, to open our imaginations to ways that we can all relate to more directly, without money mediating and intervening, and hence setting the terms of engagement. That work, and this book, are part of a larger project to help men brainstorm and create all manner of new institutions and practices to enjoy with each other. Such attempts open our minds to new ways of being with each other.

There is no end to the mischief we can dream up to line each other's lives with love, if we but set our minds to it.

We must love one another, or die.
   —W. H. Auden

We began here by pondering the paradox: If we are such a tribe of loving men, why have we built a public culture that smothers the revolutionary love that called us to each other in the first place? Whom does that serve? We have moved to the core question of whether the world we've crafted is the one we most want to enjoy with one another. If, as the previous pages suggest, our gay spheres have evolved unique habits, distinctive forms that operate differently, we must not forget that they were largely crafted by us. Nobody handed us the queer lives we enjoy. We hewed them from the hard rock of a homophobic world. Clearly, inventing a new future is a task we know how to do.

After all, consider how often we have invented new futures before. We did it in American cities after World War II. We invented a new kind of queer future with the Mattachine Society and the Stonewall Rebellion.

We do it anew with each legal challenge and each art and cultural statement. Personally, we invent a new future for ourselves each time we come out. The men who moved to mecca neighborhoods and those connected to rural queer networks, those who live in vogueing houses and Fire Island houses, who camp with the Faeries or camp in drag, all are pioneering new forms of a future with each other. In the last two decades, we drastically reinvented our sexual, volunteer, and caregiving cultures around AIDS.

This is work we know well. One of our deepest culturally ingrained habits is to constantly be inventing new ways to be together, keeping an eye out, cueing off each other, trying to understand who we are with each other and, through that, to find meaning, connection, fun, love. As we have seen, we do that bonding and connecting in powerful and unprecedented ways already. Today we are challenged to use those talents in new ways. We are blessed to have a shared queer society which is uncommonly self-created, and which grants an exceptional permission to innovate. We have, in recent times, taken it as our challenge to be out in a society that says we shouldn't exist, and to be freely sexual in a society that takes a dim view of sex. For some thirty years, this has led to a discourse of rights and entitlements, our action focused outward to power. We have stood in a circle and spoken outward to "them." It has been necessary, productive work, the path of heroes.

Now we are called to a new kind of work with each other. It is a moment to turn to face each other, the challenge to meet each other's eyes more fully across this charmed circle we have formed. We can remind ourselves, in word and deed, of some truths we have long known, but often forgotten. *At this millennial moment in culture, gay men's truly radical act is no longer simply to claim our sexuality, but to reclaim our hearts within it.*

This phase of work must happen among us. As gay men built our culture, we can reshape it. We need not accept cultural rules that we must compete and deride, that attitude serves us better than affection, that we endanger one another or cannot publicly embrace our most loving natures. We can transcend those lies, as we have transcended others. We have already rewritten the rules of men in enormous and sweeping ways. Our current challenge is to dismantle another set of givens, all the more potent because we ourselves imposed them. We can shift the discourses around beauty and body; channel new archetypes, create new language, and adopt new habits and rituals. It has been said that: "You are never given a wish without also being given the power to make it come true." We are our own wish, and our own power, and they are the same: to stop impeding love and start manifesting it.

We are caught between the world that created us and a future we have yet to create.
 —Vinita Srivastava

Much proof shows that we are already doing many magnificent things—that is our story, half-told. Now our challenge is to bring the love that moves in our private relationships into full radiance in our common culture. That is our world, half-made. We have a chance to remove the shroud around our better souls, celebrate our highest natures, and proclaim fully what it is we are already doing—those acts of heart we now commit when we don't think the world is watching.

As the evidence shows, we do this in many uncommon and remarkable ways already. What we don't do so easily is recognize it. That suggests we face an archeological task, less to instill these values from scratch than to unveil those already there. Metaphorically, ours is a whole population poised to move to a new quantum level of love. Now our work is to magnify our best impulses into common practice. We have a unique potential to create a public sphere whose norms and traditions radiate the most transformational values we enact in private.

That project starts with some questions. We must ask with open hearts if some of our accustomed institutions are vestigial, perhaps more helpful at an earlier stage of our cultural evolution than they are now. For example, are bars the best default institution we would choose for ourselves now? What other forms can our meeting places take? Are our learned behaviors in such gathering places the ones that most nourish us? Do you find that our public media and discourse with each other speak to your values? Are the ways you spend your time and money with other gay men the most satisfying? Can we see parts of our stories we could tell differently for a change? Think about the ways we connect with each other. Are the relationships we have names for the only ones we want to have? Do they bring you the riches you hoped for? How well do your sexual and social habits work for you? In short, how well do our cultural practices meet the values of our hearts? Where they fall short, what can we envision and invent to replace them?

Framing these questions is the start of reframing our lives. It is possible to take public the parts of ourselves that evidence suggests we practice so abundantly in private. As we will see in the closing pages, there are concrete steps we can devise to help our worlds of men more fully embrace this vision of ourselves. We can conduct our *public* lives and fashion a *public* culture as though we trusted this part of our natures. What shape does that take next Tuesday in the chat room? Or Saturday night at the bar? How does it look with a trick? With your boyfriend? With someone *else's* boyfriend? Clearly the answers are complex and layered. At this phase of the project, the first step is to begin asking each other these questions in new ways.

People can tolerate two homosexuals they see leaving together, but if the next day they're smiling, holding hands, tenderly embracing each other, then they cannot be forgiven. It is not the departure for pleasure that is unacceptable, it is waking up happy.
    —Michel Foucault

That's the real question, isn't it? Just how do we wake up happy? This is the next step of our collective hero's journey, to subvert cynicism and manifest love. Simply, that is, to learn again to be each other's best hope and more fully inhabit the hearts we have been given. Only by living in a brotherhood of men that unabashedly manifests our love for each other can we fully manifest our deepest gifts to culture.

10 | MEN FOR A NEW MILLENNIUM

While they are boys, they are fond of men,
and enjoy lying with them and embracing them,
and these are the best of boys because they are naturally bravest.
Some call them shameless, but that is false;
no shamelessness makes them do this, but boldness and courage
*   and a manly force. . . .*
Here is a great proof: When they grow up, such as these alone are
*   men in public affairs.*
    —Plato, *Symposium*, 193

We have seen that over the last three decades, worlds of self-identified gay men have quietly launched a series of unstructured social experiments. But if Plato was right, and we are the best of boys and the bravest of men, we remain largely unaware of it. We have been helped to neglect the meanings of the behaviors we see all around us, and to disregard the ways our lives differ. So we often remain blind to the larger purpose of what we as a people are enmeshed in.

How can we best understand the meaning of the practices queer male communities have evolved? What is behind this spontaneously occurring social evolution in which so many of us participate unaware? Why have widespread subcultures of men adopted communal customs reflecting some of the highest aspirations of ethical teachings, many of which stand in such marked contrast to the dominant cultural habits of men in the larger culture? Just what is going on here?

If the day is coming when Love is at last to take its rightful place as the binding and directing force of society . . . and society is to be transmuted in consequence to a higher form, then undoubtedly . . . the Uranians {a nineteenth-century term for gay men} will have an important part to play in the transformation.

　　—Edward Carpenter, British social philosopher

The most intriguing possibilities are the big ones, namely that the cultural changes are just the tip of a far larger iceberg. These differences might best be understood as evidence for a natively occurring, non-formalized, mass spiritual reformation. In many cultures, gender-variant men like us have long been viewed as channeling beauty, ritual, and myth into culture. In fact, this tribal work may go far deeper. We may channel a kind of love into culture, a love beyond *eros* to *agape*, a radically transformational form of social communal relation. It is precisely that sort of love made manifest in the wide variety of social innovations involving distinct practices of care and nurturance, habits of nonviolence and gentleness, new forms of sexuality, intimacy, and community, and altered relations of gender and power.

At the same time, we are now seeing a limited but fascinating body of studies accumulating in genetics, neural anatomy, field biology, psychology, and performance that offer tantalizing glimpses into deep-seated—some have even claimed hard-wired—differences that exist among some individuals in these populations, both human and animal. They raise a provocative possibility. We may in fact be witnessing the discovery of a biological species variant, caught at a moment in its evolution. Whatever the cause, we must entertain the radical possibility that gay men are now playing an unseen, deeply transformational role in the shared spiritual and ethical life of the societies where we live. What is beyond question is that we can learn much from this set of social experiments. In our social, political, spiritual lives, we offer new models for males in a new millennium. We are creating a whole new way of life, one with deep implications—for us, with each other, for our happiness as men, and for the larger world. But that cannot be realized until we do some work with ourselves.

It is time we beheld ourselves, and witnessed what we are up to. In almost every chapter, we have seen how narratives of gay life we have unwittingly adopted obscure a set of larger truths about our lives. We have, for complex reasons, told ourselves only a part of our story. We have become our own worst narrators, only too glad to recapitulate the least kind, least generous, most crimped view of our patterns and possibilities.

For too long, we have lied about our best selves. We have colluded in a series of discussions which tell half-truths. Some are self-inflicted, others sanctioned by the dominant culture, still others frankly concocted by those who would see us die. By rote we rag about too many drugs, moan over meaningless sex, complain over too many muscles and too much competition, censure the circuit; decry shallowness, bitch over body obsession, posit that the gay world makes "no place for my size/ethnicity/color/age/style/weight." We say gay men are dogs and replay the "came-out-got-disappointed-got-depressed-got-infected-got-bitter" litany. No wonder we're depressed. It's a wonder we haven't all slit our wrists long ago.

And we've had enormous help doing it. For years, it has seemed that the most common tale we have told—that most easily published, promoted, and promulgated—is a relentless, dour criticism. It has its approved canon of permissible topics and stands: muscles (bad), too much sex (bad), too little sex (bad), circuit and substances (bad and worse), barebacking (REALLY bad), dating disappointment (sad), sex addiction, Internet addiction, cigarette addiction, tawdry public sex, communal shortcomings, exclusion, and oh, did I mention body fascism? All in all, it's a litany of Familiar Dismals, each with its kernel of truth. Most derive from our fondest hopes, betrayed. Yet together they provide a received narrative as factually incomplete as it is grossly misleading. More important, when they become the only story we know to tell about ourselves, they become our reality.

To maintain our accustomed stance, we have had to agree to omit large parts of what we know to be true about our lives. How often do we discuss with friends the ways we're different with women? Or why we don't have to worry about fights in our bars? How often do we reflect on the ways our friends are our family? What you and your fuck buddy mean to each other? Where you find meaning, or why you volunteer? How you understand the roommate you've shared an apartment with for seven years, or his boyfriend, whom you used to date? Where do we speak of how we might imagine an old age we'd actually relish? Or what kinds of touch friends might best give each other? So we discuss Ecstasy, but not ecstasy; body fascism, not affectionate touch. We swap sexual war stories but rarely voice the radical hopes for our friendships with each other.

How have we failed to notice that such discussion has vanquished our celebration, and in so doing, threatens to vanquish our selves?

The time is coming when spiritual questions will take center place, as opposed to discussions of rights. I want to be on the front lines when the spiritual turnaround happens.

—Harvard chaplain Peter Gomes, discussing the gay movement

We now return with different eyes to a quote in the first chapter. Michel Foucault argued that openly gay worlds offered "unique historic opportunities for an elaboration of personal and ethical creativity analogous to that practiced by certain moral athletes in classical antiquity. Only now such creativity need not be restricted to a social elite or a single, privileged gender, but could become the common property of an entire subculture."[1]

Understanding how we do that, to more fully recognize the values we demonstrate in our actions, has been the goal of this inquiry. This first step has been to name those special parts of being gay that we don't usually talk about. This does not imply an uncritical or simplistic queer rah-rah boosterism. Nothing in this book is intended to "build esteem" or "create" pride or "show our best face to the world." The goal has been simply to tell the whole truth we know in our lives, and what we may feel in our gut. That is, to widen the analytic lens to view more of ourselves and our practices. We need to recount our wisdoms as well as we do our warts, or we're telling only half a truth. Yet all that truth-telling is just preparation for work in the real world. Because it turns out that if you seek to feel love manifest with those in your life, you need to manifest love.

I really do believe that we as gay people have an involved role in the world.
I see gays as a kind of perpetual Peace Corps.
We are meant for something far beyond ourselves and our own selfish concerns.
This is a part of the meaning of being gay.
—Reverend Malcolm Boyd

The national project by that name, Manifest Love, is a whole new kind of project for gay/queer men. It exists to help gay men find new ways to be with and for each other. Men who take part get a chance to explore our shared patterns, look at our values around community, nurturance, and affection. We offer concrete new ways to experience ourselves and conduct our relationships. By helping frame more nurturant patterns with each other, we envision and create the more sustaining queer world we want to live in.

There is no simple box for what we do. It is part social movement, part applied spirituality. Our gatherings are not encounter weekends, human potential groups, some dating service or sect. Nobody will ask you to loan your life's savings or tell you how to vote. You can go to the bathroom as often as you want and do whatever you want, when you're there.

The Manifest Love movement invites a range of queer men to create a new kind of world together, one that better reflects our best values and aspirations. Our focus is to craft the lives—social, intimate, sexual, communal, voluntary, moral—that we want to experience with each other. Call it a great gay experiment in applied affection. To date, about 1,800 of us have taken part in these events from San Francisco to Providence; from Ukiah, California, to Ellsworth, Maine. You may have heard something of the discussions of these ideas now bubbling at gay gatherings and conferences. If so, you may already be familiar with the basic thrust of this work. Men come because they are hungry for some changes in how we are with each other and what we can be for each other.

This work tries to link ethical analysis to action, to more mindfully foster creative forms of beloved community. Local chapters work to promote critical understanding of our cultural innovations—to continue the discussions of this book—and to find concrete ways to manifest sustaining values in our communities. A key focus is on creating individual and collective acts to help us reflect, experience, and practice values of care and nurture in new ways. We call them Loving Disturbances.

Loving Disturbances are just that: innovations and experiments in applied affection. They are concrete real-world experiments devised to nudge the patterns and practices of gay lives in more affirming and humane directions. They are social actions that bring values into being, and are the action core of Manifest Love's local work. They may happen at a bar, on the street, or in a meeting, between friends or tricks or neighbors. They may happen alone or with others. The point is to broaden the habitual patterns of queer men's cultures to help us meet and interact in new ways, and have fun doing it. A Loving Disturbance aims to leave a corner of queer world just a little better off—a tad more affectionate or less defended, slightly more in line with the values discussed here, a moment aglow with an aura of promise fulfilled.

In local groups, we devote much time to helping men brainstorm all manner of new institutions and practices we could create with each other, to enlarge the possibilities of our interactions. In Providence, a group decided to do a "gang affection bang" when a gaggle of friends teamed up on one of their own to cook him a meal, bake him cookies, clean his house, give him massage, walk his dog, sing him a serenade, take him to a movie, and generally celebrate his presence in their lives. The Minneapolis troop invented the idea of a "group date." Troops in Boulder and Atlanta have experimented with creating various events for voluntary, nonsexual, naked touch that are free and available to all. In San Francisco, men experimented with using their eyes differently to cruise for affection, not just sex. (If you want some more examples, take a look at our webpage: www.manifestlove.org.) Each Loving Disturbance is an example of that shameless kind of love Plato talked about.

Work in local troops affords a chance to reflect on yourself and the givens of your gay world, why you sought it out in the first place, and how it's working for you. Most important, it is a chance to reflect on what all of us are doing here together, at a deeper level than we usually think about it. If the ideas here have struck a chord with you, you are invited to join the ongoing conversations of men talking with each other, seeking new ways of being for and with each other.

These pages are a doorway to invite you into a conversation already begun by many of your brothers. The goal here is to ignite person-to-person and group inquiry about what we mean to and for each other, how the patterns of our gay worlds work and don't work with each other, and what we might want from each other. If you have not yet attended any of these events, or do not have a Manifest Love troop near you, these pages aim to provide a working tool for you and others, a text to support local discussions of these ideas. I hope you will feel moved to discuss these ideas with your friends. And to take action with them.

In an interview with a French gay magazine, Foucault once made this observation:

{Homosexuality} would make us work on ourselves and invent, I do not say discover, a manner of being that is still improbable.[2]

It is to the invention of improbability we are now called. Its exact shapes and forms depend on us. But basically, it comes down to this: If we want to rewrite the code of conduct in this Queer Kingdom, everybody has to grab a pen. The only way to get a more trusting and affectionate queer men's world is to make it. Because, it turns out, when we're all being that way with each other, the next thing you know . . . that's what we are to each other.

Be the change you wish to see in the world.
—Mahatma Gandhi

Shortly before he died, John Preston, famed gay pornographer and philosopher, wrote: "Gay men have no automatic lineage. Unlike straight men, who can be initiated into the rituals of manhood by their fathers and brothers, we must create our own models and our own rites of passage. We must self-consciously assume the roles of teacher and student, mentor and protégé." Those words have never been more true. What, exactly, is our lineage? If we are models, what are we modeling? As mentors and teachers, what truths do we teach? If we are self-conscious, what does that consciousness stand for?

Many of us strain to find meaning in the givens and habits long associated with our chosen queer cultures. At the millennium, we find ourselves having to make sense of the new communal landscape we inhabit. We live in a time inaccurately termed "post-AIDS" where the daily toll of HIV illness and death in the United States epidemic has ebbed remarkably, and in a time some even call "post-gay." We are left to pick up the reins of our lives, wonder what our future might now look like, where we fit in, and what's ahead, individually and collectively.

We are on a collective search for meaning and connection. All of us are asking what we can expect from each other. We will answer that by inventing gay cultural customs that call us to a common value of love with one other. Not habits of cattiness or bitchiness, nor customs of sarcasm and attitude, not gorgeous bodies sheltering aching hearts, nor dramas of loneliness and exclusion. But something wholly different, and much more courageous.

Instead, can our great gay imagination conjure a day in 2015 when an eighteen-year-old can walk into his first gay space and meet a profoundly different experience? A venue where he can expect to meet the open embrace of affectionate strangers, and be valued for the size of his heart as much as the size of his basket? Might he, and we, understand that this young man is graced to belong to a group of men whose special genius lies not just in how much we fuck, but in how beautifully we love? It's a tall order, one that suggests that we have big work to do with each other. But we have many times discarded, reframed, and refashioned other people's ideas about who we are. We can now renew our own ideas, as well. As we do, we may transform our culture's ideas of the possibilities for us, as for all men.

{Gay men} have the burden and enjoyment of being survivors, being outside and being aware that every day they live is a kind of triumph. This they should cling to. They should make no effort to join society. They should stay right where they are and give their name and serial number and wait for society to form itself around them, because it most certainly will.
—Quentin Crisp

We cannot yet know what will happen when this confederacy of beloved men unabashedly claims our values before the world. If we better understood and celebrated our best practices, gay lives would never look the same. Then, of course, all hell might break lose. In a world beset by violence, with male nurturance and caretaking in short supply, for a society confused and guilty in its sexuality, where practices of intimacy and the pursuit of pleasure are viewed with suspicion, where relations between the sexes are fraught with risk and confusion—in such a straining world, might not the lessons of such men help us all? As our distinct habits diffuse, how might that change the life of our larger culture?

Who knows what it could look like if our gender were less prone to violent solutions; if new varieties of communalism and caretaking now seen in many of our lives were a broader norm; if celebratory sexual exploration were a more accepted feature of our culture, enjoyed and explored, not hidden and lied about; if we structured our intimate communities in more inclusive ways; if our national life included more freely loving, publicly altruistic men; if we could find new understandings across gender lines. In a dozen demonstrable ways, our habits have the potential to shift the most deeply held values of the majority culture. How might that transform the experiences and fears of women, of children, and of men? What promise does it hold to sweeten the shared life of our planet?

These are the questions these pages have sought to open. They have attempted to lay out a series of questions and a vision for a radically enlarged view of ourselves and our lives, both as we are with each other and as we shape the larger culture. More personally, to inspire a process of thinking about your own life—and our shared lives—in a different way. It is, in short, intended to start some trouble.

If, as facts suggest, society harbors a hidden army of lovers in its midst, the challenge is to celebrate and nurture these gifts, this genius. It is a cultural patrimony we can offer to our shared life as a nation. Equally important, it is a gift to ourselves that will transform our own experience with and for each other. For now we know only this. A resolute community of fiercely loving males can only heal the world. We, whom Plato called the best of boys, the bravest of men, can compose his army of lovers. When we more fully manifest love in word and deed and we live out the values of our hidden hearts, the larger culture can only follow. It always has.

> *If we could somewise contrive to have a city or an army*
> *composed of lovers and those they loved . . . when fighting side by side,*
> *one might almost consider them able to make*
> *even a little band victorious over all the world.*
>   —Plato, *Symposium*

Reader's Note on Nomenclature for the Theoretically Inclined

For those interested in Queer Theory, dear postmodern reader under thirty-five, this note is especially for you. If that's not you, feel free to skip this note and continue reading chapter 1. (I'd also suggest you scan chapter 9 before wandering through the rest of the book . . . just a thought.) But if you *are* the sort who hears the word "Butler" and thinks "Judith" before you think "Jeeves," we need to take a theory moment to frankly acknowledge the limits of our terms. Lest you suspect that I slept through Queer Studies (both times I took it), we need to belly up to the question of fag nomenclature: What do men like us properly call ourselves?

Surely by now, all of us worth our dog-eared copies of *History of Sexuality*, vol. 1, can deconstruct the "g" word as easily as we slip on a cockring. The art of dissecting one's subject-position (the phrase itself sheer gibberish just a generation ago) may be the one truly novel gay social skill to evolve in the last few years. If you don't count lying shamelessly in a chat room. For two decades, the reigning queer academic chatter— uh, sorry, discourse—has been like a really smart terrier worrying a bone, in this case the bone called "gay." More properly, what has come to be called "gay subjectivity." For a while now, many Big Thinkers of gaydom have brought to gay subjectivity the same rapt attention that a cow brings to its cud. Chewing it over has settled into a known and comforting habit, one offering persistent activity, yet somehow nourishing less with each regurgitated mouthful.

Those who follow this debate might stipulate straight off that "gay" is an illusory, privileged, white-derived, Western, urban-commercialized pseudo-identity. Some might say "queer" is too, just with a few added piercings. That "q" word, which began as a bravura embrace of diverse, non-normative sexual identification, has morphed from something once political into a term now as self-evident to one generation as it is repellent to another. Across that age divide, we might get wide consensus that "homosexual," with its clinical and pathologizing connotations, is definitely out. It is more likely found today on tongues of rightist 'phobes (pronounced "hhhhoh-moh-SEX!!!-ewels") or in the sterile-speak of academic journals than among our own kind. While we're at it, may we have consensus—raise your hands, please—to bury that hideous *"MSM"* for men who have sex with men. That one is a real triumph of category over common sense, a term so behaviorally precise that no flesh-and-blood person actually claims it as an identity or sees his face reflected in its mirror. (Or my personal nomenclatural nemesis, its evil spawn, MSM–NGI—MSM–Non Gay Identified.) Clearly, all this babble doesn't even make a place for the bi's, those of transgender experience, or the habitually questioning.

Were all this mess not bad enough, theorists point out rightly that any such label is doomed as transhistorical, culturally bound, and hopelessly contingent. It's far safer, they counsel, for us to view these terms as placeholders of meaning, chits in a vast social parlor game. They are best understood as artifacts of a powerful symbolic social order rather than representing any objective or objectifiable fact or universal identity, let alone any essential attributes of who we are.

Of course, there's just one small problem. Someone forgot to tell the gay guys. The fact remains that outside the thought groves of academe—in places like Portland, Maine, and Chelsea, in Cincinnati and Des Moines and West Hollywood and Chicago—tens of millions of the queer citizenry persist in the folk notion that these labels do, in fact, mean something. Maybe even something important about who they are, something they have fought for and struggled to value. They persist in the cozy habit of calling themselves gay. To those millions, the "g" or "q" or "h" word actually describes themselves or important parts of their worlds, something that somehow coheres. Despite the word's admitted theoretical inadequacy, people still go to what they call gay bars and gay bookstores, march in what they think of as Gay Pride marches, belong to gay hiking clubs, churches, and swim teams, subscribe to gay magazines to read gay personal ads to find gay tricks. They seek out urban gay neighborhoods, go on gay cruises, belong to suburban gay networks, and attend rural gay gatherings. On streets called Castro, Christopher, Commercial, and Collins, people use "gay" to in some way denote their friends and hangouts, their customs and (albeit contested) communities, some ineffable or hoped-for "us"—even as they ferociously dispute its glaring limits and frailties.

Ironically, even where the term "gay" is most contested, it has solidi-fied. It is the "g" word, of course, that makes the cover of *Newsweek* and drips from Pat Robertson's thunder-rants of bigotry. Gay men of color have offered some of the most trenchant critiques of white gay monocul-turism. Yet even there, the now-familiar dichotomy of dispossession is often framed as the tension between being of color in "the" gay world and being gay in one's ethnic community of origin. The point is not that the divide is not very real, but once again, that it is the g-word—less often queer, almost never two-spirited—which is chosen as the habitually counterposed term of opposition. It is the term that defines the tension.

In these pages I use the word "gay" as conceptual shorthand, for two reasons. First, many of the chapters draw on published social science studies, where "gay" and "homosexual men" are the most commonly used terms. By using the terms these authors do, I hope to stay as close to what they actually said about who they really studied, even while acknowledging that many different researchers use the term to mean many different things.

But far more important than the language of the studies is the language of men's real lived experience. "Gay" is the word used most comfortably and frequently among the men I encounter, interview, and describe. No other term is shared by the Radical Faeries of Tennessee, the leather men on Long Island, the dowager queens of Indiana, the guys at Mainely Men. None is more likely to be heard at Club Lauderdale, the Houston Log Cabin Club, or the Rocky Mountain Gay Men's Club, among the gymrats of Chelsea, the Gay Men of African Descent, the cruisers of Boystown and the tourists of Rehoboth Beach. "Gay" simply trumps by force of custom. It is what we most often call ourselves, for better and worse. For all its lim-its, it reflects the dominant social practice of these communities that have come together to invent their new ways of being.

Obviously, the word "gay" does not cover all who are homosexually active or inclined. The pages of this work focus on self-identified gay men, to explore the social and ethical potential of our subcultures. This book does not treat lesbian culture nor pretend to. Lesbians and gay men inhabit radically differing worlds, with different issues, situations, and historical moment. Lesbian and queer women's cultural innovations, while as deeply important and richly complex as gay men's, are so dis-tinct that to suggest otherwise would be to blur profound differences and do injustice to those in both groups.

So as you read "gay" in these pages, please keep in mind that the term is imperfect and shivers with intrinsic contradictions. It should not be taken to describe in one clear semantic hue a mix of identities drawn in overlapping shades of pastel. In choosing it, I do not mean to slight the intellectual critiques of that or other identities, to obscure the radical questions of race, class, and gender inclusion raised by rejecting the notion of a monolithic white gay-male culture, or to seem tone-deaf to important questions of transgression posed by those who identify as queer. I mean no disrespect to the power of the transgendered to perturb our most cherished illusions of a gender binary, nor do I wish to slight the very real struggle and vision of those who march beneath banners of bi rights and queer solidarity in the name of a greater and more humane inclusion. All of those struggles are vital. Their discourses and debates are essential to our progress, and their challenges inspire our unfolding humanity.

Still and all, in this arbitrary business of naming, one must land somewhere. For me and the men described in these pages, that somewhere is "gay." This book is less concerned with the deeper arguments of queer theory. The thinkers who labor in those vineyards, being far queerer than I, do it far better. Rather, it offers a more sociological view, in order to open an ethical and spiritual inquiry. Of interest are the radiant and inventive cultures of heart, body, and soul created by those men who call themselves gay, and the worlds they are in the process of fashioning. In their very diversity, those worlds remind us that "gay" is, at root, a word in search of endless refilling, a perpetual work in progress, as are the myriad communities it denotes.

Indeed, that is the very point of us, as we have seen.

Chapter 1: Unseen Hearts and Habits

1. S. O. Murray, "Components of Gay Community in San Francisco," in *Gay Culture in America*, ed. G. Herdt (Boston: Beacon Press, 1992, 107–146).
2. G. Herdt, ed., *Gay Culture in America: Essays from the Field* (Boston: Beacon Press, 1992).
3. D. Halperin, *Saint Foucault: Towards a Gay Hagiography* (Oxford and New York: Oxford University Press, 1995).

Chapter 2: Our Peaceable Kingdom

1. C. Sowar, *Computer-Aided Distress Report* (Denver, Colo.: Denver Police Department, 1997–2000).
2. B. Williams, Washington, D.C. Police Department, Third District. Personal communication, 2000.
3. L. H. Ellis; Harry Hoffman; and D. M. Burke, "Sex, Sexual Orientation, and Criminal and Violent Behavior," *Personality and Individual Differences* 11(12) (1990): 1207–1212.
4. P. M. Nardi and R. Bolton, "Gay-bashing: Violence and Aggression Against Gay Men and Lesbians," in *Targets of Violence and Aggression* (1991): 349–400; A. R. D'Augelli, "Lesbian and Gay Male Undergraduates' Experiences of Harassment and Fear on Campus," *Journal of Interpersonal Violence* 7(3) (1992): 383–395; G. M. Herek, "Documenting Prejudice Against Lesbians and Gay Men on Campus: The Yale Sexual Orientation Survey," *Journal of Homosexuality* 25(4) (1993): 15–30; W. P. Norris, "Liberal Attitudes and Homophobic Acts: The Paradoxes of Homosexual Experience in a Liberal Institution," *Journal of Homosexuality* 22(3–4) (1991): 81–120; B. Slater, "Violence Against Lesbian and Gay Male College Students," *Journal of College Student Psychotherapy* 8(1–2) (1993): 177–202; J. Hunter, "Vio-

lence Against Lesbian and Gay Male Youths," *Journal of Interpersonal Violence* 5(3) (1990): 295–300.

5. Ellis, (1990) op. cit.

6. J. Harry, "Parental Physical Abuse and Sexual Orientation in Males," *Archives of Sexual Behavior* 18(3) (1989): 251–261.

7. D. L. Island and Patrick Letellier. *Men Who Beat the Men Who Love Them: Battered Gay Men and Domestic Violence* (Binghamton, N.Y.: The Hawthorne Press, 1991).

8. C. M. Renzetti, "Violence in Lesbian and Gay Relationships," *Gender Violence: Interdisciplinary Perspectives* (New York: New York University Press, 1997), 285–293; C. M. Renzetti and C. H. E. Miley, ed., *Violence in Gay and Lesbian Domestic Partnerships* (New York: Harrington Park Press/Haworth Press, 1996) xiii, 121; G. S. Merrill, "Understanding Domestic Violence Among Gay and Bisexual Men," in *Issues in Intimate Violence,* ed. Raquel Kennedy Bergen, (Sage Publications, 1998) 129–141.

9. J. Leland, "Silence Ending About Abuse in Gay Relationships," *New York Times,* Nov. 6, 2000: A18.

10. L. K. Waldner-Haugrud; L. V. Gratch; and B. Magruder, "Victimization and Perpetration Rates of Violence in Gay and Lesbian Relationships: Gender Issues Explored," *Violence and Victims* 12(2) (1997): 173–184.

11. S. LeVay, "A Difference in Hypothalamic Structure in Heterosexual and Homosexual Men," *Science,* v. 253, 1991: 1034–1037.

12. D. H. Hamer, et al., "A Linkage Between DNA Markers on the X Chromosome and Male Sexual Orientation," *Science,* v. 261, 1993: 321–327.

13. L. S. Allen and R. A. Gorski, "Sexual Orientation and the Size of the Anterior Commissure in the Human Brain," *Proceedings of the National Academy of Sciences of the United States of America* 89 (1992): 7199–7202.

14. D. McFadden and E. G. Pasanen, "Comparison of the Auditory Systems of Heterosexuals and Homosexuals: Click-Evoked Otoacoustic Emissions," *Proceedings of the National Academy of Sciences of the United States of America* 95(5) (1998): 63–72.

15. M. Reite, "Cerebral Laterality in Homosexual Males: Preliminary Communication Using Magnetoencephalography," *Archives of Sexual Behavior* 24(6) (1995): 585–593.

16. J. Michael Bailey and Richard C. Pillard, "A Genetic Study of Male Sexual Orientation," *Archives of General Psychiatry* 48 (1993): 1089–1096; F. L. Whitam et al., "Homosexual Orientation in Twins: A Report on 61 Pairs and Three Triplet Sets," *Archives of Sexual Behavior* 22(3) (1993): 187–206.

17. J. A. Y. Hall and D. Kimura, "Dermatoglyphic Asymmetry and Sexual Orientation in Men," *Behavioral Neuroscience* 108(6) (1994): 1203–1206.

18. R. Blanchard et al., "Measuring Physical Aggressiveness in Heterosexual, Homosexual, and Transsexual Males," *Archives of Sexual Behavior* 12(6) (1983): 511–524.

19. C. Tavris, "Masculinity," *Psychology Today,* 10 (1977), 34–42.
20. P. D. Wayson, "Personality Variables in Males As They Relate to Differences in Sexual Orientation," *Journal of Homosexuality* 11(1–2) (1985): 63–73.
21. R. Blanchard et al., (1983) op. cit.
22. R. Green, "Childhood Cross-gender Behavior and Subsequent Sexual Preference," *American Journal of Psychiatry,* 136(1) (1979): 106–108; R. Green, "Specific Cross-gender Behaviour in Boyhood and Later Homosexual Orientation," *British Journal of Psychiatry,* 151 (1987): 84–88.
23. R. C. Friedman and L. O. Stern, "Juvenile Aggressivity and Sissiness in Homosexual and Heterosexual Males," *Journal of the American Academy of Psychoanalysis* 8(3) (1980): 427–440; L. H. Ellis; Harry Hoffman; and D. M. Burke, op. cit.; P. J. O'Connor, "Aetiological Factors in Homosexuality as Seen in Royal Air Force Psychiatric Practice," *British Journal of Psychiatry,* 110(466) (1964): 381–391.
24. F. L. Whitam and M. Zent, "A Cross-cultural Assessment of Early Crossgender Behavior and Familial Factors in Male Homosexuality," *Archives of Sexual Behavior* 13(5) (1984): 427–439; F. L. Whitam, "Culturally Invariable Properties of Male Homosexuality: Tentative Conclusions from Crosscultural Research," *Archives of Sexual Behavior* 12(3) (1983): 207–226.
25. G. Murdock and C. Provost, "Factors in the Division of Labour by Sex: A Cross-Cultural Analysis," *Ethnology* 12(2) (1973): 203–225.
26. R. C. Friedman and L. O. Stern, (1980) op. cit.
27. G. Dörner, "A Neuroendocrine Predisposition for Homosexuality in Men," *Archives of Sexual Behavior* 4(1) (1975): 1–8.
28. G. Schmidt and U. Clement, "Does Peace Prevent Homosexuality?" *Journal of Homosexuality* 28 (3–4) (1995): 269–75.
29. S. N. Haynes and L. J. Oziel, "Homosexuality: Behaviors and Attitudes," *Archives of Sexual Behavior* 5(4) (1976): 283–289.
30. M. E. Lumby, "Homophobia: The Quest for a Valid Scale," *Journal of Homosexuality* 2(1) (1976): 39–47.
31. T. J. Ficarrotto, "Racism, Sexism, and Erotophobia: Attitudes of Heterosexuals Toward Homosexuals," *Journal of Homosexuality* 19(1) (1990): 111–116.
32. H. E. Adams; L. W. Wright; and B. A. Lohr, "Is Homophobia Associated with Homosexual Arousal?" *Journal of Abnormal Psychology* 105 (1996): 440–445.
33. S. L. Corbett; R. R. Troiden; and R. A. Dodder, "Tolerance as a Correlate of Experience with Stigma: The Case of the Homosexual," *Journal of Homosexuality* 3(1) (1977): 3–13.
34. C. A. Mallen, "Sex Role Stereotypes, Gender Identity, and Parental Relationships in Male Homosexuals and Heterosexuals," *Journal of Homosexuality* 9(1) (1983): 55–74.
35. N. J. Beran, "Attitudes Toward Minorities: A Comparison of Homosexuals and the General Population," *Journal of Homosexuality* 23(3) (1992): 69–83.

36. S. M. White and L. R. Franzini, "Heteronegativism? The Attitudes of Gay Men and Lesbians Toward Heterosexuals," *Journal of Homosexuality* 37(1) (1999): 65–69.

37. G. K. Bliss and M. B. Harris, "Teachers' Views of Students with Gay or Lesbian Parents," *Journal of Gay, Lesbian, & Bisexual Identity* 4(2) (1999): 149–171.

38. E. Goffman, *Stigma: Notes on the Management of a Spoiled Identity* (New York: Fawcett Columbine, 1988).

39. L. K. Waldner and B. Magruder, "Coming Out to Parents: Perceptions of Family Relations, Perceived Resources, and Identity Expression as Predictors of Identity Disclosure for Gay and Lesbian Adolescents," *Journal of Homosexuality* 37(2) (1999): 83–100.

40. F. A. Ernst; R. A. Francis; and H. Nevels, "Condemnation of Homosexuality in the Black Community: A Gender-Specific Phenomenon?" *Archives of Sexual Behavior* 20(6) (1991): 579–585.

41. M. E. Kite and B. E. Whitley, Jr., "Do Heterosexual Women and Men Differ in Their Attitudes Toward Homosexuality? A Conceptual and Methodological Analysis," *Stigma and Sexual Orientation: Understanding Prejudice Against Lesbians, Gay Men, and Bisexuals* (Thousand Oaks, Calif.: Sage Publications, 1998).

42. M. E. Kite, "Sex Differences in Attitudes Toward Homosexuals: A Meta-analytic Review," *Journal of Homosexuality* 10(1–2) (1984): 69–81.

43. T. Pratte, "A Comparative Study of Attitudes Toward Homosexuality: 1986 and 1991," *Journal of Homosexuality* 26(1) (1993): 77–83.

44. C. R. Logan, "Homophobia? No, Homoprejudice," *Journal of Homosexuality* 31(3) (1996): 31–53.

45. M. Johnson; C. Brehms; and P. Alford-Keating, "Personality Correlates of Homophobia," *Journal of Homosexuality* 34(1) (1997): 57–69.

46. L. LaMar and M. Kite, "Sex Differences in Attitudes Toward Gay Men and Lesbians: A Multidimensional Perspective," *Journal of Sex Research* 35(2) (1998): 189–196.

47. D. A. Jones, "Discrimination Against Same-sex Couples in Hotel Reservation Policies," *Journal of Homosexuality* 31(1–2) (1996): 153–159.

48. A. S. Walters and M. C. Curran, "'Excuse Me, Sir? May I Help You and Your Boyfriend?' Salespersons' Differential Treatment of Homosexual and Straight Customers," *Journal of Homosexuality* 31(1–2) (1996): 135–152.

49. R. E. Hellman, "Childhood Sexual Identity, Childhood Religiosity, and 'Homophobia' as Influences in the Development of Transsexualism, Homosexuality, and Heterosexuality," *Archives of General Psychiatry* 38(8) (1981): 910–915; R. Seltzer, "The Social Location of Those Holding Antihomosexual Attitudes," *Sex Roles* 26(9–10) (1992): 391–398; J. D. Oldham and T. Kasser, "Attitude Change in Response to Information That Male Homosexuality Has a Biological Basis," *Journal of Sex and Marital Therapy* 25(2) (1999): 121–124.

50. A. H. Lilling and R. C. Friedman, "Bias Towards Gay Patients by Psycho-analytic Clinicians: An Empirical Investigation," *Archives of Sexual Behavior* 24(5) (1995): 562–570.

51. W. Marsiglio, "Attitudes Toward Homosexual Activity and Gays as Friends: A National Survey of Heterosexual 15- to 19-year-old Males," *Journal of Sex Research* 30(1) (1993) 12–17; E. S. Nelson and S. L. Krieger, "Changes in Attitudes Toward Homosexuality in College Students: Implementation of a Gay Men and Lesbian Peer Panel," *Journal of Homosexuality* 33(2) (1997): 63–81; E. G. Schellenberg; J. Hirt; and A. Sears, "Attitudes Toward Homo-sexuals Among Students at a Canadian University," *Sex Roles* 40(1–2) (1999): 139–152; G. M. Herek, (1993) op. cit.; W. P. Norris, (1991) op. cit.

52. J. J. Mohr and A. B. Rochlen, "Measuring Attitudes Regarding Bisexuality in Lesbian, Gay Male, and Heterosexual Populations," *Journal of Counseling Psychology* 46(3) (1999): 353–369; P. Irwin and N. L. Thompson, "Accep-tance of the Rights of Homosexuals: A Social Profile," *Journal of Homosexu-ality* 3(2) (1977): 107–121; R. Seltzer, (1992) op. cit.

53. M. Johnson and C. Brehms, (1997) op. cit.

54. W. Marsiglio, (1993) op. cit.

55. R. Woodworth, "Within These Walls" (New York: New York City Lesbian and Gay Community Services Center, 1987).

56. Gay and Lesbian Alliance Against Defamation, "Christian Radio Host Urges Death to Gay People" (New York: Gay and Lesbian Alliance Against Defamation, 1997).

57. P. J. Peters, "INTOLERANCE OF, DISCRIMINATION AGAINST AND THE DEATH PENALTY FOR HOMOSEXUALITY is prescribed in the Bible" (LaPorte, Colo.: Scriptures for America, 1992).

58. F. X. Clines, "Slaying of a Black Gay Spurs Call for Justice," *New York Times*, July 15, 2000: A16.

59. J. Leland, (2000) op. cit.

60. G. R. Bailey, Jr., "Treatment of Domestic Violence in Gay and Lesbian Relationships," *Journal of Psychological Practice* 2(2) (1996): 1–8

61. J. Bernhardt, *New York Times*, Jan. 2, 2001: F3. Letters to the Editor

Chapter 3: Communities of Caring

1. D. J. Allen and T. Oleson, "Shame and Internalized Homophobia in Gay Men," *Journal of Homosexuality* 37(3) (1999).

2. S. Folkman; M. A. Chesney; and A. Christopher-Richards, "Stress and Cop-ing in Caregiving Partners of Men with AIDS," *Psychiatric Clinics of North America* 17(1) (1994): 35–53.

3. D. Johnston; R. Stall; and K. Smith, "Reliance by Gay Men and Intra-venous Drug Users on Friends and Family for AIDS-related Care," *AIDS Care* 7(3) (1995): 307–319.

4. H. A. Turner; J. A. Catania; and J. Gagnon, "The Prevalence of Informal Caregiving to Persons with AIDS in the United States: Caregiver Charac-

teristics and Their Implications," *Social Science and Medicine* 38(11) (1994): 1543–1552; J. A. Catania, "Coping with Death Anxiety: Help-seeking and Social Support Among Gay Men with Various HIV Diagnoses," *AIDS* 6(9) (1992): 999–1005; R. B. Hays, "Help-seeking for AIDS-related Concerns: A Comparison of Gay Men with Various HIV Diagnoses." *American Journal of Community Psychology* 18(5) (1990): 743–755.

5. H. A. Turner, J. A. Catania, and J. Gagnon, "The Prevalence of Informal Caregiving to Persons with AIDS in the United States: Caregiver Characteristics and Their Implications," *Social Science and Medicine* 38 (11) (1994): 1543–1552.

6. Turner, (1994) op. cit.

7. J. B. Cassel and S. Ouellette, "A Typology of AIDS Volunteers," *AIDS Education & Prevention* 7(5 Supp) (1995): 80–90.; S. C. Ouellette, "GMHC Volunteers and the Challenges and Hopes for the Second Decade of AIDS." *AIDS Education & Prevention* 7(Supp) (1995): 64–79; M. Snyder and A. M. Omoto, "Volunteerism and Society's Response to the HIV Epidemic," *Current Directions in Psychological Science* 1(4) (1992): 113–116; Marie A. Brown; and Gail M. Powell-Cope, "AIDS Family Caregiving: Transitions Through Uncertainty," *Nursing Research* 40(6) (1991): 338–345; C. S. Sipes, "The Experiences of Gay Male Caregivers Who Provided Care for Their Partners with AIDS," *Dissertation Abstracts International: Section B: The Sciences & Engineering,* 58(12-B) (1998): 6492.

8. A. R. D'Augelli and L. D. Garnets, "Lesbian, Gay, and Bisexual Communities," *Lesbian, Gay, and Bisexual Identities over the Lifespan: Psychological Perspectives* (New York: Oxford University Press, 1995).

9. M. Snyder and A. M. Omoto, op. cit.; P. M. Kayal, *Bearing Witness: Gay Men's Health Crisis and the Politics of AIDS* (Boulder, Colo.: Westview Press, 1993); A. M. Omoto and M. Snyder, "Basic Research in Action: Volunteerism and Society's Response to AIDS," *Personality and Social Psychology Bulletin* 16(1) (1990): 152–165; A. M. Omoto and M. Snyder, "Sustained Helping Without Obligation: Motivation, Longevity of Service, and Perceived Attitude Change Among AIDS Volunteers," *Journal of Personality and Social Psychology* 68(4) (1995): 671–686.

10. L. A. Wardlaw, "Sustaining Informal Caregivers for Persons with AIDS," *Families in Society* 75(6) (1994): 373–384.

11. S. Folkman, "Caregiver Burden in HIV-positive and HIV-negative Partners of Men with AIDS," *Journal of Consulting and Clinical Psychology* 62(4) (1994): 746–756.

12. B. Miller and L. Cafasso, "Gender Differences in Caregiving: Fact or Artifact?" *Gerontologist* 32(4) (1992): 498–507.

13. B. J. Kramer and S. Kipnis, "Eldercare and Work-role Conflict: Toward an Understanding of Gender Differences in Caregiver Burden," *Gerontologist* 35(3) (1995): 340–348.

14. C. S. Sipes, (1998) op. cit.

15. S. M. Allen, "Gender Differences in Spousal Caregiving and Unmet Need for Care," *Journals of Gerontology* 49(4) (1994): s187–s195.

16. S. Folkman; M. Chesney; and A. Christopher-Richards, (1994) op. cit.

17. A. Christopher-Richards, "Altruistic Behavior and Caregiving in the AIDS Epidemic" (paper presented at the Center for AIDS Prevention Studies, 1992).

18. E. C. Clipp, "Informal Caregivers of Persons with AIDS," *Journal of Palliative Care* 11(2) (1995): 10–18.

19. R. J. Montgomery and M. M. Datwyler, "Women and Men in the Caregiving Role," *Generations* 14(3) (1990): 34–38.

20. L. Badgett, "Creating Communities: Giving and Volunteering by Gay, Lesbian, Bisexual, and Transgender People" (Amherst, Mass.: Working Group on Funding Lesbian and Gay Issues / Institute for Gay and Lesbian Strategic Studies, 1998).

21. W. Jessdale, personal communication.

22. The Advocate Poll, in *The Advocate,* Jan. 16, 2001, 35.

23. D. Link, "Should Gay Men Be Allowed to Donate Blood?" *GMHC Treatment Issues* 14(11–12) (2000): 1–6.

24. G. A. Irving; R. Bor; and J. Catalan, "Psychological Distress Among Gay Men Supporting a Lover or Partner with AIDS: A Pilot Study," *AIDS Care* 7(5) (1995): 605–617; S. Folkman; M. Chesney; and A. Christopher-Richards, (1994) op. cit.; S. Folkman, "Postbereavement Depressive Mood and Its Prebereavement Predictors in HIV+ and HIV-Gay Men," *Journal of Personality and Social Psychology* 70(2) (1996): 336–348.

25. I. M. Shuff, "Volunteers Under Threat: AIDS Hospice Volunteers Compared to Volunteers in a Traditional Hospice," *The Hospice Journal*, 7(1–2) (1991): 85–107.

26. B. A. Koblin, "The Feasibility of HIV-1 Vaccine Efficacy Trials Among Gay/Bisexual Men in New York City: Project ACHIEVE," *AIDS* 10(13) (1996): 1555–1561; S. Buchbinder, "Feasibility of HIV Vaccine Trials in Homosexual Men in the United States: Risk, Behavior, Seroincidence, and Willingness to Participate," *Journal of Infectious Diseases* 174 (1996): 71–78.

27. "Vaccine Trials," in *The Advocate,* Jan. 18, 2000: 59.

28. "Trial by Virus," in *POZ,* Oct. 1999: 71.

29. "Vaccine Trials," in *The Advocate,* Jan. 18, 2000: 59.

30. B. A. Koblin, "Readiness of High-risk Populations in the HIV Network for Prevention Trials to Participate in HIV Vaccine Efficacy Trials in the United States," *AIDS* 12(7) (1998): 785–793.

31. R. K. Hays and S. Kegeles, "Factors Related to Willingness of Young Gay Men to Participate in Preventive HIV Vaccine Trials," *Journal of Acquired Immune Deficiency Syndromes and Human Retrovirology* (2) (1999): 164–171.

32. D. Salais and R. B. Fischer, "Sexual Preference and Altruism," *Journal of Homosexuality* 28(1–2) (1995): 185–196.

33. D.S. Nieto, "Who Is the Male Homosexual? A Computer-mediated Exploratory Study of Gay Male Bulletin Board System (BBS) Users in New York City," *Journal of Homosexuality* 30(4) (1996): 97–124.

34. A. Taylor, "Conceptions of Masculinity and Femininity as a Basis for Stereotypes of Male and Female Homosexuals," *Journal of Homosexuality* 9(1) (1983): 37–53.

35. J.J. Bigner and R.B. Jacobsen, "Parenting Behaviors of Homosexual and Heterosexual Fathers," *Journal of Homosexuality* 18(1–2) (1989): 173–186.

36. W.M. Burdon, "Deception in Intimate Relationships: A Comparison of Hetereosexuals and Homosexal/Bisexuals," *Journal of Homosexuality* 32(1) (1996): 77–91.

37. J.F. Barba, "Sexual Orientation and Capacity for Intimacy," *Dissertation Abstracts International: Section B: The Sciences & Engineering*, 58(10-B) (1998): 5635.

38. Y.B. Chung and L.W. Hanson, "The Career Interests and Aspirations of Gay Men: How Sex-role Orientation Is Related," *Journal of Vocational Behavior* 45(2) (1994): 223–239; M.V.L. Badgett, "Tolerance, Taboos, and Gender Identity: The Occupational Distribution of Lesbians and Gay Men," *Institute for Gay Lesbian Strategic Studies Abstracts* 1 October 1999.

39. J. Blandford, "Gay and Lesbian Career Choices," personal communication.

40. J.D. Weinrich, "Biological Research on Sexual Orientation: A Critique of the Critics," *Journal of Homosexuality* 28(1–2) (1995): 197–213; J.D. Weinrich, "A New Sociobiological Theory of Homosexuality Applicable to Societies with Universal Marriage," *Ethology and Sociobiology* 8(1) (1987): 37–47; J.A.W. Kirsch and J.D. Weinrich, "Homosexuality, Nature, and Biology: Is Homosexuality Natural? Does It Matter?" *Homosexuality: Research Implications for Public Policy* (Newbury Park, Calif.: Sage Publications, 1991); E.O. Wilson, *Sociobiology* (Cambridge, Mass.: Belknap Press of Harvard University Press, 1975); C. Badcock, *Evolution and Individual Behavior: An Introduction to Human Sociobiology* (Oxford: Blackwell, 1991).

41. D.M. Seaborg, "Sexual Orientation, Behavioral Plasticity, and Evolution," *Journal of Homosexuality* 10(3–4) (1984): 153–158.

42. S. Folkman; M. Chesney; and A. Christopher-Richards, (1994) op. cit.

43. T.A. Richards and S. Folkman, "Spiritual Aspects of Loss at the Time of a Partner's Death from AIDS," *Death Studies* 21 (1997): 527–552.

44. A. Humm, "Brother's Keeper," *POZ,* June 2000: 61–62; M. Boyd, "Telling a Lie for Christ," *Gay Spirit: Myth and Meaning,* ed. Mark Thompson (New York: St. Martin's Press, 1987).

45. C.S. Sipes, (1998) op. cit.

Chapter Four: Dogs, Pigs, and Altruists

1. D. Binson, et al., "Prevalence and Social Distribution of Men Who Have Sex with Men: United States and Its Urban Centers," *Journal of Sex Research* 32(3) (1995): 245–254.

2. G. Marks, "Anal Intercourse and Disclosure of HIV Infection Among Seropositive Gay and Bisexual Men," *Journal of Acquired Immune Deficiency Syndrome* 7(8) (1994): 866–869.

3. J. P. Paul; R. Stall; and F. Davis, "Sexual Risk for HIV Transmission Among Gay/Bisexual Men in Substance-abuse Treatment," *AIDS Education and Prevention,* 5(1) (1993): 11–24.

4. T. W. Mayne, et al., "Beyond 2000 Sexual Health Survey: Sexual Health and Practices of Gay, Bisexual and Homosexually Active Men in New York City," New York: Gay Men's Health Crisis, 1999.

5. R. Voigt, "Increasing Condom Use but Stable Numbers of Casual and Regular Partners in a Cohort of Gay Men (1987–91)," *The Vancouver Lymphadenopathy–AIDS Study (VLAS) Group. International Conference on AIDS* 8(2) (1992): C261.

6. M. L. Ekstrand and T. J. Coates, "Maintenance of Safer Sexual Behaviors and Predictors of Risky Sex," *San Francisco Men's Health Study* 80 (1990): 973–977.

7. S. F. Posner and G. Marks, "Prevalence of High-risk Sex Among HIV-positive Gay and Bisexual Men: A Longitudinal Analysis," *American Journal of Preventive Medicine* 12(6) (1996): 472–477.

8. G. K. Prestage, et al. *Sydney Gay Community Periodic Survey* (Sydney, Australia: University of New South Wales, 1996).

9. A. Silvestre, et al. "Changes in HIV Rates and Sexual Behavior Among Homosexual Men, 1984 to 1988/92." *American Journal of Public Health* (4) (1993): 578–583.

10. A. J. Hunt et al. "Changes in Condom Use by Gay Men," *AIDS Care* 5(4) (1993): 439–448.

11. J. Dawson, "The HIV Test and Sexual Behaviour in a Sample of Homosexually Active Men," *Social Science and Medicine* 32(6) (1991): 683–688.

12. F. Moreau-Gruet and F. Dubois-Arber, "AIDS Prevention in Homosexuals in Switzerland: Adaptation to Risks According to Type of Partner," *Sozial- und Praventivmedizin* 41(1) (1996): 1–10.

13. R. A. Roffman; S. A. Kalichman; and J. A. Kelly, "HIV Antibody Testing of Gay Men in Smaller US Cities," *AIDS Care* (1995): 405–413.

14. D. H. Osmond, et al., "HIV Infection in Homosexual and Bisexual Men 18 to 29 Years of Age: The San Francisco Young Men's Study," *American Journal of Public Health* (12) (1994): 1933–1937.

15. T. Myers and G. Godin, "Sexual Risk and HIV-testing Behavior by Gay and Bisexual Men in Canada," *AIDS Care* 8(3) (1996): 297–309.

16. D. O. Perkins, "Psychosocial Predictors of High-Risk Sexual Behavior Among HIV-Negative Men," *AIDS Education and Prevention* 5(2) (1993): 141–152.

17. C. R. Waldo; R. D. Stall; and T. J. Coates, "Is Offering Post-exposure Prevention for Sexual Exposures to HIV Related to Sexual Risk Behavior in Gay Men?" *AIDS,* 14(8) (May 2000): 1035–1039.

18. J. A. Kelly, "Factors Predicting Continued High-risk Behavior Among Gay Men in Small Cities: Psychological, Behavioral, and Demographic Characteristics Related to Unsafe Sex," *Journal of Consulting and Clinical Psychology* 63(1) (1995): 101–107.

19. D. Kanouse et al., *AIDS-Related Knowledge, Attitudes, Beliefs, and Behaviors in Los Angeles County* (Santa Monica, Calif.: Rand, 1991).

20. S. L. Steiner; L. Audi; and R. A. Roffman, "Risk Behavior for HIV Transmission Among Gay Men Surveyed in Seattle Bars," *Public Health Reports* 109(4) (1994): 563–566.

21. H. I. Meyer and L. Dean, "Patterns of Sexual Behavior and Risk Taking Among Young New York City Gay Men," *AIDS Education and Prevention* 7(Supp.) (1995): 13–23.

22. M. Bochow et al., "Sexual Behaviour of Gay and Bisexual Men in Eight European Countries," *AIDS Care* 6(5) (1994): 533–549.

23. K. W. Schmidt, "Sexual Behaviour Related to Psycho-social Factors in a Population of Danish Homosexual and Bisexual Men," *Social Science and Medicine* 34(10) (1992): 1119–1127.

24. J. A. Kelly, "Community AIDS/HIV Risk Reduction: The Effects of Endorsements by Popular People in Three Cities," *American Journal of Public Health* 82(11) (1992): 1483–1489.

25. D. T. Ridge, "Young Gay Men and HIV: Running the Risk?" *AIDS Care* 6(4) (1994): 371–378.

26. J. A. Kelly, "Acquired Immunodeficiency Syndrome/Human Immunodeficiency Virus Risk Behavior Among Gay Men in Small Cities," *Archives of Internal Medicine* 152(11) (1992): 2293–2297.

27. S. Kippax et al., "Sustaining Safe Sex: A Longitudinal Study of a Sample of Homosexual Men," *AIDS* 7(2) (1993): 257–263.

28. F. C. Hickson et al. "No Aggregate Change in Homosexual HIV Risk Behaviour Among Gay Men Attending the Gay Pride Festivals, United Kingdom, 1993–1995," *AIDS* 10(7) (1996): 771–774.

29. G. J. Wagner; R. H. Remien; and A. Carballo-Dieguez, " 'Extramarital' Sex: Is There an Increased Risk for HIV Transmission? A Study of Male Couples of Mixed HIV Status," *AIDS Education & Prevention* 10(3) (1998): 245–256.

30. D. Binson, (1995) op. cit.

31. F. Molitor; M. Facer; and J. D. Ruiz, "Safer Sex Communication and Unsafe Sexual Behavior Among Young Men Who Have Sex with Men in California," *Archives of Sexual Behavior* 28(4) (1999): 335–343.

32. J. Kelly et al., "Psychological Factors That Predict AIDS High-Risk vs. AIDS-Precautionary Behavior," *Journal of Consulting Clinical Psychology* 58 (1990): 117–120.

33. J. Wang, "HIV Testing History Among Gay/Bisexual Men Recruited in Barcelona: Evidence of High Levels of Risk Behavior Among Self-reported HIV+ Men," *Social Science and Medicine* 44(4) (1997): 469–477.

34. L. H. McKusick et al., "Tailoring AIDS Prevention: Differences in Behavioral Strategies Among Heterosexual and Gay Bar Patrons in San Francisco," *AIDS Education & Prevention* 3(1) (1991): 1–9.

35. D. L. Higgins et al., "Evidence for the Effects of HIV Antibody Counseling and Testing on Risk Behaviors," *Journal of the American Medical Association* 266(17) (1991): 2419–2429.

36. J. A. Catania et al., "Prevalence of AIDS-related Risk Factors and Condom Use in the United States," *Science* 258(5085) (1992): 1101–1106.

37. J. D. Fisher and W. A. Fisher, "Changing AIDS Risk Behavior," *Psychological Bulletin* 111(3) (1992): 455–474.

38. M. Dolcini, et al., "Demographic Characteristics of Heterosexuals with Multiple Partners: The National AIDS Behavioral Surveys (NABS)," *Family Planning Perspectives* 25 (1993): 208–214.

39. K. Tanfer et al., "Condom Use Among U.S. Men, 1991," *Family Planning Perspectives* 25(2) (1993): 61–66.

40. J. A. Catania, "Risk Factors for HIV and Other Sexually Transmitted Diseases and Prevention Practices Among US Heterosexual Adults: Changes from 1990–1992," *American Journal of Public Health* 85(11) (1995): 1492–1499.

41. K.-H. Choi and J. A. Catania, "Changes in Multiple Sexual Partnerships, HIV Testing, and Condom Use Among U.S. Heterosexuals 18 to 49 Years of Age, 1990 and 1992," *American Journal of Public Health* 86(4) (1996): 554–556.

42. A. Avins et al., "HIV Infection and Risk Behaviors Among Heterosexuals in Treatment Programs," *Journal of the American Medical Association* 271 (1994): 515–518.

43. P. E. Dziuk, "A Comparison of Students' AIDS-related Attitudes, Knowledge, and Sexual Behaviors at a Southwestern University Between 1989 and 1993," *Dissertation Abstracts International: Section B: The Sciences & Engineering* 55(11-B) (1995); J. D. Fisher, (1992) op. cit.

44. K. H. Choi; J. A. Catania; and M. M. Dolcini, "Extramarital Sex and HIV Risk Behavior Among US Adults: Results from the National AIDS Behavioral Survey," *American Journal of Public Health* 84(12) (1994): 554–556.

45. Doreen Rosenthal; Madeline Fernbach; and Susan Moore, "The Singles Scene: Safe Sex Practices and Attitudes Among At-risk Heterosexual Adults," *Psychology and Health* 12(2) (1997): 171–182.

46. M. J. Rotheram-Borus; W. D. Marelich; and S. Srinivasan, "HIV Risk Among Homosexual, Bisexual, and Heterosexual Male and Female Youths," *Archives of Sexual Behavior* 28(2) (1999): 159–177.

47. S. Moore and A. P. Halford, "Barriers to Safer Sex: Beliefs and Attitudes Among Male and Female Adult Heterosexuals Across Four Relationship Groups," *Journal of Health Psychology* 4(2) (1999): 149–163.

48. M. Levine and K. Siegel, "Unprotected Sex: Understanding Gay Men's Participation," *The Social Context of AIDS* (Newbury Park, Calif.: Sage Publications, 1992).

49. R. D. Stall; T. J. Coates; and C. Hoff, "Behavioral Risk Reduction for HIV Infection Among Gay and Bisexual Men: A Review of Results from the United States," *American Psychologist* 43(11) (1988): 878–885.

50. S. C. Kalichman et al. "Risk for HIV Infection Among Bisexual Men Seeking HIV-prevention Services and Risks Posed to Their Female Partners," *Health Psychology* 17(4) (1998): 320–327.

51. L. S. Doll and C. Beeker, "Male Bisexual Behavior and HIV Risk in the United States: Synthesis of Research with Implications for Behavioral Interventions," *AIDS Education & Prevention* 8(3) (1996): 205–225.

52. D. Binson, (1995) op. cit.

53. R. M. Diaz et al., "HIV Risk Among Latino Gay Men in the Southwestern United States," *AIDS Education & Prevention* 8(5) (1996): 415–429; J. L. Peterson et al., "High-risk Sexual Behavior and Condom Use Among Gay and Bisexual African-American Men," *American Journal of Public Health* 82(11) (1992): 415–429; J. L. Peterson, "AIDS-Related Risks and Same-sex Behaviors Among African-American men," *AIDS, Identity, and Community* (Thousand Oaks, Calif.: Sage Publications, 1995); E. H. Johnson et al., "What Is the Significance of Black-White Differences in Risky Sexual Behavior?" *Journal of the National Medical Association* 86(10) (1994): 745–759; D. Binson, (1995) op. cit.

54. "Young, Gay, Black, and HIV-positive," *The Advocate*, March 13, 2000.

55. J. M. Dawson et al., "Awareness of Sexual Partners' HIV Status as an Influence upon High-risk Sexual Behaviour Among Gay Men," *AIDS* 8(6) (1994): 837–841.

56. A. S. News, "AIDS/STD News Report: Reckless Sexual Habits of Young Gays Threaten to Start New Wave of HIV" (Silver Spring, Md.: CD Publications, 1996).

57. National Highway Traffic Safety Administration, "Increasing Seat Belt Use Among Part-Time Users: Messages and Strategies" (Washington, D.C.: Office of Research and Traffic Records, National Highway Traffic Safety Administration, 1996).

58. S. Russell, " 'Russian Roulette' Sex Parties: Rise in Fringe Group's Unsafe Practices Alarms AIDS Experts," *San Francisco Chronicle,* Jan. 29, 1999: A1.

59. A. C. Seibt, et al., "Relationship Between Safe Sex and Acculturation into the Gay Subculture," *AIDS Care* 7 (Supplement 1) (1995): S85–S88.

60. J. A. Catania, et al., "Changes in Condom Use Among Homosexual Men in San Francisco," *Health Psychology* 10(3) (1991): 190–199; S. M. Kegeles et al., "Community Mobilization Reduces HIV Risk Among Young Gay Men: A Two Community Study," *International Conference on AIDS* 11(1) (1996): 52; D. T. Ridge, (1994) op. cit.

61. M. J. Chapple; S. Kippax; and G. Smith, " 'Semi-straight Sort of Sex': Class and Gay Community Attachment Explored Within a Framework of Older Homosexually Active Men," *Journal of Homosexuality* 35(2) (1998): 65–83.

62. P. Davies, et al., *Sex, Gay Men and AIDS* (London, Falmer Press, 1993).

63. M. Pollak, "Homosexual Rituals and Safer Sex," *Journal of Homosexuality* 25(3) (1993): 307–317.

64. M. Bochow, (1994) op. cit.

65. G. J. Van Griensven et al., "Impact of HIV Antibody Testing on Changes in Sexual Behavior Among Homosexual Men in the Netherlands," *American Journal of Public Health* 78 (1988): 1575–1577.

66. J. Wang, (1997) op cit.; J. G. Zapka et al., "Psychosocial Factors and AIDS-related Behavior of Homosexual Men: Measurement and Associations," *Evaluation and the Health Professions* 13(3) (1990): 283–297; J. Dawson, (1991) op. cit.; R. Wolitski et al., "HIV-Seropositive Men's Perceived Responsibility for Preventing the Transmission of HIV to Others," International Conference on AIDS, 1998, 12:413–414 (abstract no. 23361); I. H. Frazer et al., "Influence of Human Immunodeficiency Virus Antibody Testing on Sexual Behaviour in a 'High-risk' Population from a 'Low-risk' City," *Medical Journal of Australia* 149(7) (1988): 365–368; L. McKusick; T. J. Coates; and S. Morin, "Longitudinal Predictors of Reductions in UAI Among Gay Men in San Francisco," *American Journal of Public Health* 80(8) (1990): 978–983; T. J. Coates et al., "AIDS Antibody Testing: Will It Stop the AIDS Epidemic? Will It Help People Infected with HIV?" *American Psychologist* 43(11) (1988): 859–864; C. Hoff; R. Stall; and J. Paul, "Differences in Sexual Behavior Among HIV Discordant and Concordant Gay Men in Primary Relationships," *Journal of Acquired Immune Deficiency Syndromes and Human Retrovirology* 14(1) (1997): 72–78; J. McCusker et al., "Effects of HIV Antibody Test Knowledge on Subsequent Sexual Behaviors in a Cohort of Homosexually Active Men," *American Journal of Public Health* 78(4) (1988): 462–467.

67. D. L. Higgins, (1991) op. cit.

68. R. Wolitski, (1998) op. cit.

69. D. Nimmons and S. Folkman, "Other-sensitive Motivation for Safer Sex Among Gay Men: Expanding Paradigms for HIV Prevention," *AIDS and Behavior* 3(4) (1999): 313–324.

70. T. W. Mayne, 1999, op. cit.

71. M. R. Bartos; H. Middleton; and G. Smith, "Gay Men in Regular Relationships and HIV Risk," International Conference on AIDS, 1996 11(1): 384 (abstract no. 8); M. Levine and Karolynn Siegel, "Unprotected Sex: Understanding Gay Men's Participation. The Social Context of AIDS," in *The Social Context of AIDS*, eds. Joan Huber and Beth E. Schneider (Newbury Park, Calif.: Sage Publications, 1992), 306; G. Marks et al., "Self-disclosure of HIV Infection: Preliminary Results from a Sample of Hispanic

Men," *Health Psychology* 11(5) (1992): 300–306; G. Marks et al., "Self-disclosure of HIV Infection to Sexual Partners," *American Journal of Public Health* 81(10) (1991): 1321–1322; M. W. Otten and A. A. Zaidi, "Changes in Sexually Transmitted Disease Rates After HIV Testing and Posttest Counseling, Miami, 1988 to 1989," *American Journal of Public Health* 83(4) (1993): 529–533; S. F. Posner and G. Marks, "Prevalence of High-risk Sex Among HIV-positive Gay and Bisexual Men: A Longitudinal Analysis," *American Journal of Preventive Medicine* 12(6) (1996): 472–477; G. M. Powell-Cope, "The Experiences of Gay Couples Affected by HIV Infection," *Qualitative Health Research* 5(1) (1995): 36–62; K. Siegel and M. Glassman, "Individual and Aggregate Level Change in Sexual Behavior Among Gay Men at Risk for AIDS." *Archives of Sexual Behavior* 18(4) (1989): 335–338; B. Tindall, C. Swanson, et al., "Sexual Practices and Condom Usage in a Cohort of Homosexual Men in Relation to Human Immunodeficiency Virus Status," *Medical Journal of Australia* 151(6) (1989): 318–322; G. J. Wagner et al., (1998) op. cit.; C. Hoff, L. McKusick, and B. Hilliard, "Changes in Gay Relationships Before the AIDS Epidemic and Now," VII International Conference on AIDS, Amsterdam, 1992.

72. San Francisco AIDS Foundation Survey, "A Qualitative Interview Study of 92 Gay and Bisexual Males Regarding the Risk of HIV and Sexual Behavior." San Francisco AIDS Foundation, 1997; S. Kippax et al., "Sustaining Safe Sex: A Longitudinal Study of a Sample of Homosexual Men," *AIDS* 7(2) (1993): W. P. Sacco and R. L. Rickman, "AIDS-relevant Condom Use by Gay and Bisexual Men: The Role of Person Variables and the Interpersonal Situation," *AIDS Education and Prevention* 8(5) (1996): 430–443; T. Exner, H. F. Meyer-Bahlberg, and A. A. Ehrhardt, "Effects of Individual and Partner Sero-status on Condom Use," VII International Conference on AIDS, Amsterdam, 1992; B. Tindall et al., (1989) op. cit. 318–322; C. C. Hoff et al., "Impact of HIV Antibody Status on Gay Men's Partner Preferences: A Community Perspective," *AIDS Education and Quarterly* 4 (1992): 318–322; C. C. Hoff, (1997) op. cit.

73. F. F. Hamers, H. A. Buehler, and T. A. Peterman, "Communication of HIV Serostatus Between Potential Sex Partners in Personal Ads," *AIDS Education and Prevention* 9(1) (1997): 42–48; S. M. Kegeles, J. A. Catania, and T. J. Coates, "Intentions to Communicate Positive HIV-antibody Status to Sex Partners," *Journal of the American Medical Association* 259(2) (1988): 216–217; R. R. Stempel, J. M. Moulton, and A. R. Moss, "Self-disclosure of HIV-1 Antibody Test Results: The San Francisco General Hospital Cohort," *AIDS Education and Prevention* 7(2) (1995): 116–123; D. J. Schnell et al., "Men's Disclosure of HIV Test Results to Male Primary Sex Partners," *American Journal of Public Health* 82(12) (1992): 1675–1676; G. Marks, J. L. Richardson, and N. Maldonado, "Self-disclosure of HIV Infection to Sexual Partners," *American Journal of Public Health* 81(10) (1991): 1321–1322.

74. F. Muscarella, "The Homoerotic Behavior That Never Evolved," *Journal of Homosexuality* 37(3) (1999): 1–18.
75. C. Zahn-Waxler, E. M. Cummings, and R. Iannotti, "Altruism and Aggression: Biological and Social Origins," *Cambridge Studies in Social and Emotional Development* (Cambridge: Cambridge University Press, 1986).
76. C. D. Batson and L. L. Shaw, "Encouraging Words Concerning the Evidence for Altruism," *Psychological Inquiry* 2(2) (1991): 159–168.
77. D. M. Seaborg, "Sexual Orientation, Behavioral Plasticity, and Evolution," *Journal of Homosexuality* 10(3–4) (1984): 153–158.

Chapter 5: Alive and Well in Sexual Madagascar

1. M. Zuckerman, "Sensation Seeking in Homosexual and Heterosexual Males," *Archives of Sexual Behavior* 12(4) (1983): 347–356.
2. D. Binson et al., "Prevalence and Social Distribution of Men Who Have Sex with Men: United States and Its Urban Centers," *Journal of Sex Research* 32(3) (1995): 245–254.
3. G. Herdt, "Culture, History, and Life Course of Gay Men," in *Gay Culture in America: Essays from the Field* (Boston: Beacon Press, 1992).
4. S. Schaefer, "Sociosexual Behavior in Male and Female Homosexuals: A Study in Sex Differences," *Archives of Sexual Behavior* 6(5) (1977): 355–364.
5. J. Harry, "Gay Marriages and Communities of Sexual Orientation," *Alternative Life Styles* (2) (1979): 177–200.
6. M. Mendola, *The Mendola Report: A New Look at Gay Couples* (New York: Crown, 1980).
7. L. A. Peplau and S. D. Cochran, "Value Orientations in the Intimate Relationships of Gay Men," *Journal of Homosexuality* 6(3) (1981): 1–19.
8. A. A. Deenen, L. Gijs, and A. X. Van Naerssen, "Intimacy and Sexuality in Gay Male Couples," *Archives of Sexual Behavior* 23(4) (1994): 421–431.
9. A. K. T. Yip, "Gay Male Christian Couples and Sexual Exclusivity," *Sociology* 31(2) (1997): 289–306.
10. L. McKusick, T. J. Coates, and S. Morin, "Longitudinal Predictors of Reductions in UAI Among Gay Men in San Francisco," *American Journal of Public Health* 80(8) (1990): 978–983.
11. G. J. Wagner, R. H. Remien, and A. Carballo-Dieguez, " 'Extramarital' Sex: Is There an Increased Risk for HIV Transmission? A Study of Male Couples of Mixed HIV Status," *AIDS Education & Prevention* 10(3) (1998): 245–256.
12. D. P. McWhirter and A. M. Mattison, *The Male Couple* (Englewood Cliffs, N.J.: Prentice-Hall, 1984).
13. R. T. Michael et al., *Sex in America: A Definitive Survey* (New York: Warner Books, 1994).
14. W. M. Burdon, "Deception in Intimate Relationships: A Comparison of Heterosexuals and Homosexual/Bisexuals," *Journal of Homosexuality* 32(1) (1996): 77–91.

15. R. O. Hawkins, "The Relationship Between Culture, Personality, and Sexual Jealousy in Men in Heterosexual and Homosexual Relationships," *Journal of Homosexuality* 19(3) (1990): 67–84.

16. R. G. Bringle, "Sexual Jealousy in the Relationships of Homosexual and Heterosexual Men: 1980 and 1992," *Personal Relationships* 2(4) (1995): 313–325.

17. R. G. Bringle and L. A. Bunk, "Extradyadic Relationships and Sexual Jealousy," in *Sexuality in Close Relationships* (Hillsdale, N.J.: Lawrence Erlbaum Associates, 1991); J. W. Engel and M. Saracino, "Love Preferences and Ideals: A Comparison of Homosexual, Bisexual and Heterosexual Groups," *Contemporary Family Therapy: An International Journal* 8(3) (1986): 241–250.

18. R. O. Hawkins, (1990) op. cit.

19. F. C. Hickson et al., "Maintenance of Open Gay Relationships: Some Strategies for Protection Against HIV," *AIDS Care* 4(4) (1992): 409–419.

20. S. Kippax, et al., "Sexual Negotiation in the AIDS Era: Negotiated Safety Revisited," *AIDS* 11(2) (1997): 191–197; A. E. Grulich et al. "HIV Serostatus of Sexual Partners of HIV-positive and HIV-negative Homosexual Men in Sydney," *AIDS* 12(18) (1998): 2508.

21. R. T. Michael et al., (1994) op. cit.

22. R. O. Hawkins, (1990) op. cit.

23. A. A. Deenen, L. Gijs, and A. X. Van Naerssen, "Intimacy and Sexuality in Gay Male Couples," *Archives of Sexual Behavior* 23(4) (1994): 421–431.

24. L. A. Kurdek and J. P. Schmitt, "Relationship Quality of Gay Men in Closed or Open Relationships," *Journal of Homosexuality* 12(2) (1985): 85–89.

25. A. Hodges and D. Hutter, *Downcast Gays* (London: Pomegranate Press, 1974).

26. D. P. McWhirter and A. M. Mattison, (1984) op. cit.

27. S. Schaefer, "Sociosexual Behavior in Male and Female Homosexuals: A Study in Sex Differences," *Archives of Sexual Behavior* 6(5) (1977): 355–364.

28. A. K. T. Yip, (1997) op. cit.

29. L. A. Kurdek and J. P. Schmitt, (1985) op. cit.

30. D. P. McWhirter and A. M. Mattison, (1984) op. cit.

31. P. Frieberg, "Couples Study Shows More Strengths," *Washington Blade*, March 16, 2000, A1.

32. W. M. Burdon, "Deception in Intimate Relationships: A Comparison of Hetereosexuals and Homosexal/Bisexuals," *Journal of Homosexuality* 32(1) (1996): 77–91.

33. J. W. Ramey, "Emerging Patterns of Behavior in Marriage," *Journal of Sex Research* 8(1) (1972): 6–30.

34. M. Shernoff, "Monogamy and Gay Men," *Family Therapy Networker,* March-April (1999): 63–71; A. K. T. Yip, (1997) op. cit.; L. A. Kurdek and J. P. Schmitt, (1985) op. cit.; D. Blasband and Peplau, L. A. "Sexual Exclusivity Versus Openness in Gay Male Couples," *Archives of Sexual Behavior* 14(5), (1985).

35. J. A. Lee, "Forbidden Colors of Love: Patterns of Gay Love and Gay Liberation," *Journal of Homosexuality* 1(4) (1976): 401–418.

36. R. O. Hawkins, (1990) op. cit.

37. A. Pryce, "Researching Eros—Revisiting Ethnographic Chronicles of Male Sex in Public Places," *Sexual and Marital Therapy* 11(3) (1996): 321–334.

38. M. Graham and M. Litt, "Identity, Place, and Erotic Community Within Gay Leather Culture in Stockholm," *Journal of Homosexuality* 35(3–4) (1998): 163–183.

39. G. Chauncey, *Gay New York* (New York: Basic Books, 1994).

40. M. Pollak, "Homosexual Rituals and Safer Sex," *Journal of Homosexuality* 25(3) (1993): 307–317.

41. R. Bolton, J. Vincke, and R. Mak, "Gay Baths Revisited—An Empirical Analysis," *GLQ: A Journal of Lesbian and Gay Studies* 1(3) (1994): 66–78.

42. C. Moore, "Poofs in the Park—Documenting Gay Beats in Queensland, Australia," *GLQ: A Journal of Lesbian and Gay Studies* 2(3) (1995): 24–34.

43. C. Moser, "S/M (Sadomasochistic) Interactions in Semi-public Settings," *Journal of Homosexuality* 36(2) (1998): 19–29.

44. A. Pryce, (1996) op. cit.

45. A. Nilsson, "Creating Their Own Private and Public: The Male Homosexual Life Space in a Nordic City During High Modernity," *Journal of Homosexuality* 35(3–4) (1998): 81–116.

46. M. Child et al., "Personal Advertisements of Male-to-female Transsexuals, Homosexual Men, and Heterosexuals," *Sex Roles* (1996): 34 (5–6) 447–455.

47. M. R. Laner and G. L. Kamel, "Media Mating I: Newspaper 'Personals' Ads of Homosexual Men," *Journal of Homosexuality* 3(2) (1977): 149–162.

48. J. A. Lee, (1976) op. cit.

49. K. Deaux and R. Hanna, "Courtship in the Personals Column: The Influence of Gender and Sexual Orientation," *Sex Roles* 11(5–6) (1984): 363–375.

50. D. Klinkenberg and S. Rose, "Dating Scripts of Gay Men and Lesbians," *Journal of Homosexuality* 26(4) (1994): 23–35.

51. J. W. Wells, "Sexual Language Usage in Different Interpersonal Contexts: A Comparison of Gender and Sexual Orientation," *Archives of Sexual Behavior* 18(2) (1989): 127–143; J. W. Wells, "The Sexual Vocabularies of Heterosexual and Homosexual Males and Females for Communicating Erotically with a Sexual Partner," *Archives of Sexual Behavior* 19(2) (1990): 139–147.

52. J. A. Lee, (1976) op. cit.

53. N. J. Beran et al., "Attitudes Toward Minorities: A Comparison of Homosexuals and the General Population," *Journal of Homosexuality* 23(3) (1992): 65–83.

54. D. Schemo, "Sex Education with Just One Lesson: No Sex," *New York Times,* November 28, 2000: A1.

55. S. N. Haynes and L. J. Oziel, "Homosexuality: Behaviors and Attitudes," *Archives of Sexual Behavior* 5(4) (1976): 283–289.

56. J. A. Lee, "Going Public: A Study in the Sociology of Homosexual Liberation," *Journal of Homosexuality* 3(1) (1977): 48–78; A. Spengler, "Manifest Sadomasochism of Males: Results of an Empirical Study," *Archives of Sexual Behavior* 6(6) (1977): 441–446.

57. N. Breslow, L. Evans, and J. Langley, "Comparisons Among Heterosexual, Bisexual, and Homosexual Male Sado-masochists," *Journal of Homosexuality* 13(1) (1986): 83–107.

58. J. A. Lee, (1977) op. cit.; N. K. Sandnabba, P. Santilla, and N. Nordling, "Sexual Behavior and Social Adaptation Among Sadomasochistically Oriented Males," *Journal of Sex Research* 36(3) (1999): 273–282.

59. M. Pollak, "Homosexual Rituals and Safer Sex," *Journal of Homosexuality* 25(3) (1993): 307–317.

60. R. W. Connell, et al., "Danger and Context: Unsafe Anal Sexual Practice Among Homosexual and Bisexual Men in the AIDS Crisis," *Australian and New Zealand Journal of Sociology* 26(2) (1990): 187–208; D. H. Osmond et al., "HIV Infection in Homosexual and Bisexual Men 18 to 29 Years of Age: The San Francisco Young Men's Study," *American Journal of Public Health* (12) (1994): 1933–1937; C. C. Hoff et al., "Differences Between Gay Men in Primary Relationships and Single Men: Implications for Prevention," *AIDS Education and Prevention* 8(6) (1996): 546–559; C. Hoff, R. Stall, and J. Paul, "Differences in Sexual Behavior Among HIV Discordant and Concordant Gay Men in Primary Relationships," *Journal of Acquired Immune Deficiency Syndromes and Human Retrovirology* 14(1) (1997): 72–78; S. F. Posner and G. Marks, "Prevalence of High-risk Sex Among HIV-positive Gay and Bisexual Men: A Longitudinal Analysis," *American Journal of Preventive Medicine* 12(6) (1996): 472–477; R. D. Stall, T. J. Coates, and C. Hoff, "Behavioral Risk Reduction for HIV Infection Among Gay and Bisexual Men: A Review of Results from the United States," *American Psychologist* 43(11) (1988): 878–885; J. Kelly et al., "Psychological Factors That Predict AIDS High-Risk vs. AIDS-Precautionary Behavior," *Journal of Consulting and Clinical Psychology* 58 (1990): 117–120; L. Valleroy et al., "Prevalence and Predictors of Unprotected Receptive Anal Intercourse for 15–22-Year-Old Men Who Have Sex with Men in Seven Urban Areas, USA," International Conference on AIDS, Geneva, 1998; L. A. Gaies, W. P. Sacco, and J. A. Becker, "Cognitions of Gay and Bisexual Men in Sexual Situations: Development of the Sex and AIDS Thought Scale (SATS)," *AIDS Education and Prevention* 7(6) (1995): 513–522; R. H. Remien, A. Carballo-Dieguez, and G. Wagner, "Intimacy and Sexual Risk Behaviour in Serodiscordant Male Couples," *AIDS Care* 7(4) (1995): 429–438; M. Morris and L. Dean, "Effect of Sexual Behavior Change on Long-term Human Immunodeficiency Virus Prevalence Among Homosexual Men," *American Journal of Epidemiology* 140(3) (1994): 217–232; J. A. Kelly, J. S. St. Lawrence, and T. L. Brasfield, "Predictors of Vulnerability to AIDS Risk Behavior Relapse," *Journal of Consulting and Clinical Psychology* 59(1)

(1991): 163–166; A. Prieur, "Norwegian Gay Men: Reasons for Continued Practice of Unsafe Sex," *AIDS Education & Prevention* 2(2) (1990): 109–115; S. Kippax et al., "Cultures of Sexual Adventurism as Markers of HIV Sero-conversion: A Case Control Study in a Cohort of Sydney Gay Men," *AIDS Care* 10(6) (1998): 677–688; P. R. Appleby, L. C. Miller, and S. Rothspan, "The Paradox of Trust for Male Couples: When Risking Is Part of Loving," *Personal Relationships* 6(1) (1999): 81–93; H. I. Meyer and L. Dean, (1995) op. cit.; J. L. McNeal, "The Association of Idealization and Intimacy Factors with Condom Use in Gay Male Couples," *Journal of Clinical Psychology in Medical Settings* 4(4) (1997): 437–451; U. Davidovich, "Steady Partners Are Main Source of HIV Infection Among Young Gay Men," *AIDS* 15 (2001): 1303–1308.

Chapter 6: Permissible Intimacies

1. M. Foucault, "Friendship as a Way of Life," *Foucault Live: Interviews 1961–1984* (New York: Semiotext(e), 1996).

2. K. Weston, *Families We Choose: Lesbians, Gays, Kinship* (New York: Columbia University Press, 1991); W. Pequenat and J. Szapoczniik, *The Role of Families in Preventing and Adapting to HIV/AIDS* (Centers for Disease Control report, 2000).

3. P. M. Nardi and D. Sherrod, "Friendship in the Lives of Gay Men and Lesbians," *Journal of Social & Personal Relationships* 11(2) (1994): 185–189; P. M. Nardi, "Friends, Lovers, and Families: The Impact of AIDS on Gay and Lesbian Relationships," *Changing Times: Gay Men and Lesbians Encounter HIV/AIDS* (Chicago: University of Chicago Press, 1997); P. M. Nardi, *Gay Men's Friendships: Invincible Communities* (Chicago: University of Chicago Press, 1999).

4. M. W. DeLozier and J. Rodrigue, "Marketing to the Homosexual (Gay) Market: A Profile and Strategy Implications," *Journal of Homosexuality* 31(1–2) (1996): 203–212.

5. R. M. Berger, "Passing and Social Support Among Gay Men," *Journal of Homosexuality* 23(3) (1992): 85–97.

6. R. A. Dorfman, K. Walters, and P. Burke, "Old, Sad and Alone: The Myth of the Aging Homosexual," *Journal of Gerontological Social Work* 24(1–2) (1995): 29–44.

7. J. Stacey, "Gay and Lesbian Families: Queer Like Us," *All Our Families: New Policies for a New Century* (New York: Oxford University Press, 1998).

8. A. A. Nesmith, D. L. Burton, and T. J. Cosgrove, "Gay, Lesbian, and Bisexual Youth and Young Adults: Social Support in Their Own Words," *Journal of Homosexuality* 37(1) (1999): 95–107; L. M. Diamond, R. C. Savin-Williams, and E. M. Dube, "Sex, Dating, Passionate Friendships, and Romance: Intimate Peer Relations Among Lesbian, Gay, and Bisexual Adolescents," *The Development of Romantic Relationships in Adolescence* (Cambridge: Cambridge University Press, 1999); L. A. Kurdek and J. P.

Schmitt, "Perceived Emotional Support from Family and Friends in Members of Homosexual, Married, and Heterosexual Cohabiting Couples," *Journal of Homosexuality* 14(3–4) (1987): 57–68.

9. L. A. Kurdek, "Perceived Social Support in Gays and Lesbians in Cohabitating Relationships," *Journal of Personality and Social Psychology* 54(3) (1988): 504–509.

10. S. C. Boies, "Community Participation, Identity Development, and Psychological Well-being in Young Gay Men: Exploring Expressions of Gay Self-concept in Community Interactions," *Dissertation Abstracts International: Section B: The Sciences & Engineering* 58(11-B) (1998) 6277.

11. S. O. Murray, "Components of Gay Community in San Francisco," *Gay Culture in America,* ed. G. Herdt (Boston: Beacon Press, 1992).

12. F. R. Lynch, "Non-ghetto Gays: A Sociological Study of Suburban Homosexuals," *Journal of Homosexuality* 13(4) (1987): 13–42; C. Silverstein, *Man to Man: Gay Couples in America* (New York: Quill, 1981).

13. D. Johnston, R. Stall, and K. Smith, "Reliance by Gay Men and Intravenous Drug Users on Friends and Family for AIDS-related Care," *AIDS Care* 7(3) (1995): 307–319.

14. J. A. Catania et al., "Coping with Death Anxiety: Help-seeking and Social Support Among Gay Men with Various HIV Diagnoses," *AIDS* 6(9) (1992): 999–1005.

15. R. B. Hays et al. "Help-seeking for AIDS-related Concerns: A Comparison of Gay Men with Various HIV Diagnoses," *American Journal of Community Psychology* 18(5) (1990): 743–755.

16. H. A. Turner and J. A. Catania, "Informal Caregiving to Persons with AIDS in the United States: Caregiver Burden Among Central Cities Residents Eighteen to Forty-nine Years Old," *American Journal of Community Psychology* 25(1) (1997): 35–59; S. Folkman, M. Chesney, and A. Christopher-Richards, "Stress and Coping in Caregiving Partners of Men with AIDS," *Psychiatric Manifestations of HIV Disease* 17(1) (1994): 35–53; H. A. Wayment, R. C. Silver, and M. E. Kemeny, "Spared at Random: Survivor Reactions in the Gay Community," *Journal of Applied Social Psychology* 25(3) (1995): 187–209.

17. R. E. Goss, A. Strongheart, and S. Adams, "Our Families, Our Values: Snapshots of Queer Kinship," *Haworth Gay and Lesbian Studies* (New York: Harrington Park Press/The Haworth Press, 1997); H. A. Turner, R. B. Hays, and T. J. Coates, "Determinants of Social Support Among Gay Men: The Context of AIDS," *Journal of Health and Social Behavior* 34(1) (1993): 37–53.

18. M. Rucker, A. Freitas, and O. Huidor, "Gift-giving Among Gay Men: The Reification of Social Relations," *Journal of Homosexuality* 31(1–2) (1996): 43–56.

19. W. M. Burdon, "Deception in Intimate Relationships: A Comparison of Heterosexuals and Homosexual/Bisexuals," *Journal of Homosexuality* 32(1) (1996): 77–91.

20. J. W. Engel and M. Saracino, (1986) op. cit.

21. E. M. Gorman, "The Pursuit of the Wish: An Anthropological Perspective on Gay Male Subculture in Los Angeles," *Gay Culture in America*, ed. G. Herdt (Boston: Beacon Press, 1992); D. Binson et al., "Prevalence and Social Distribution of Men Who Have Sex with Men: United States and Its Urban Centers," *Journal of Sex Research* 32(3) (1995): 245–254.

22. E. M. Gorman, (1992) op. cit.; P. M. Nardi, (1999) op. cit; F. R. Lynch, "Nonghetto Gays: An Ethnography of Suburban Homosexuals," *Gay Culture in America* ed. G. Herdt (Boston: Beacon Press, 1992); F. R. Lynch, "Non-ghetto Gays: A Sociological Study of Suburban Homosexuals," *Journal of Homosexuality* 13(4) (1987); P. J. Cody and P. L. Welch, "Rural Gay Men in Northern New England: Life Experiences and Coping Styles," *Journal of Homosexuality* 33(1) (1997): 51–67.

23. A. R. D'Augelli and M. M. Hart, "Gay Women, Men, and Families in Rural Settings: Toward the Development of Helping Communities," *American Journal of Community Psychology* 15(1) (1987): 79–83.

24. K. Weston, (1991) op. cit.

25. J. Stacey, "Gay and Lesbian Families: Queer Like Us," in *All Our Families: New Policies for a New Century*, ed. Mary Ann Mason and Arlene Skolnick (New York: Oxford University Press, 1998), 117–143.

26. J. Scanzoni, "Wider Families as Primary Relationships," *Marriage and Family Review* 17(1–2) (1991): 117–133.

27. R. A. Dorfman, (1995), op. cit.

28. R. Bellah, et al. *Habits of the Heart* (Berkeley and Los Angeles: University of California Press, 1985).

29. G. Herdt, *Gay Culture in America* (Boston: Beacon Press, 1992).

Chapter 7: Unlikely Bedfellows: The Love of Gay Men and Straight Women

1. M. Thompson, *Gay Spirit: Myth and Meaning* (New York: St. Martin's, 1987).

2. W. Roscoe, "Bibliography of Berdache and Alternative Gender Roles Among North American Indians," *Journal of Homosexuality* 14(3–4) (1987): 81–171.

3. Midwest Institute of Sexology, *Survey, July 2000* (Southfield, Mich.: Midwest Institute of Sexology, 2000).

4. M. E. Lumby, "Homophobia: The Quest for a Valid Scale," *Journal of Homosexuality* 2(1) (1976): 39–47.

5. J. M. Bailey and M. Oberschneider, "Sexual Orientation and Professional Dance," *Archives of Sexual Behavior* 26(4) (1997): 433–444.

6. P. M. Nardi, *Gay Men's Friendships: Invincible Communities* (Chicago: University of Chicago Press, 1999).

7. "Tammy Faye," *The Advocate*, July 18, 2000, 36.

8. A. R. Spangler, "The Politics of Disease: Social Movement Responses to AIDS, Breast Cancer, and Prostate Cancer in the United States" (graduate thesis, Department of Sociology, Columbia University, 2000).

9. J. Saslow, "Crossing the Categories," in *Gay Spirit: Myth and Meaning*, ed. Mark Thompson (New York: St. Martin's, 1987), 134–137.

Chapter 8: A Flagrant Joy: Outlaws in Search of Bliss

1. C. Bagley and P. Tremblay, "On the Prevalence of Homosexuality and Bisexuality, in a Random Community Survey of 750 Men Aged 18 to 27," *Journal of Homosexuality* 36(2) (1998): 1–18.
2. N. McConaghy, N. Buhrich, and D. Silove, "Opposite Sex–linked Behaviors and Homosexual Feelings in the Predominantly Heterosexual Male Majority," *Archives of Sexual Behavior* 23(5) (1994): 565–577.
3. R. L. Sell, J. A. Wells, and D. Wypij, "The Prevalence of Homosexual Behavior and Attraction in the General Population," *Archives of Sexual Behavior* 24 (1995): 235–248; Nathaniel McConaghy, "Heterosexuality/ homosexuality: Dichotomy or Continuum?" *Archives of Sexual Behavior* 16 (1987): 411–424.
4. J. R. Bemporad, "Epigenesis and Sexual Orientation: A Report of Five Bisexual Males," *Journal of the American Academy of Psychoanalysis* 27(2) (1999): 221–237.
5. A. L. Walsh and E. B. Crepeau, " 'My Secret Life': The Emergence of One Gay Man's Authentic Identity," *American Journal of Occupational Therapy* 52(7) (1998): 563–569.
6. L. A. Lewis and M. W. Ross, "The Gay Dance Party Culture in Sydney: A Qualitative Analysis," *Journal of Homosexuality* 29(1) (1995): 41–70.
7. Simmons, *Simmons Gay and Lesbian Consumer Survey Index* (New York: Simmons Research, 1996).
8. L. A. Lewis and M. W. Ross, (1995) op. cit.
9. L. A. Lewis and M. W. Ross, (1995) ibid.
10. S. F. Philipp, "Gay and Lesbian Tourists at a Southern U.S.A. Beach Event," *Journal of Homosexuality* 37(3) (1999): 69–86.
11. G. Herdt, *Rituals of Manhood: Male Initiations in Papua New Guinea* (Berkeley and Los Angeles: University of California Press, 1982).
12. L. A. Lewis and M. W. Ross, (1995) op. cit.
13. L. A. Lewis and M. W. Ross, (1995) ibid.
14. L. A. Lewis and M. W. Ross, (1995) ibid.; W. Bogoras, "Shamanistic Performance in the Inner Room," *Comparative Religion: An Anthropological Approach* (New York: Harper and Row, 1979).
15. J. M. Bailey and M. Oberschneider, (1997) op. cit.
16. F. L. Whitam, "Culturally Invariable Properties of Male Homosexuality: Tentative Conclusions from Cross-cultural Research," *Archives of Sexual Behavior* 12(3) (1983): 207–226.
17. M. Diamond, "Homosexuality and Dance: Relation to AIDS and Hawai'i," *Archives of Sexual Behavior* 26(4) (1997): 459–461.
18. J. M. Bailey and M. Oberschneider, (1997) op. cit.

19. J. Demb, "Are Gay Men Artistic? A Review of the Literature," *Journal of Homosexuality* 23(4) (1992): 83–92.
20. M. Willmott and H. Brierley, "Cognitive Characteristics and Homosexuality," *Archives of Sexual Behavior* 13(4) (1984): 311–319.
21. Blandford. Personal communication, July 1, 2000.
22. M. Willmott and H. Brierley, (1984) op. cit.
23. Y. B. Chung and L. W. Hamon, "The Career Interests and Aspirations of Gay Men: How Sex-role Orientation Is Related," *Journal of Vocational Behavior* 45(2) (1994): 223–239.
24. J. Demb, (1992) op. cit.
25. A. Freitas, S. Kaiser, and T. Hammidi, "Communities, Commodities, Cultural Space, and Style," *Journal of Homosexuality* 31(1–2) (1996): 83–107.
26. J. Saslow, (1987) op. cit.
27. D. Romesberg, "Guerrilla Queer Bar," *The Advocate*, August 14, 2001, 45–51.
28. Romesberg, ibid.
29. J. H. Duckitt and L. duToit, "Personality Profiles of Homosexual Men and Women," *Journal of Psychology* 123 (1989): 497–505.
30. C. Barker, "Gods and Monsters," *The Advocate*, Jan. 18, 2000, 107.
31. Robert Mellors, Papers, Hall-Carpenter Archives, London, U.K.
32. R. Wright, *The Moral Animal: Why We Are the Way We Are* (New York: Pantheon Books, 1994).
33. D. J. Futuyma and S. J. Risch, "Sexual Orientation, Sociobiology, and Evolution," *Journal of Homosexuality* 9(2–3) (1983): 157–168; E. O. Wilson, *Sociobiology* (Cambridge, Mass.: Belknap Press of Harvard University Press, 1975); M. Ruse, "Are There Gay Genes? Sociobiology and Homosexuality," *Journal of Homosexuality* 6(4) (1981): 5–34; W. Byne, "Science and Belief: Psychobiological Research on Sexual Orientation," *Journal of Homosexuality* 28(3–4) (1995): 303–344; R. Herrn, "On the History of Biological Theories of Homosexuality," *Journal of Homosexuality* 28(1–2) (1995): 31–56; M. Dickemann, "Reproductive Strategies and Gender Construction: An Evolutionary View of Homosexualities," *Journal of Homosexuality* 24(3–4) (1993): 55–73.
34. M. Dickemann, "Wilson's Panchreston: The Inclusive Fitness Hypothesis of Sociobiology Re-examined," *Journal of Homosexuality* 28(1–2) (1995): 147–183; W. Byne, (1995) op. cit.

Chapter 9: Mind the Gap: When Private Hearts and Public Habits Collide

1. R. S. F. Stall, AIDS Foundation interviews (Center for AIDS Prevention Studies, San Francisco AIDS Foundation, 1998).
2. Yankelovitch Partners, *Perspective on Gays and Lesbians* (New York: Yankelovitch Partners, 1994).

3. Thanks to Ken Hanes and his wonderful book, *Speaking Out: 425 Gay Men Explain It All For You* (New York: Random House, 1998), a collection of ordinary gay men's observations about their lives, for many of the quotes in this chapter.
4. K. Hanes, (1998) op. cit.
5. S. C. Boies, (1998) op. cit.
6. L. A. Lewis and M. W. Ross, (1995) op. cit.
7. K. Hanes, (1998) op. cit.
8. A. Freitas, S. Kaiser, and T. Hammidi, (1996) op. cit.

Chapter 10: Men for a New Millennium

1. D. Halperin, (1995) op. cit.
2. M. Foucault, (1996) op. cit.

INDEX